COMPILED FROM HOT ROD MAGAZINE

Mustang Restoration
TIPS & TECHNIQUES

Compiled by R M Clarke from articles published in the
Hot Rod Automotive Performance Series

ISBN 0 948 207 973

Published by
Brooklands Books with permission of Petersen Publishing Company
Printed in Hong Kong

CONTENTS

ACKNOWLEDGEMENTS

Bruce Caldwell and the editors of Hot Rod have earned an enviable reputation over the years for publishing clear, informative, technical articles covering automotive upkeep, repair and restoration. Among these fine pieces have been many on Mustangs, a car they greatly admire. They were amongst the first to recognise that the early Mustangs were modern classics and fulfilled their readers needs by writing a series of stories that helped them maintain and improve their vehicles.

Armed with their easy-to-follow picture sequences and comprehensive instructions many a timid owner has been encouraged to tune his 289 or improve the handling of his 350GT.

Unfortunately todays owners of Mustangs find it almost impossible to locate these early articles and with this in mind we have collected what we think are the most useful and valuable of the series and combined them into a book. We are indebted as always to Lee Kelley and the management of Petersens Publishing Company for their understanding and for allowing us to reprint their copyright stories.

R.M. Clarke

DISTRIBUTED BY

Motorbooks International
Osceola
Wisconsin 54020
USA

Brooklands Books Distribution Ltd
Holmerise, Sevenhills Road
Cobham, Surrey KT11 1ES
England

HOW TO BUY A USED MUSTANG

WHAT TO LOOK FOR (AND AVOID) IN YOUR NEXT PURCHASE *BY JIM SCHMIDT*

ABOUT THE AUTHOR: Jim Schmidt is well-qualified to write about Mustangs as he is the owner and driving force behind the three National Parts Depot Mustang parts stores. Jim presently owns several beautiful Mustangs, and has had his share in the past as well. He has been involved in show-quality restorations of Mustangs and Thunderbirds, so he knows first-hand that what looks like a small problem at the time of purchase can actually be a major expense. Completely restoring a Mustang is a sure way to learn about the time and costs involved.

If you are anxious to become the owner of an early Mustang or you would like to replace your present 'Stang with a better one, you will probably welcome some advice on what to look for and how to estimate restoration costs on a specific car. Primarily, you'll need a lot of ''horse-sense'' and a keen eye to spot the problems that others have tried to cover up.

Body rust is the most difficult problem for an amateur restorer to handle, and the most expensive problem to cure professionally. Keep in mind that the Mustang is a unibody vehicle which has no actual frame. Various support members and the floorpan/transmission tunnel are spot-welded together at the factory to form a strong but lightweight underbody assembly. When rust attacks this underbody structure, the result is weak or totally rusted-out floorboards, trunk floors, frame rails, and inner rocker panels (these help form the rigid alignment necessary to enable the doors to close properly).

You usually can't see this form of rust damage by walking around outside the car. Take a jack, use a hoist, crawl under the car, or do whatever it takes to inspect it closely. At the same time, be alert for signs of collision damage.

Look closely at the floorboards; tap them lightly and listen for a solid ring. Also check the inner rocker panel by tapping. It should sound solid and you should not hear the sound of rust scale falling inside the rocker panel assembly. It's important to check the lower portion of the front rails from the firewall on back as these are rust-prone. The rear of the rear frame rail is also very rust-prone. If these rails need to be replaced, they must be properly welded into the unibody, and the floor areas which they are welded to must be strong.

Be cautious if you find a thick undercoat which prevents you from seeing the condition of the underbody. Many times this is a cover for severe rust or amateur repairs such as sheet aluminum or sheetmetal fastened by brazing or sheetmetal screws. These repairs can cover a hole, but will not restore strength to the unibody. Sections to properly repair all common underbody rust areas are available from National Parts Depot. When properly fitted and welded, strength and appearance are restored. Floorpans average $200 per set, frame rails about $100 a pair, inner rockers on convertibles about $125 per pair. Professional labor to fit and weld these items can run between $400-$2000, depending on the shop and the extent of rust replacement required. A cheap Mustang that needs extensive underbody repairs may not be a bargain at all!

Be alert to both rust and collision damage in the interior/exterior sheetmetal, and look for signs of previous repair for either reason. Open the hood and carefully inspect the leading edge of it for rust holes and other damages; a new hood will run over $200, and good used hoods are hard to find. Inspect the sheetmetal panels that form the engine compartment. These are prone to rust and are good indicators of past front end collisions; new fenders may have been installed, but metal in the engine compartment is usually just rough-straightened.

Rust in the battery area is common, and this sheetmetal can be replaced for about $35 plus labor. The driver's side front section and the radiator support are also generally obtainable for most years. However, the rear portion of the inner fender between the shock tower and the firewall (which provides some of the vertical rigidity) is not available as a new or reproduced part. It's also very difficult to remove and install, so it's best to pass if the prospective Pony needs this area replaced.

Check the lower rear corner of the front fenders for rust repairs. This area is one of the first to rust through, and is commonly filled with Bondo. Repair sections are made to replace this section and the lower portion of the brace behind it. If the rust condition exists and the fender is weak along the top edge or has collision damage, consider replacing it with a new ($200) or used ($100) front fender. Front fenders bolt on and require very little labor, so many times it's actually cheaper to replace a bad fender than it is to repair it.

The front lower stone deflector (va-

You aren't likely to find a used Mustang GT Enduro for sale, but the standard GTs are a great used car value.

An early V8 coupe is a common Mustang to find for sale. This one was offered at a California swap meet.

The late-model Mustang convertibles are popular now, and they stand to be collector cars as they get older. Find a low-mileage example and watch your investment grow.

When shopping for rare Mustangs like this '71 Boss 351, your choices are limited by the number of cars available.

When checking a Mustang, put it up on a hoist and look for rust in the floorpan. The rust is moving right along.

People will actually buy even a badly damaged early Mustang convertible like this one. It was hit in the left rear quarter and needs extensive bodywork.

It is common to find rust around the battery because it is so corrosive. Remove the battery and check for damage underneath the battery tray.

Rust shows up in some of the most unexpected places like underneath the front lip of the hood (arrows).

Putting a car up on the hoist is an easy way to check for any rust or collision damage on the support braces under the radiator.

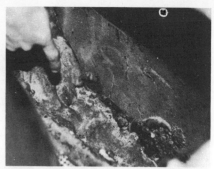

The trunk is a sure place to detect rear end damage. Repairs are often done with body filler, and the damage can be seen inside the trunk. This area is also prone to rust.

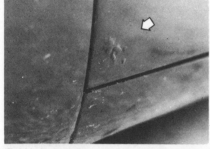

Bubbles under the paint (arrow) indicate rust trouble. When the paint is removed you will probably find more rust than expected.

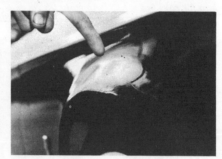

This front fender was poorly repaired. The owner just painted right over the hastily repaired damage.

Alignment problems such as on this hood can be easily corrected, but they may indicate a past accident. See if minor adjustments will cure the problem.

lance) is usually much the worse-for-wear. Since it unbolts and is hard to straighten, it's best to just replace it with a new one for about $70 plus labor.

One of the worst rust problems (and the least anticipated) is cowl rust in '65-'68 models. The design is such that air enters through the grille in the cowl behind the hood for fresh interior air and for the heater. Unfortunately, so does rainwater, road salt, leaves, and pine needles. This causes the basin of the cowl to rust severely. When you feel water dripping on your feet during the rain or outside air entering the passenger compartment, chances are this is the problem.

Various home cures include tar or fiberglass resin poured into the cowl. This stops the leak temporarily, but the rust continues to work and the leaks will reappear. The only real cure is to remove everything from the dash area, hand-form new sheetmetal areas as needed, and butt-weld them into the cowl from underneath. This takes a talented professional hours or even days to do, and can easily cost $500-$1000 to fix properly. Look for signs of rust or water under the dash area, around the heater box, or under the front carpet. If in doubt, run a slow water hose into the cowl grille and watch for leaks and signs of home cures.

Next are the doors. Believe it or not, Ford did not protect the inside of the door sheetmetal with even a coat of primer. While there is a rust repair panel made to replace the lower few inches of the outer door skin, generally the bottom and lower inner metal have rusted away as well. On '65-'68 doors the

interior metal is embossed with a leather-like grain, so there is no practical way to make a rust repair that isn't noticeable. This means a badly rusted door or one with heavy collision damage must be replaced. A used, straight, rust-free door can be located in the dry Southwest, but figure on paying at least $150 plus shipping.

The rear fender quarter panels can be repaired with available repair sections, and in many cases new factory full panels can still be found. Costs vary from $35 for a lower rear section to over $200 for a full quarter panel. Since you generally can get what you need, don't be too concerned if the car is good but the quarters need some work. Inner and outer wheel houses are readily available, and replacing both full quarters and outer wheel houses can add about $1000 to your restoration. Using specific repair sections can reduce this cost drastically.

Many cars have been hit in the rear at one time or another, and the replacement of a taillight panel runs about $100 plus welding labor. The rear valance unbolts, and is easily replaceable at approximately $50.

Trunk lids are rust-prone along their lower rear, and some new lids are available for about $200, while good used lids run $75-$150. Generally, rust repairs don't last in a trunk lid, so it's better to spend money replacing it rather than repairing it over and over again.

Now you can see why it's so important to look closely at the sheetmetal. If you purchase a Mustang inexpensively, knowing it needs bodywork, be aware that it can add substantially to the cost of your car.

Next, take a look inside. Almost every interior trim item is available from National Parts Depot for '65-'68 models, and a good selection for the '69-'73 models as well. However, check the seats to be sure they're correct for the year and model of the car. Used seats in restorable condition cost $50-$100 to obtain. Also, although newer radios are better, if the dash has been cut or holes drilled to accept a new radio and accessories, it's difficult to restore and the car's value is reduced. Be sure that the shifter is the correct factory unit. If not, and the floorpan was modified, the value is reduced.

An original interior can be replaced with duplicate seat upholstery, door panels, carpet, headliner, and armrests for approximately $500-$700, depending on the year and model. A new dash pad runs $175-$250. The interior is where the least amount of money will make the most improvement. Most people can install duplicate interiors themselves with a little professional help. A car with a perfect interior is worth at least $500 more than the same car with a poor interior.

Chrome is one more area where it doesn't cost too much to go first-class. The chrome and trim molding on most Mustangs can be replaced with new factory parts, and an average of $500 will replace the bumpers, grille, and hood moldings, rocker moldings, taillight trim, emblems, and script. It is generally cheaper to buy the parts new instead of re-chroming, but inspect the stainless moldings that rim the windshield and rear window for damage from tools or careless sanding. Only a few of these are available new, and the

A good taillight panel is important on a potential Mustang. Repair panels are available, but they aren't easy to add on.

The front of this early Mustang is damaged, but the parts aren't difficult to come by. This damage should lower the purchase price to an amount equal to the cost of repairs.

Check alignment of body styling lines such as between the doors and fenders. The door hinges may be worn, or misalignment may mean the car was damaged.

Check to be sure the fender has the correct rolled lip as found on original Boss 302s.

On a collectible Mustang like a Shelby GT350 the optional wheels can be a big bonus. These rare mags were made by Cragar and fitted with a CS center cap.

The Magnum 500 wheels that were available on the Boss 302s were often discarded in favor of expensive mags. Now they are the hot item.

A modified Mustang that has been lowered, painted, and equipped with custom wheels and tires is a good compromise between wild and stock.

Modified Mustangs like this blown fastback are tough to price. The modifications cost plenty, but the selling price depends on taste.

Semi-rare Mustangs like the California Specials are great everyday drivers that will appreciate if you take care of them.

Optional equipment can make a substantial difference in the price of two similar cars. This GT coupe has the driving lights and rare bench seat.

cost to straighten and polish stainless steel parts is much higher than the cost of chroming. A car with perfect chrome and trim is worth about $500 more than one with rusty or pitted chrome, and the bumpers account for $200 of the total.

Rubber weatherstripping usually requires replacement, and this shouldn't affect your decision in purchasing a car. Rubber parts or weatherstripping are available for most years. Each part on a coupe or fastback is about $200-$400, while on a convertible it increases to $300-$500.

The condition of the glass is a valid concern. Windshields are readily available new, but some door glasses such as on early convertibles are not easily found. Inspect for cracks, chips, and scratches, and deduct about $200 if a windshield needs replacement and at least $100 for each bad door glass.

Mechanical considerations can vary with the car, so for our purposes we'll stick to original specs as the basis of value in a classic Mustang. (If you prefer the modified street approach and feel that the modified car in question has been properly built, then you must judge what the value may be on your own.) I have seen countless Mustangs that appear to be stock but they actually had many changes that made them less valuable. It's often hard to tell—until it's too late.

The primary change is the engine swap. The most common swap is a newer 302 installed in place of the original 289. Aside from not being original, these newer 302s offer neither the performance or the economy of the 289. During most engine swaps, a lot of details are overlooked and original parts

such as carburetors, air cleaners, distributors, and exhaust manifolds are discarded. To convert back to an original engine requires locating a suitable complete engine from a salvage source. This costs about $300, then a custom rebuild runs an additional $600-$1000.

Each engine originally had a stamped metal tag attached by a bolt through the intake manifold. The tag lists production codes plus the displacement and year of the engine, and if this tag is missing or doesn't match what the car should be, chances are the engine has been swapped.

If the transmission and/or original shifter have been swapped, it may be difficult to replace, since in many cases these were engineered for Mustang models only.

Rearends also get swapped, but this is less prevalent in regular Mustangs than in high-performance cars. If you no longer have the correct rearend in a Boss car, figure on some heavy looking and at least $500 for a used unit.

Several areas deserve special attention when mechanically evaluating a car. If you can swing it, run a compression and vacuum test on the engine, or at least put it on a scope. If such tests aren't feasible, listen to the tailpipe for an even, solid cadence at idle. Hold a light rag or handkerchief just behind the tailpipe and see if it flutters evenly. Smell the tailpipe exhaust for excessive richness. Check the color of the residue inside the pipe; white/gray is good, black/sooty is not. Typically, rebuilding a weak engine will run about $600-$1000, so allow heavily if it sounds like it needs immediate attention.

Test drive the car to see how the

transmission shifts and sounds. Listen for rearend whine, particularly on deceleration; it may just be an inexpensive wheel bearing, but it may be a whole lot more. It is easy to spend hundreds repairing a poor transmission or noisy rearend.

Try some steering and braking situations, and see if the car pulls to one side if you relax your grip on the steering wheel when driving or braking. Approach these tests carefully, and don't be surprised if every component of the front suspension and steering are long overdue for replacement.

To get an indication of the condition of the steering, have someone inside the car move the steering wheel slowly back and forth, and watch the action of the pivot joints. No noticeable free-play should exist. Grab the top of a front end tire and push it until you hear it start to clunk to get an idea of the adjustment and condition of the wheel bearings. Next, using the front bumper, push down and lift up to set the suspension in motion. Listen for squeaks and groans which indicate dry lubrication points and worn parts. If the shocks are particularly bad, the suspension parts are probably worn even more than normal. Rebuilding a complete front end will cost $300-$500 plus labor.

Brakes, even if bad, are relatively cheap and easy to repair. Generally, $100 will bring all four wheels up to par, so don't factor brakes as an important value in your purchase.

Take a look at the radiator for signs of rusty water. If so, the engine has probably overheated, and it may have been damaged. If the fan runs into the

The owner of this '69 GT350 convertible has the production number of his rare 'Stang on the license plate.

If you just want good economical transportation, consider a '67 or '68 Mustang coupe. Prices on the plain Janes are still quite reasonable.

The Mustang six-cylinder engine won't give you any nosebleeds, but it will get you everywhere you need to go.

Interiors are an important consideration when buying a used Mustang. Most items can be fixed or replaced with excellent reproduction upholstery.

This '70 Mustang has the correct seats in good condition and the factory center console, but the steering wheel is a cheap aftermarket item.

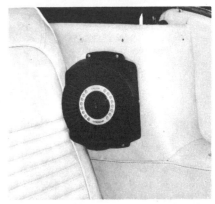

The addition of big stereo speakers should be considered a liability.

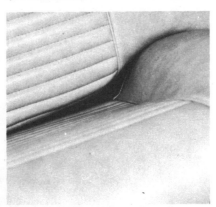

There is a big gap between the cushions on this back seat; either the springs are worn-out or it was poorly reupholstered.

Convertible tops are available, but they aren't cheap. The weatherstripping on this top is sagging and should be replaced.

On a Boss 302, the engine is imperative. A Boss 302 without a Boss 302 engine is just a Mustang with fancy stripes.

Chances of finding a late-model Mustang 302 with the wrong engine are slim, but you should have a mechanic give it a clean bill of health.

A sound engine is an important factor. Look for an original engine with most of the factory parts because it can always be rebuilt.

The interior of this early convertible is thrashed. The factory radio opening has been hacked to fit an aftermarket radio.

A modified Mustang in unfinished condition can be a good buy if you like the work that has been done so far. Metal fender flares like these are expensive to build.

radiator fins or the radiator has been replaced with something from a Volkswagen, consider a new radiator. It costs just a little more than re-coring (figure $100-$200).

If the wiring in the engine compartment running to the taillights, back-up lights, or parking lights has been spliced, hand-wired, burned, cut, or taped off, this indicates a need to replace it. Also check for what caused the problem, and be sure it was properly repaired. It's not unusual to find difficulty in obtaining harnesses as very few are currently available, so deduct value accordingly.

Another bad swap is the six-cylinder to V8 or vice-versa. On the early models in particular, six-cylinder cars had their own lighter-duty brakes, springs, wheels, steering linkage, transmissions, and rearends. Unless all of these components are swapped, you have a real hybrid car that is not an improvement in any way. Be wary of buying such a car; there are more around than you would suspect.

It takes an hour to inspect each prospective Mustang purchase following these guidelines. With these tips in hand you should be able to select a good base car that you can feel confident in and be proud of. *M*

Little items can make the difference between a show-quality and so-so Mustang. The windshield weatherstripping (arrows) on this convertible has deteriorated.

Parking lots of swap meets and old car meets are a good place to look for Mustangs. Many people just take their Mustang and put a "For Sale" on it.

When you have the Mustang on the hoist, check all the suspension components.

The trunk of a project Mustang can be a treasure chest of usable parts. Every part you don't have to buy is money saved.

There are reproduction rear deck lid spoilers available for '69 and '70 Mustangs, but an original adds $100-$200 to a car.

Automotive swap meets are an excellent place to find Mustangs for sale. This '70 Boss 302 had low mileage and was mostly original, but the hood scoop was incorrect.

Swap meets are a good place to find Mustangs in a wide variety of conditions and prices. You can also find parts.

If a Mustang has a V8 engine and four-lug wheels, you can be sure the car previously had a six-cylinder engine.

SHEETMETAL SURGERY

HOW TO REPAIR RUST THE RIGHT WAY

BY BRUCE CALDWELL

That treacherous villian, rust, is almost impossible to evade. In many parts of the country rust is taken for granted, but even supposedly rust-free West Coast cars have been known to fall victim to its ugly ravages. We happen to know because we bought a relatively straight, one-owner '70 Mustang fastback with a see-through trunk. The rear lower back panel (which contains the taillights and gas filler neck) was rusting badly around the edges of the taillights.

You can always do a crude repair by stuffing the holes full of body filler, but the correct way to fix the problem is to remove the damaged sheetmetal and replace it with new material. In the case of our taillight panel, replacement was

CONTINUED ON PAGE 17

1 This was the starting point for our panel replacement job. The taillight panel on this '70 Mustang doesn't look too bad, but the arrows point to the rust-out.

2 A closer look shows that there was more rust under the taillights. Then, after the car was disassembled, even more rust-out was found.

3 Remove the bumper by taking out the four bolts, which are reached from inside the trunk. Don't separate the bumper from the brace that goes between the bumper and the body.

4 Take off the quarter panel extensions; do this by unscrewing the three nuts inside the trunk.

5 With the extensions removed, rust becomes increasingly visible.

6 Take the taillight housing and lens out from the trunk after you remove the light socket.

7 The pot metal outer part of the taillight will come right off after you remove the taillight housing.

8 With the taillight removed you see how much rust was hidden. Only the small hole on the lower right was visible before.

SHEETMETAL SURGERY

9 With a Phillips screwdriver, remove the rubber strip that goes between the body and the bumper over the license plate light.

10 The lower splash pan is held in place with Phillips screws. Leave the back-up lights in place and let the panel hang out of the way on the wiring to the lights.

11 The license plate light is screwed to the bumper and the wire goes into the trunk via a push-in grommet in the taillight panel. Disconnect the male/female wire connector in the trunk and use a screwdriver to pry out the grommet.

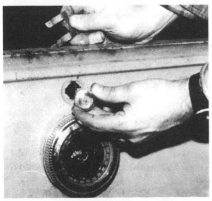

12 Take out the key assembly after you remove the U-shaped clip in the trunk.

13 Several sheetmetal screws hold the outer gas neck filler flange to the taillight panel. Use a ¼-inch drive ratchet to remove the screws.

14 The cable retainer for the gas cap has a threaded stud that goes through the panel to a nut inside the trunk.

15 Loosen the hose clamp on the piece of rubber tubing inside the trunk and pull out the gas filler neck.

16 As soon as you remove the filler neck, stuff a wet rag in the part of the filler neck leading to the gas tank. Wrap duct tape over the end of the filler neck and use the original hose clamp to secure the tape. It's very important that no sparks or flames get near the gas tank.

17 Here's the brand-new taillight panel from National Parts Depot. The panel comes in red oxide primer ready to install.

18 The factory taillight panel was spot-welded in place by machines, so it's easier to find the welds if you grind away the paint.

19 Some of the machine-made welds are pretty thick. Drill through the weld on the outside of the panel to separate the panel from the body.

20 There are two places on each side of the trunk lip where the taillight panel meets the main body; sever these with a hack saw.

SHEETMETAL SURGERY

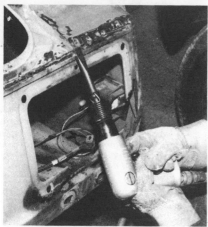

21 *With the spot-welds drilled through on the outer surface, it's easy to break the underlying welds with an air chisel. Be sure to wear gloves and goggles.*

22 *When drilling out the spot-welds on the lower part of the panel, use care to just break the welds. You don't want to drill into the gas tank.*

23 *It might take a little prying to make sure all the welds have been broken, but once they are the old panel will slide out. The panel is also welded (arrows) to the lock supports.*

24 *The old panel (top) and the National Parts Depot panel (bottom) are identical, except for their condition.*

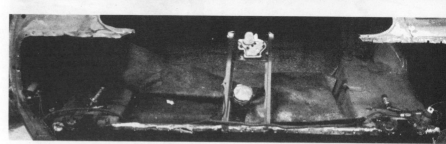

25 *The Mustang with its trunk exposed. Notice the lower panel is suspended by the back-up light wires. Leave the trunk-lock supports attached to the body; separate supports at the top two welds.*

26 *With the taillight panel removed, you'll notice a lot of white seam filler. Remove this with a utility or putty knife before any welding is done.*

27 *Use a grinder to remove the rest of the sealant.*

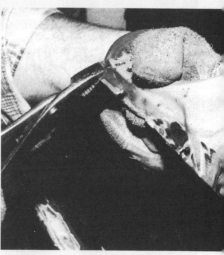

28 *In the process of breaking the old spot welds and prying out the taillight panel, the lip on the body might get bent. Use a pair of pliers to get the lip back into shape.*

29 *Now use a hammer and dolly to make the lip flat in preparation for welding in the new panel.*

30 *Grind the paint (to bare metal) on the lip of the new panel where the welds will be made.*

31 *Put the new taillight panel in as carefully as possible to avoid bending it. Put one side in first.*

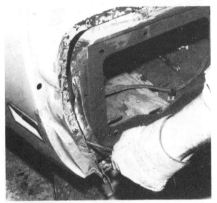

32 *Pry out the body just enough on one side to fit the new panel.*

33 *Hammer the pried-out section into shape, and overlap the edge of the new panel.*

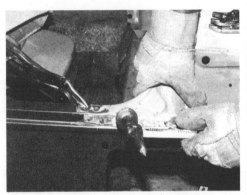

34 *Secure the two pieces (with Vise Grip pliers) where the body meets the new panel at the trunk lip.*

35 *Hold the new panel in place while you do additional hammer and dolly work. Make everything fit as well as possible before doing any welding.*

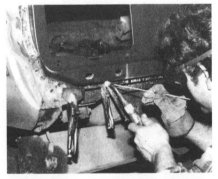

36 *Clamp the new panel securely in place and braze the four corners. After checking that the panel is still correctly aligned, weld the rest of the panel.*

37 *Notice how close the Vise Grip pliers are to each other. Brian Kennedy clamps them on each side of where he wants to weld to help control warpage.*

38 *Put the quarter panel extensions on to see how the car looks after you weld the new panel in place. The basic repair is done, but there's still a lot of finish work to go.*

39 *Seal the seams between the panel and the body. We used Auveco body sealer from the H.C. Fastener Company.*

SHEETMETAL SURGERY

40 Before applying the sealer, grind the seams and welds with a wire brush. It's important to use a grinder to remove the flux left from the brazing rod so the paint will adhere properly.

41 While an air grinder is the quick and easy method, an ordinary wire brush and a lot of elbow grease will also get the job done.

42 Apply the Auveco body sealer inside and out with a chaulking gun.

44 The right corner after the body sealer was applied. You must use a sealer that can be painted over.

45 Smooth all low spots where the trunk-lock supports were attached to the panel. We used Ditzler 999 body filler.

46 After the filler is dry, sand with 100-grit paper; do this with a long sanding board.

48 After the primer is dry, apply paint. We wanted a super nice job, so even the lower edges were well-painted with Ditzler acrylic enamel.

49 Paint the areas under the quarter panel extensions, too. There will be a slight gap between the extensions and the main body, so paint that area.

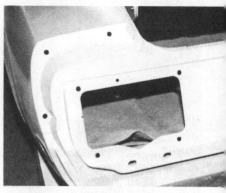

50 The new taillight panel after painting. Quite an improvement from when we first disassembled the car.

51 The big gasket around the taillight housing was caked with rusted metal. We used a putty knife and a wire brush to make the gasket serviceable again.

52 There's a big difference between the cleaned lens and gasket on the left and the rusty, dirty one on the right.

53 With the lights and bumper back in place, the taillight panel looks just as good as new.

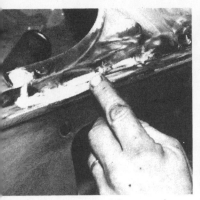

3 *Work the sealer into the seams by hand.*

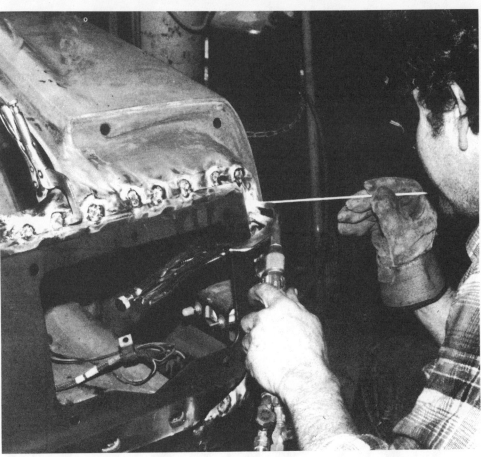

7 *Scuff the new panel and the original surrounding body with a Scotch-Brite pad before applying (with a touch-up gun) Ditzler Red Oxide Primer.*

CONTINUED FROM PAGE 12

the only answer because there was even more hidden rust found after we disassembled the car.

Fortunately for Mustang owners, there are a lot of fine repair and replacement panels on the market. Depending on the amount of rust (or other damage), you can either get a complete panel or opt for just a patch panel. We got our new taillight panel from the extensive selection at National Parts Depot. Their catalog lists lots of factory-original parts including complete fenders, hoods, quarter panels, and patch panels for every problem area known to Mustangs. National Parts Depot is based in Florida (3101 SW 40th Blvd., Gainesville, FL 32608, 800/874-7595 or 904/378-2473). They also conveniently have a West Coast store located in California (1495-C Palma Dr., Ventura, CA 93003, 800/235-3445 or 800/342-3614), and a Michigan outlet (12780 Currie Ct., Livonia, MI 48150, 800/521-6104 or 313/591-1956), so

they can handle Mustang customers from coast to coast. The taillight panel arrived promptly, and it was an exact match to the original.

Ace bodyman Brian Kennedy performed the metal surgery as we followed along. Ditzler products were used to fill some of the less visible depressions and to prime and paint the panel back to match the rest of the car. Besides being welded, the panel must be sealed to keep out water, so we used Auveco automotive body sealer for the seams. It's important to use a sealer that can be painted over, such as Auveco. We got it through the mail from the H.C. Fastener Company, P.O. Box P, Alvarado, TX 76009.

Our only complaint about this repair is that the back panel looks so much better than the rest of the car that we'll have to paint and repair the whole thing soon. Follow along as we show you how to substitute new sheetmetal for old. ☐

RUST REDEMPTION

HOW TO REPAIR THAT PONY'S SHEETMETAL

BY BRUCE CALDWELL

If an original rust-free California Mustang is at the top of your dream list, it stands to reason that a clapped-out rust bucket from the Northeast is at the bottom of the list. Unfortunately for most Mustang lovers, the latter seems to be in significant abundance. .

A Mustang with rust is a fact of life for many enthusiasts, even ones who live in California. If you think there's no such thing as a rusty California car, check out a few gems from the many beach cities—what the salt air doesn't corrode, the smog eats. The solution to the problem is to seek the car you can afford with the least amount of rust, then learn how to fix the rust that does exist.

Customizer Eddie Paul of Customs By Eddie Paul (124 Nevada St., El Segundo, CA 90245, 213/322-0451) is a big fan of Mustangs and likes building

1 *This is a California Mustang in need of redemption. Like so many project cars, it had its share of flaws, but was well worth fixing.*

them as his personal cars. Being a bodyman, he leans toward bargain models needing repairs. This typical budget-priced, early-Mustang 2+2 had rusty doors. It would be possible to repair the damage by simply switching doors, but Eddie agreed to demonstrate

how to repair the problem when a better door isn't readily available.

The techniques used to repair the rusty door are similar to how other rusty body parts can be fixed, so follow along as we show you the basics. *M*

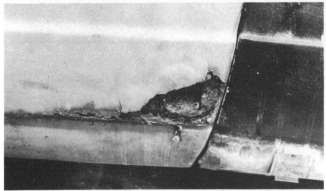

2 *An excessive amount of moisture that caused rust-out had collected in the lower door area over the years.*

3 *A way to repair a rusty door quickly would be to swap doors. This used door had some bad dents in it and was previously repaired with large amounts of body filler. Fixing the rust was easier.*

4 *Remove the door so it's easier to work on. This one was placed on a 55-gallon drum so it was flat and at a comfortable height.*

5 *Grind off the paint surrounding the damaged area to determine the extent of the rust. Clean, bare metal is necessary for welding in the replacement patch panel.*

6 *Notice the door was previously repaired with body filler (arrow), but the repair didn't last. Break the lower seam to remove the damaged section of metal. A chisel or body grinder will do the trick.*

7 *Use an air chisel to quickly and neatly cut out the rusty sheetmetal.*

8 *There was some rust under the door skin, but the area was still structurally strong so the rust was removed by grinding.*

9 *Use a carpenter's square and a metal scribe to mark a rectangular patch panel on a sheet of metal.*

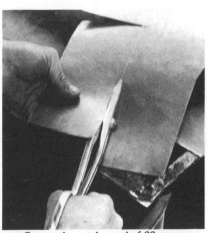

10 *Cut out the patch panel of 22-gauge sheetmetal; use tin snips for this.*

RUST REDEMPTION

11 *If there are any small holes after the rust on the main part of the door is ground smooth, you can braze them with a welding rod.*

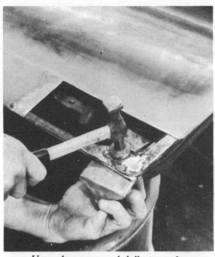

12 *Use a hammer and dolly to make sure the brazed area is flat. Grind smooth the excess welding material.*

13 *Fit the patch panel in place. It's easier to cut slightly large and then trim, than having too small a patch panel.*

16 *Grind the welds smooth with a coarse-grit disc on a body grinder.*

17 *Gas-weld the bottom seam of the door shut. Pack both sides of the seam with Moist Bastos first; this material is like clay and helps keep the area cool to prevent warping from the heat of the torch.*

18 *Remove the Moist Bastos and grind the excess welding material away.*

20 *Grind the soldered seam smooth with a sanding disc; a coarse-grinding disc is too rough.*

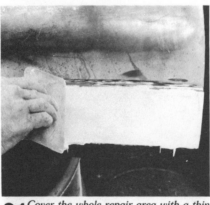

21 *Cover the whole repair area with a thin coat of plastic body filler to take care of any low spots or waves.*

22 *Use a cheesegrater file to remove the excess body filler.*

14 *Slowly and carefully tack-weld the repair panel in place to minimize warpage.*

15 *Work the welds over with a hammer and dolly to make the door smooth and flat.*

19 *Use a heavy-duty soldering iron and acid-core solder to fill the tiny imperfections left after the welds are ground down. Here there were a few holes made where the arc welder was improperly adjusted.*

23 *Sand, prime, and touch up the whole area with spot putty, then sand again and cover with a final coat of primer.*

24 *This car still needs work, but the door is just fine. The rust was removed and replaced with good, strong sheetmetal.*

Mustang Ranchero

(1) The roof and trunk sections are removed from the coupe and separated along the line which will form the rear compartment. Fourteen inches are taken out of the roof to make room for the large 3-foot 4-inch x 4-foot 5-inch area.

(2) Once cut to size, the roof is welded back into position well forward of its original location. The roof is molded to follow the lines of the classic Mustang.

TEXT & PHOTOGRAPHY: CAM BENTY

WHEN THIS PONY HAULS, IT HAULS

The classic Mustang came in many forms—convertibles, coupes, and fastbacks—but none came from the factory in the form designed by J. Brunk at Beverly Hills Mustang (9280 Alden Dr., Beverly Hills, CA 90210, 213/276-2036). He masterminded the "Ranchero Mustang," a classic Mustang with the load-carrying capabilities of a shortbed pickup.

To achieve this unique result, the trunk and part of the roof are removed from the body, moving the rear windshield 14 inches in front of its original position. The new two-passenger Ranchero-style Mustang has a large 3-feet 4-inch by 4-feet 5-inch aft compartment. The rear compartment comes with a snug-fitting tonneau cover, chrome railings, a protective bed mat, and a locking storage compartment. A Mustang never had it so good—neither did a Mustang owner.

(4) These four pieces form the basis for the rear compartment. A great deal of trial fitting is necessary to make the pieces mate to the original Ford bodywork.

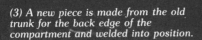

(3) A new piece is made from the old trunk for the back edge of the compartment and welded into position.

Ranchero

(5) Andy Hill shows how the panels fit together. Each panel is riveted into place once a satisfactory fit is achieved.

Starting with the base Ranchero Mustang from Beverly Hills Mustang, this machine goes a step beyond with Shelby striping, Bill Stroppe custom rollbar, and Marchal lighting package.

(6) A locking storage compartment is found in the forward portion of the storage area—perfect for storing tools.

(7) From the inside, the conversion is finished off neatly with a vinyl-covered package tray/compartment separator and carpeting from one side to the other.

PHOTOGRAPHY: JERRY HEASLEY

In the Spring 1983 issue of HOT ROD's *Mustang* we went through the procedure for painting your vintage Mustang. We've gone a step further, and now we'll demonstrate how to repair a minor dent on the same '66 coupe.

The '66 ponycar was Wimbledon White, painted with Ditzler's new Acrylic Urethane. We chose this paint because like other brands of urethane (and polyurethane), it has the toughness and high gloss of an enamel, with the easy-to-spray characteristics of a lacquer. With Ditzler, we could also buy an exact color match as factory blend, and of OEM quality (meeting or exceeding the original equipment manufacturer).

Keep in mind that our instructions are detailed for a modern "catalysed" finish—a urethane with hardener added. Generally, the steps would apply to any type of paint, allowing for certain differences in product application (check on the back of the can for undercoat/topcoat compatibility and drying times).

1 *Here's the damage—a deep scratch and a small dent on the left rear quarter panel.*

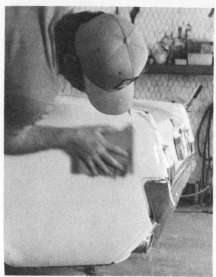

2 *First, clean the entire quarter panel with soap and water to remove the dirt.*

Many steps are required to complete a spot repair. In fact, painting an entire car involves less work than fixing a minor dent. Follow along as we show how to do this complicated procedure, then try it yourself. Just remember to take your time, be careful, and follow instructions! *M*

QUICK FIX

HOW TO MAKE SPOT DENT REPAIRS

BY JERRY HEASLEY

3 *Next, use a wax and grease remover like Ditzler DX-330 to remove any wax, road tar, or oil. Any traces of wax or grease will prevent the new coat of paint from sticking.*

4 *Begin the straightening process next. For our minor dent, we used an all-purpose body dolly and a tacking hammer.*

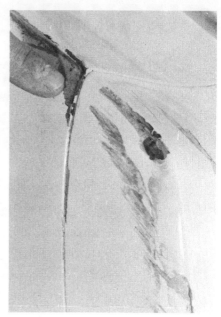

5 *Here's a closeup of the body damage after working the metal as straight as possible. Of course, very few dents can be perfectly popped back into place.*

6 *Leveling is next; begin by rough-sanding the worked metal with a #24-grit disc. This removes the paint from the damaged area.*

7 *Switch to #80-grit paper and bevel the perimeters of the damaged area to a smooth finish. Here's what the area looks like after featheredging.*

8 *Throughout the job, keep the rear quarter free of debris by blowing with compressed air. Be sure to wear a mask to protect your lungs.*

9 *Next comes the body filler. We used Ditzler Fillerup (DX-4) mixed with a cream hardener, DX-672.*

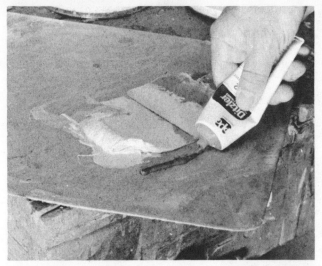

10 *The directions recommend a ratio of about a golf ball-size mass of filler to a two-inch strip of hardener.*

11 *Mix the hardener into the filler, pressing down with your flat-bladed putty knife so the air is worked out.*

13 *Notice the filler is applied to the straightened area, but not to the sanded-only metal which didn't need it.*

14 *When the filler dries to the consistency of hard clay, it's ready for rough contouring with the cheesegrater file. Use this tool before the filler dries hard.*

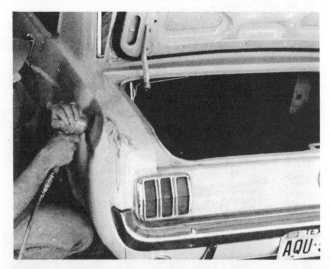

16 *Use #220-grit paper on a dual-action sander to give the bevel a smoother, less abrupt edge. Complete the featheredging around the perimeter of the repair.*

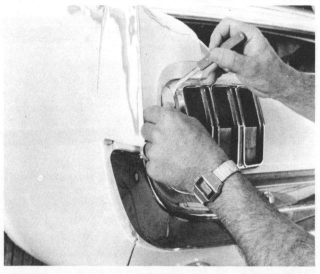

17 *Masking is next. We taped off the taillight bezels, but many painters remove the whole assembly.*

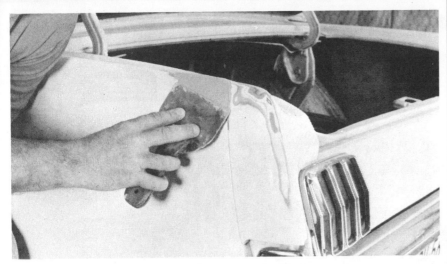

12 *Using a flexible plastic putty spreader, compress the filler into the metal, building it slightly higher than the surrounding metal.*

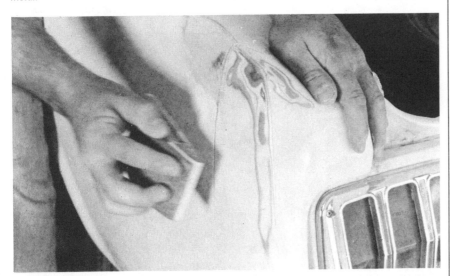

15 *Next, block-sand with #80-grit, keeping inside the repair, but featheredge the perimeter to a rather sharp, quick bevel.*

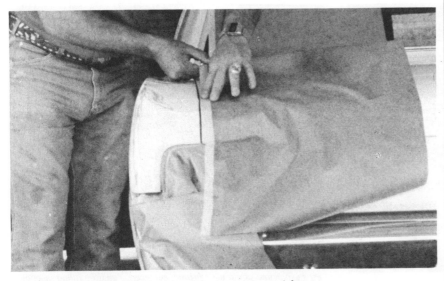

18 *Protect the rear deck lid (with masking tape and paper) from overspray.*

19 *Wheelcover skins are made to protect the tires, but you can use paper.*

20 *Spray on primer/surfacer next. We used Ditzler Kondar acrylic primer/surfacer (DZ-3), which must be mixed with DTL-16 Duracryl All-Purpose Thinner.*

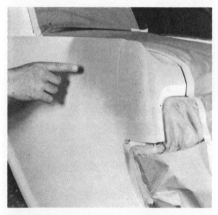

23 *Notice how we applied the primer/surfacer over the repaired area, fading it out along the edges. It's critical to let it dry completely (30 minutes in our case).*

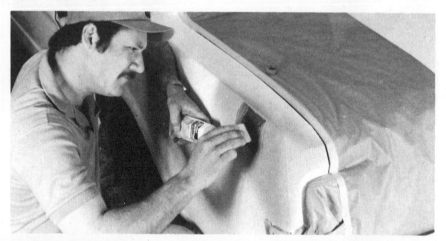

24 *Apply Spot & Glaze putty (in thin coats) next. We used DFL-17 Ditzler Red Cap, which fills the minute scratches and small imperfections left by the primer/surfacer.*

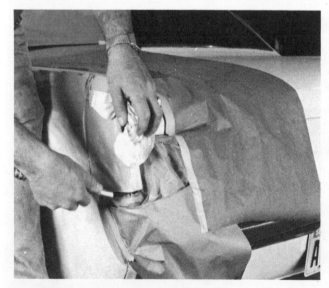

27 *Dry the area with a clean rag and compressed air.*

28 *Reprime again with primer/surfacer. You'll be filling in any tiny imperfections (with #220-grit sandpaper) that may remain after sanding the glazing putty.*

21 *The primer/surfacer, like all paint products, should be thoroughly mixed and poured through a strainer before applying.*

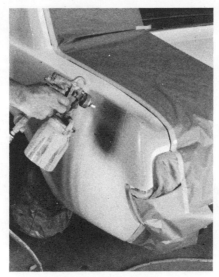

22 *Apply the primer/surfacer over the repaired area and slightly beyond.*

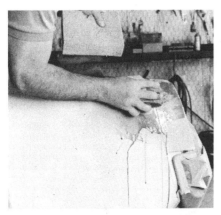

25 *After the spot putty dries, sand the surface with #320-grit wet or dry sandpaper. The sanding is faster if you use a sponge to keep the area wet and carry away the debris.*

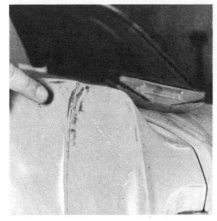

26 *Notice how you can still see some of the spot putty. At this point, it has filled in tiny scratches and nicks—the rest is smooth.*

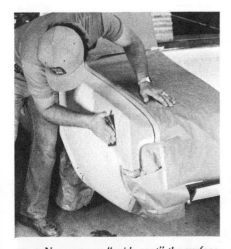

29 *Now you can "guide coat" the surface with black lacquer, then sand with fine-grit paper to make certain the surface is completely leveled—then reprime. Or, you can sand with #600-grit (dry), which is the last step before painting.*

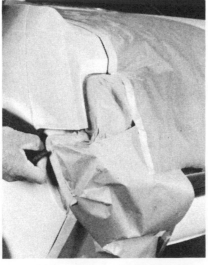

30 *Use Scotch-Brite pads to sand those hard-to-reach areas that sandpaper can't reach.*

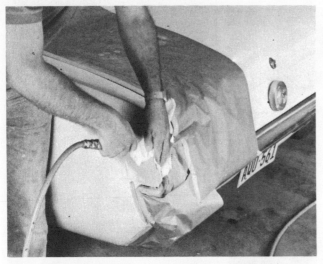

31 *Blow away the sanding debris and wipe the surface clean with a paper towel.*

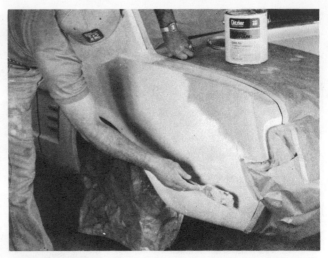

32 *Next, apply a rubbing compound (we used Ditzler DRX-55) to the primed surface edges and to a large area around it, which will be repainted.*

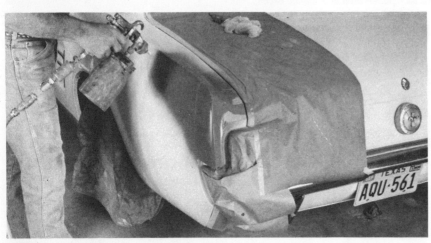

35 *Spray the sealer on the entire surface that will be repainted. The Ditzler Del-Seal comes ready to use—no mixing is required. Flash time is about 30 minutes.*

36 *A good charcoal-filter mask is necessary to protect your lungs from the paint fumes. A respirator is especially important when using urethane and two-part paints.*

39 *After the paint has flashed to dry, pull off the masking tape and paper. Peel the tape back on itself.*

40 *Allow the paint to dry overnight, then wax the edges of the new paint repair to blend it in with the old paint. The new paint on our '66 coupe matches splendidly.*

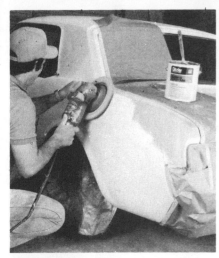

33 *Most pros prefer to machine buff when compounding. Use care so the paint doesn't get "burned."*

34 *Apply sealer to "seal" the old paint from the new and to give a good surface to which the new paint can stick. We used Ditzler Del-Seal (DAS-1980).*

37 *We sprayed on the Wimbledon White paint next. After the first coat, allow about 15-20 minutes flash time before applying the second coat. The paint should be sprayed so it overlaps the primed (sealed) area.*

38 *After the second coat is applied, immediately spray the edges of the new paint with reducer to "melt in" the old paint. Use the same-temperature reducer as with the paint mix.*

41 *The complete repair—no sign that it was ever damaged.*

QUARTER PANEL EXCHANGE

WORKING THE SHEETMETAL INTO A NEW BODY PANEL

TEXT AND PHOTOGRAPHY BY DON EMMONS

IF YOUR MUSTANG HAS BEEN THE victim of another's bumper or has fallen prey to the dreaded villian, body rot, all is not lost. The remedy is so simple it could be overlooked: Replace the body panel. In our case, we wanted to exchange a thrashed rear quarter panel on a fastback. This replacement can be a little tricky because of the way the panel fits into the top. However, don't let that stop you. Read on for some tips on how this operation can be made fast and easy.

Bob Jackson of Riverview Auto Body in Riverside, California, was assigned the task of replacing the rear quarter panel on a '70 model, and the work needed to be done very precisely so no modifications could be seen.

Bob first found a used panel to install, as new ones are no longer available. After removing the old, grimy panel, Bob leaded the joint at the roofline with Evercoat Pure Metal, a metal-like body filler that is applied and works like regular filler, except its appearance has more similarity to real lead. Eight-pound body filler should be used; experts feel that this grade works best. Another recommendation is to go easy on the catalyst; if too much is used, it sets off the filler quickly and doesn't allow enough time to do the close work in the doorjamb.

Bob certainly had his hands full with this job. The rear section was damaged and had to be reworked as the panel was installed. This professional tackled the problem head-on, and got some excellent results. So if the rear quarter panel on your Mustang has seen better days, get out some bodywork tools, a spray gun, and a compressor, then follow along. You can't go wrong if you follow our expert's instructions. *M*

1 *An abused body panel such as this takes some doing to bring back, but it's not impossible.*

2 *Begin by center punching the middle of each spot weld.*

3 *Use a spot welding tool to cut along each spot weld. Be sure to cut all of them.*

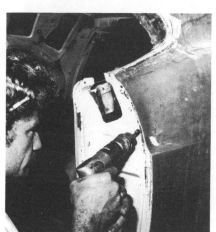

4 *Cut along the window area and leading edge of the panel.*

5 *Note factory spot welding on the lip of the window.*

6 *There are welds on the lip of the wheelwell. Cut out all welds so the panel can be removed.*

7 *This area was leaded when the top was joined to the quarter panel at the factory, and old lead must be melted out.*

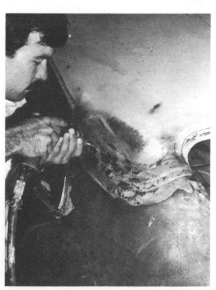

8 *Spot welds below the lead hold the two sections together.*

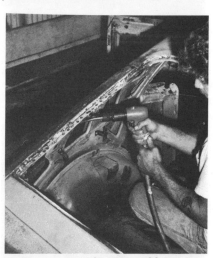

9 *Don't expect the spot weld cutter to always cut all of the weld. Run a chisel between the two pieces to break them apart.*

EXCHANGE

10 Use a chisel to cut the spot welds in the lower window panel area. Work carefully as it must be left intact.

11 Remove the panel by working a screwdriver between the two and prying them apart.

14 Ford Motor Company no longer offers new sheetmetal quarter panels, so a used one will be installed. Select a good rust-free unit, and remove from the old body.

15 Clean the replacement fenderwell in the areas that will be welded.

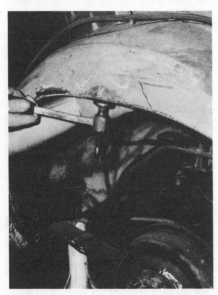

18 Work the lip on the wheelwell until it's nice and flat.

19 Grind down the top to make it clean and smooth before the new section is slipped in underneath.

12 *With all areas broken loose, remove the panel.*

13 *Check for rust. This particular Mustang is from California and rust-free, but most cars will have problems in these lower areas.*

16 *Use a hammer and dolly to straighten any areas that were bent during removal of the old panel.*

17 *Grind down the surface that will be getting the new sheetmetal. Make sure this area is very straight; it will be exposed when the job is finished.*

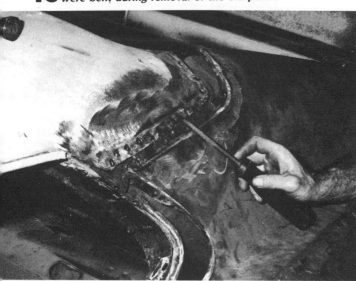

20 *Start the installation process by working the top portion of the panel in under the roof. Work the front lip in at the window opening.*

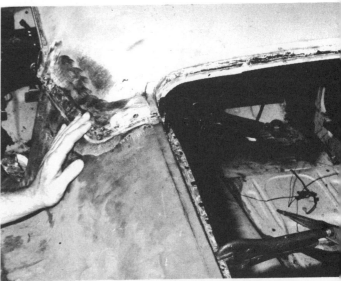

21 *Once the panel has been worked into place, secure it with several clamps. Check all areas to make sure everything lines up properly.*

EXCHANGE

22 *Measure across the back glass. It must be 43½ inches to allow enough space for the glass.*

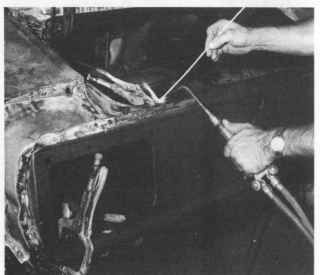

24 *While clamps hold the panels in place, tack weld together.*

25 *Before proceeding, hold the extension piece in place for a trial fit.*

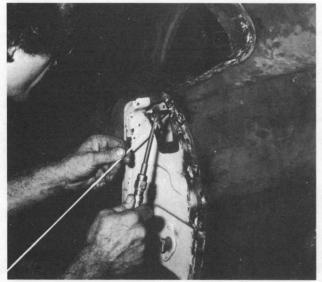

27 *After the top section has been brazed, start working the front edge.*

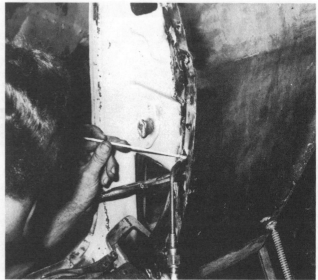

28 *Braze each hole that was cut out. A repair in this area will stick out like a sore thumb if done wrong.*

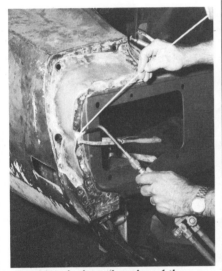

23 *Line up the rear panel with the new section. A new rear panel is used (see the Summer 1984 issue for details on this replacement).*

26 *Work along the edge of the quarter panel, brazing in the holes left by the spot weld cutter.*

29 *Braze holes along the rear window area. This portion will be covered, so it doesn't have to be perfect.*

EXCHANGE

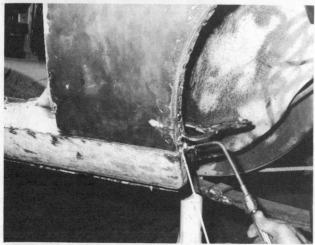

30 The rough area is the wheelwell. The factory put a patch of spot welds along the lip; they must all be filled in.

31 Grind down the welded spots along the edge and all other welds. Remember to work carefully in this area.

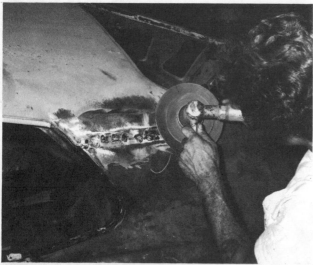

32 Grind the welds down in the area where the top meets the panel. The surface must be taken to bare metal.

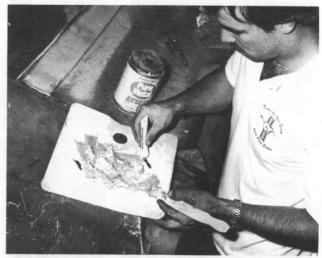

33 Bob Jackson of Riverview Auto Body uses Evercoat Pure Metal body filler to give the look of lead. Read instructions carefully and allow enough time to work the filler before it goes off.

34 The Pure Metal is slightly difficult to work with, but is applied in the same manner as other fillers. Apply just a little more than necessary.

35 Test by touching to see if the filler is ready to work. (When it cools, it's ready.)

EXCHANGE

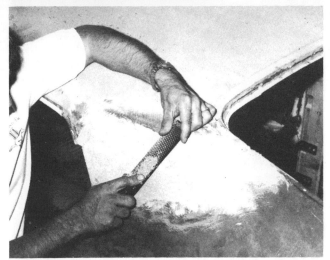

36 *As it cools, shave off the excess with a cheesegrater file.*

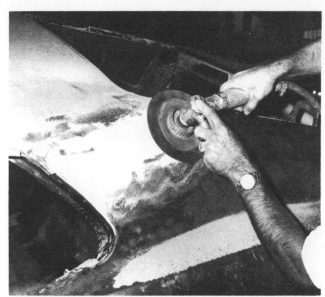

37 *After the body filler has set completely, grind to the proper contour. A second coat may be needed to fill the area completely.*

38 *Finish by using a sanding block to work the metal filler.*

39 *Spread a light coat of regular body filler over the area.*

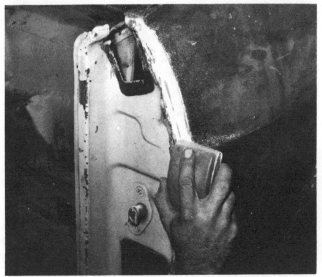

40 *Apply body filler to the front edge. Work this area carefully as it is very visible.*

41 *The edge of a small disc grinder works well for cleaning the area, and will help the job to look original.*

EXCHANGE

42 When all bodywork is complete, sand the entire area down to bare metal.

43 Apply primer to the panels (in this case, the entire car). A complete paint job is the next order of business.

44 After primer coats are finished, apply body sealer to the seams that will be covered by the quarter panel extension piece.

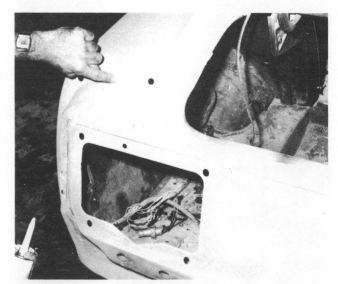

45 Work the sealer into the joints, then wipe off the excess.

46 Paint the extension pieces separately, then install.

47 Now that our 'Stang is back together and looking good, you'd never guess all it has been through.

BODY BUILDING

A POOPED-OUT PONY BECOMES A SUPER STALLION

By Bruce Caldwell

Without a doubt, the most popular post-'48 Ford product is the Mustang. It is the top choice for Ford fanatics, whether they choose to build a drag strip terror, a road racer, or a wild street machine. All early Mustangs are popular, but one stands out from the rest of the herd: the '65-'66 2 + 2 fastback. It has all the good Mustang traits plus the sleekest styling. Those factors duly noted,

we chose a 1965 fastback as the starting point for our Mustang restoration project.

Even though we chose a fastback, most of what was done to the car applies to all Mustangs. We like the fastback purely for aesthetic reasons; for someone on a tighter budget, the hardtop coupe would be a better choice since early fastbacks are skyrocketing in price and getting hard to find. Average, running examples with a V8 easily bring $2000 in Southern California,

so finding one for less than $1000 proved to be quite a chore. Our "find" was advertised in a local paper for $600—firm! However, it took $700 cash at midnight to ace out the other bidders.

The car was a real basket case. The previous owner had started to restore the 100,000-plus-mile car, completely stripping it. The body had its share of dings but was sound and rust-free. The interior was a lost cause. The engine ran just well enough to get the car home using the remaining two speeds of the 3-speed automatic transmission. The car came with a lot of new parts, and was definitely a good starting point. Besides, it was the only affordable fastback we

Our $700 starting point was this rather tired, but solid '65 Mustang fastback. The previous owner had partially disassembled the car, and the deal included a lot of spare parts.

43

BODY BUILDING

could find.

One advantage of the car's stripped state was that it was much easier to get started on the bodywork. A great deal of work would have been necessary to restore our faded fastback, so we decided to transform the body into a swoopy street machine.

The early Mustang's looks are very contemporary, even today. The long front end and short trunk, coupled with crisp lines, is a timeless body style that would be tough to improve on. Luckily, master metalman Eddie Paul had plenty of ideas on how to upgrade our Mustang. Eddie suggested some wild modifications that retained the Mustang look by employing modified Mustang parts.

We took the dreary fastback to Eddie's busy shop (Customs By Eddie Paul, 124 Nevada St., El Segundo, CA 90245, 213/322-0451), where Eddie started by removing the Mustang's dents and previous battle scars. The fender flares and front air dam all required the talents of a good bodyman like Eddie, but firms like Maier Racing (235 Laurel Ave., Hayward, CA 94541) offer a wide variety of fiberglass Mustang flares, spoilers, scoops, and air dams that are relatively easy to install.

The front flares were the easiest, so Eddie started there. Eddie figured the best way to retain the Mustang look was to use the original fender and widen it. The first step is unbolting the fender on the lower edge and at the back by the door. (Work is easier if the door is removed.) With the fender loose, split the fender along the styling seam with an air chisel. The flare will have a wedge shape, so to cover the front of the tire, the front fender lip must be brought out. This was done by separating the lip from the fender (starting at the top center of the arch) with a Rodac air chisel. The lip was then brought out 2 inches at the bottom and the gap filled with 22-gauge cold rolled steel.

The upper slit in the fender was filled with a sheetmetal wedge that

(1) The front flares were built first. Customizer Eddie Paul marked the fender for cutting. A chalk line was snapped against the fender to make the line.

(2) The fender was cut with a Rodac air chisel. The door was removed and the bottom of the fender unbolted to make the job easier.

(3) After the straight cut was made, the fender lip was cut so that the front of the wheelwell would be the same distance from the body as the rear of the fender.

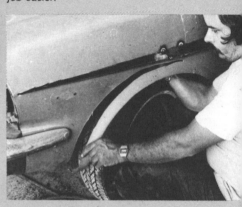

(4) Small pieces of metal and welding rod were used to properly space the fender from the body. Wedge-shaped pieces were used because the fender tapers toward the front of the car.

(5) Moistbestos was used during welding to minimize warpage. Even so, a lot of

hammer-and-dolly work was necessary to make the flare perfectly smooth.

was 4 inches wide at the end near the door. The wedge was tack-welded in place, with great care being taken to prevent warpage, and then, using lots of Moistbestos to keep the metal cool, skip-welded (like torquing a cylinder head) with a MIG welder. After the new piece

was welded to the fender, the welds were ground smooth with a Rodac air grinder, and any imperfections were filled with Ditzler body filler and then sanded and primed with Ditzler primer.

To make the inner fender cleaner, sheetmetal was formed to take

(6) The front spoiler was designed by making a template out of construction paper. The front valance was removed prior to making the spoiler.

(7) After the main shape was determined, the paper was cut to form an air scoop. Notice the notch left for the bumper bracket.

(8) The construction paper template was used to draw the pattern on 22-gauge sheetmetal.

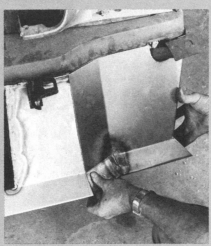

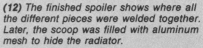

(11) Sheetmetal, 22-gauge, was used to blend the front fender flares with the spoiler. The welds are later ground and filled.

(12) The finished spoiler shows where all the different pieces were welded together. Later, the scoop was filled with aluminum mesh to hide the radiator.

(9) The center section of the spoiler is made from two identical patterns that were reversed. The scoop is for improved cooling.

(10) The outer portions of the spoiler were formed and welded in place after the center section was finished. The sharp creases were made with a metal brake.

BODY BUILDING

the place of the original fender. Eddie hand-formed this part, but a piece of an old fender could be used instead. To keep rocks from going through the flare and chipping the door, perforated aluminum was installed an inch from the back edge of the flare, after which, it was painted black.

The front flares were blended into a Trans Am-style front air dam, which Eddie hand-formed from 22-gauge sheetmetal after making a pattern out of construction paper. The spoiler was designed to retain the stock bumper, but the bumper must be removed during construction, leaving the bumper brackets in place for proper clearance. The front lower valance was no longer needed, so it was discarded.

Lots of measurements were taken when the spoiler was built so it wouldn't catch on every driveway encountered. Eddie determined that 10 inches from the top of the bumper still left ample clearance. The pattern was made in two sections, which were flopped to make the right and left pieces. The four separate spoiler sections were then welded together. To get the sharp creases, Eddie used a metal brake. The center of the spoiler was left open to duct air to the radiator and leave room for mounting driving lights. The air dam was skip-welded like the front flares. Low spots were worked up with a hammer and dolly; welds were ground smooth; and the spoiler was finished with body filler and lots of sanding.

The rear fender flares are quite unique because they were made out of Mustang quarter panels, picked up at our local Ford dealership. (Most dealers still carry many early sheetmetal parts.) The first step was enlarging the wheelwell opening to the size of the inner fenderwell. Then the new quarter panel was reduced in size so that the back edge would be 4 inches from the back of the original fender. A 4-inch section (see photos) was removed from the center of the fender above the wheelwell lip and from directly behind the well opening. Then, the two pieces were

welded back together. The top edge of the quarter panel was trimmed with a sabre saw so that the fender would be 4 inches out from the body. The front leading edge was trimmed further since it would be tapered to the body just behind the door. The area between the scoop and the top of the fender was slit to ease tapering.

Once the quarter panel was welded to the car, quite a bit of hammer-and-dolly work was required to make the top edge smooth and straight. A scoop was formed at the front of the fender following the stock Mustang styling lines. Metal had to be added to the bottom of the flare to blend it into the body. At the rear of the flare, reinforcement ribs were fashioned out of 22-gauge sheetmetal bent over ¼x½-inch bar stock. The ribs blend the rear of the flare to the car, as well as add strength. All the welds were ground smooth and the flare finished as before.

The new, wider fenders didn't look right with the stock taillights, so Eddie suggested a simple taillight swap that could easily be duplicated at home. The stockers were replaced with '67-'68 Camaro units with Rally Sport lenses. The standard Camaro lenses with the backup light included are easier to find and less expensive, but we prefer the better looking Rally Sport lenses.

Installing the Camaro lenses requires simply making the original opening wider and slightly bigger on the top and bottom. Mounting brackets must be made out of sheetmetal and tack-welded to the inside of the trunk. Eddie performed

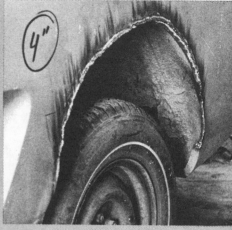

(13) The rear flares were started by enlarging the wheelwell openings. This is the time to be sure your new tires will fit the wheelwells.

(14) The rear flares were made by cutting up a pair of new rear quarter panels. Each panel was shortened 4 inches by cutting out the marked sections with a sabre saw.

(15) The fender was rewelded after the marked sections were removed. The front of the fender was slit, as shown, to allow the flare to be tapered into the body. The scoop area was also opened up.

(16) *The modified quarter panel was welded to the body, and then the scoop was formed. Extra metal was added to form the bottom of the scoop.*

(17) *Support ribs were made to fit into the opening at the back of the rear flare. The ribs were made out of 22-gauge sheetmetal and formed with a hammer over ¼x½-inch bar stock.*

(18) *The stock Mustang taillights were removed and replaced with '67-'68 Camaro units. The back panel was opened up with tin snips.*

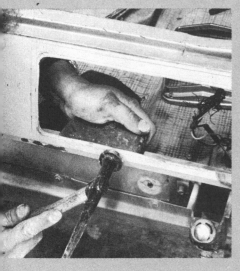

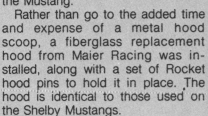

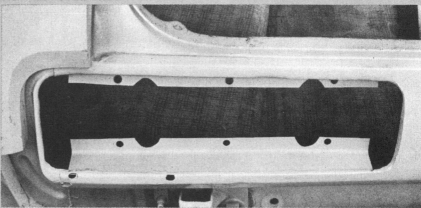

(19) *A new lip was made using a hammer and dolly. Make the new opening smaller than the taillights so that there is enough metal left to form the lip.*

(20) *Mounting brackets were made out of sheetmetal and tack-welded in place. The mounting holes are determined by the Camaro taillights.*

the swap quickly, and the Camaro lights look like they were made for the Mustang.

Rather than go to the added time and expense of a metal hood scoop, a fiberglass replacement hood from Maier Racing was installed, along with a set of Rocket hood pins to hold it in place. The hood is identical to those used on the Shelby Mustangs.

With all the welding finished, the body was gone over thoroughly with Rodac pneumatic grinders and sanders to make the surface ready for paint. The car was then covered with many coats of Ditzler primer and sanded between coats. The primer was allowed to set up for several weeks, but this step isn't absolutely necessary. However, if you have the time, it is a good idea as it takes care of any filler or primer shrinkage.

Even though the Mustang was still in primer, we couldn't stand to look at it with the skinny stock wheels and tires. Wide wheels and tires are definitely required for such

radical fender flares. We chose a dynamite combination of Uniroyal tires and Appliance mags. The tires are Uniroyal's handsome Laredo

(21) *The whole area was sanded and primed, and the Camaro taillights were installed and hooked up. They look like they were made for Mustangs.*

BODY BUILDING

R60 raised white letter tires, GR 60-15s up front and LR 60-15s in back. The wheels are Appliance's striking Diamags, which bear a strong resemblance to the very

painted black so that the thin orange and yellow stripes would really jump out. The entire paint job was then covered with Ditzler's Delclear for extra shine and protection.

The only body mods left to do were detail touches like the new bumpers and grille. (These parts also came from our local Ford dealership.) The grille is a '66, even though the car is a '65, because we prefer its horizontal bars. A cast script that says "Hotrod" was obtained from the Deuce Factory and

fastened to the grille. Driving lights from KC HiLites were installed in the front air scoop opening, and the stock mirrors were replaced with a pair of black racing mirrors from Vilem B. Haan. Haan also provided the flat black license plate frames.

The body looks great—a far cry from its previous deteriorated state. The interior is still barren, and the car barely runs. But those faults will be rectified before the renovation is through.   **HR**

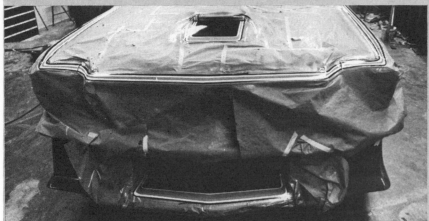

(22) The bodywork finished, the newly transformed Mustang was rolled outside the shop for some photos. The wheels and tires are a combination of Uniroyal Laredo R60 tires and Appliance Diamag wheels. At the time this photo was taken, the rear tires were GR 60-15s; they were later replaced with wider LR 60-15s.

(23) After the primer was allowed to set, the car was painted by Customs By Eddie Paul in El Segundo, California. The stock hood was replaced with a fiberglass, Shelby-style unit from Maier Racing Enterprises.

(24) The finished front end shows the new bumper, KC driving lights, '66 grille, "Hotrod" script, and Rocket hood pins.

popular Pontiac Trans Am wheels, and measure 15x7 up front and 15x8.5 in back. They feature Appliance's Roto-Lug system, which allows them to be used on different makes of cars. The wheels and tires really made the fender flares look right.

For a final color, we wanted something that would really stand out. We also wanted a factory color for ease of touching up any future scratches or nicks. One of the wildest reds around is Ditzler's Porsche Indian Red, which is what we chose. Eddie applied the acrylic enamel paint and the orange-and-yellow-over-black stripes. The area that received the stripes was first

RESTORE THAT DOOR

MAKE YOUR DOORS LOOK LIKE NEW

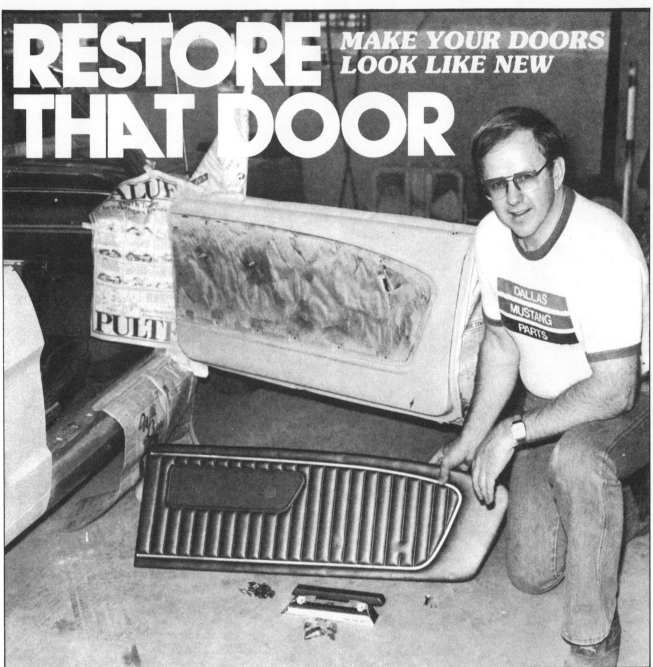

PHOTOGRAPHY: BOB McCLURG

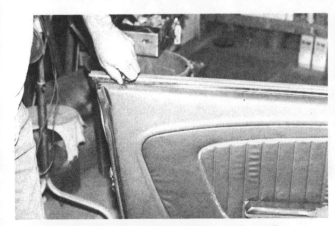

1 First, unscrew the door-lock knob and pry up the small grommet that goes around the knob.

2 Remove the armrest base by taking out the two Phillips head screws under the base on '65 and '66 Mustangs. On '67 and '68 models, use a ⅜-inch nut driver. Don't use a socket; it will get stuck in the armrest.

While not as prone to wear and tear as the seats, the interior door panels on Mustangs definitely take their share of abuse. When you restore one part of the car it looks great, but the rest looks worse than before by comparison. If you're taking the effort to replace the seat upholstery, it's a perfect time to install new door panels. While you're at it, you might as well go all the way and paint the metal parts of the door, another necessary step when changing the color of an interior.

To find out how to restore interior door panels, we went to Dallas Mustang Parts (9515 Skillman, Dallas, TX 75243, 800/527-1223 or 800/442-1047) where we watched Gene Hill restore the door panels on a '65 Mustang. The techniques shown are virtually the same for all '64½-'68 Mustangs. Dallas Mustang Parts offers exact reproduction door panels for under $100 a pair. The panels are die-cut with die-electric embossing and they come in the full Mustang color range.

The biggest difference between the model years is the method of attaching items such as armrests and door handles. Inspection should reveal the method of attachment, or you can consult a shop manual.

Follow along as Dallas Mustang Parts demonstrates how to restore that door. *M*

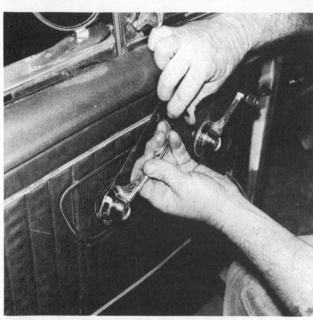

3 Remove the door and window handles. The '64½ and early-'65 models need a clip-retainer tool to release the little horseshoe-shaped clip. Other models just have a Phillips head screw on the handles.

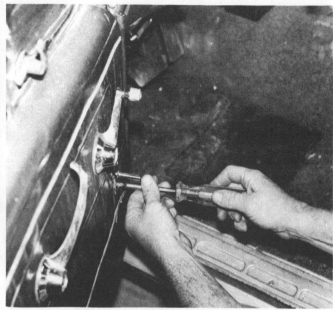

4 Our demonstration vehicle had the remote-control mirror. The base plate is simply unscrewed.

5 On '65 and '66 remote-control mirrors, you must remove the three control wires from the control unit. This step isn't necessary on '67s and '68s.

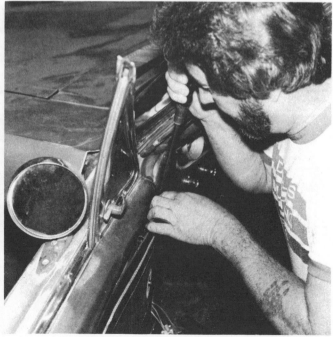

6 Use a large, flat-tipped screwdriver to gently pry loose the door panel. The panel is held in place with clips that are spring loaded.

7 *Notice the location of the door panel clips (arrows). Don't lose the two coil springs that fit around the door and window handles.*

8 *If the inner weatherstrip is to be replaced, remove it now by prying it loose with a flat-tip screwdriver.*

9 *Use a wire brush in an electric drill to remove the old paint from the door. Be careful around the chrome and rubber.*

10 *Take care when doing the top part of the door. You don't want to damage the outer part of it. A good idea is to cover the outer door edge with masking tape.*

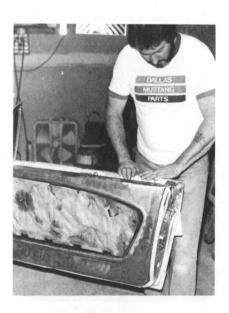

11 *Clean the weatherstripping with wax and grease remover or lacquer thinner so the masking tape will stick better, then mask off the door with newspaper and tape. Notice how the newspaper is inserted down by the glass and folded over the edge of the door. The vent window is completely wrapped and the doorjamb is well-protected.*

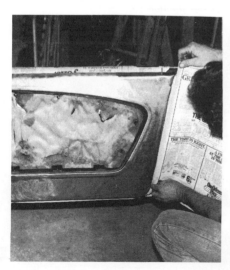

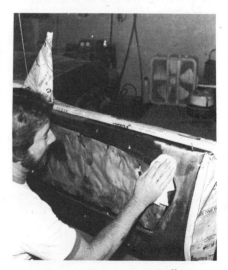

12 *When everything is masked off, wipe down the metal to be painted with wax and grease remover.*

13 *If you don't have access to a regular spray gun and compressor, you can use this self-contained aerosol sprayer made by Preval. The color of your choice goes in the glass container.*

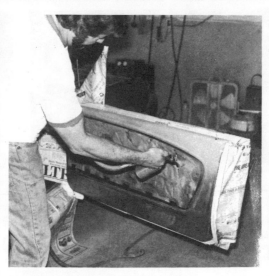

14 *First cover the door with primer. Let the primer dry thoroughly before applying the color coats.*

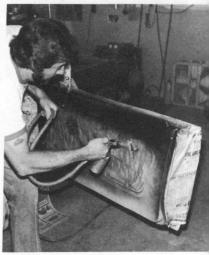

15 *If you have a touch-up gun and a compressor use it, or try the Preval spray bottle. The paint is a semi-gloss lacquer. Dallas Mustang Parts carries all the colors.*

19 *Punch two holes for the armrest-base screws.*

20 *Install the old door panel retaining clips, or new ones if necessary.*

21 *The door panel is now ready for installation. Start at the lower front corner and work across the bottom, pushing in one clip at a time.*

25 *The type of door handles with the clips just snap into place with a good push. The other style is screwed into place.*

26 *Install the new lock grommet. Be careful not to scratch the new paint.*

27 *The finished project looks like a b new door.*

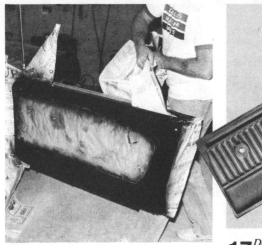

16 *After the paint is dry, carefully remove the paper and masking tape.*

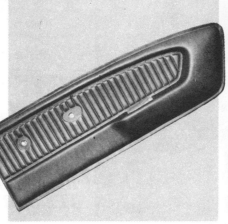

17 *Dallas Mustang Parts' optional door panels for cars equipped with the Pony-interior option.*

18 *Use an X-acto knife to cut out the openings for the door handle and window crank on the back side of the new upholstery panel. Cut the openings a little on the small side.*

22 *Replace the door handle and window-crank springs before securing the top clips on the door panel.*

23 *A new armrest pad and base should be assembled before being installed on the door.*

24 *Re-install the armrest.*

A Fender With Flare

INSTALLING STEEL FENDER FLARES

TEXT & PHOTOGRAPHY: CAM BENTY

One major complaint among Mustang owners is the lack of fenderwell clearance. Installing oversized tires and wheels presents some problems; the tires are unsightly hanging out of the wheelwells, and flying dirt and rocks can harm the exterior paint. Custom fender flares solve these problems, and they do it with style.

Though there are a number of ways to go, steel fender flares have to be the ultimate for their durability and good looks. Customs By Eddie Paul (124 Nevada St., El Segundo, CA 90245, 213/322-0451) deals daily with Mustang customizations, and steel fender flares are one of their specialties.

The techniques demonstrated in this article can be adapted to any steel-bodied car requiring virtually unlimited tire clearance. All materials used in the basic structure of the fender are steel, including the fenderwell lip and the fender panels, making the new fender stronger than the original. Durability and styling—a winning combination. 𝓜

(1) While steel fender flares are certainly desirable, they require a lot of time and effort to install correctly. These are the tools Eddie Paul uses for the installation of his custom flares. The arc welder and gas welder are certainly the most exotic tools used; however, they do make a sound and durable flare possible.

(2) The stock Mustang fenderwell is indeed small, especially on early-model Mustangs.

(3) Brian Hatano cuts the original fender away, leaving a full inch between the bottom of the cut and the point where the new fender will be attached. A zip gun makes cutting the sheetmetal a simple task.

(4) The freshly cut fenderwells leave plenty of room for the largest of tires and wheels.

(5) Using ½-inch cold-rolled steel for the outer lip of the custom fender, Brian bends it to the correct shape using the hammer and vise method.

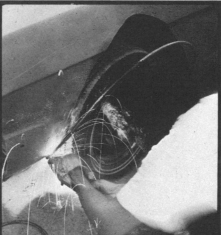

(6) The bar is then arc-welded to the front and rear points of the fender.

(7) The fender is marked with a grease pencil to ensure that the contours of the new fender are correct as it is assembled.

(8) A grinder is used to cut away the paint where the fender sections will attach to the car.

(9) Using 12-gauge sheet steel, Brian cuts out the fender sections two at a time to make sure both sides of the car have matching fender flares.

(10) A shrinking machine compacts the metal to form the bend of the fender without crimping the metal. Using a hammer and solid block of metal in a vise can accomplish the same thing, but it takes longer to come up with the same results.

(11) The panel is tack-welded to the body and then trimmed to the correct length with tin snips.

(12) The trimmed panel is positioned atop the fenderwell lip (bar) and tack-welded in position.

(13) After each piece of the fender has been tack-welded in place, a gas welder is used to finish-weld the panels together. Moist Bastos is used to absorb the heat from the gas welder which could distort the metal and hurt the flare's final appearance.

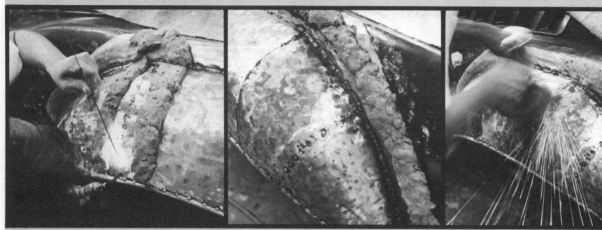

(14) When welding the panels, start at the lowest point and work up to improve the final appearance of the weld.

(15) An arc-welder is used at the point where the flare meets the body and where the individual panels attach to the fender lip. Again, the weld starts at the lowest point and moves up the fender. Notice the use of the Moist Bastos again.

(16) Once the welding is complete, the grinder is used to smooth out the rough welding spots.

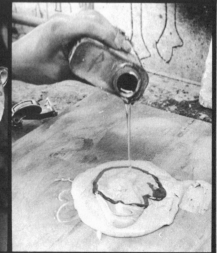

(17) The inside of the fender must be cleaned up to avoid cutting your new tires. The first step is to hammer the two sides as flat as possible.

(18) A piece of steel (similar to the steel used in the fender panels) is cut to cover the joint and tack-welded on top of the point where the two panels meet.

(19) Along with the normal mix of plastic body filler and hardener, fiberglass resin is added to help cut down on pinholes which form in dried body filler panels.

(20) Thin layers of body filler are laid on the fender in several coats. Ensure that each layer is fully dry before the next is applied. It is important to apply the filler along the flow of the fender and along the point where the fender meets the car, shaping the fender as you go. This is the final step in designing the custom flare.

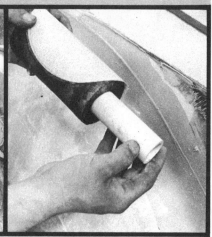

(21) Between each layer, a cheesegrater file is used to roughen the surface for the next coat to adhere to.

(22) Using 240-grit sandpaper, the fender is smoothed out.

(23) A 240-grit sandpaper disc is attached to a section of rubber tubing around a piece of plastic tubing, allowing the sanding disc to mold to the shape of the crease where the fender meets the car.

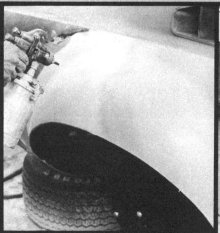

(24) The final paint procedure starts with a light coat of gray primer sanded smooth with 360-grit paper. This process is repeated with finer and finer-grit paper until a satisfactory finish is achieved. The fender is then painted the desired color.

(25) The final product; even N50-15s fit in this fenderwell!

CANDY COUPE

A custom-car painter without good examples of his handiwork could have trouble getting jobs, but that isn't a problem for Rob Taylor of Lemon Grove, California. Rob drives his calling card every day. Everywhere he goes, his beautiful '65 Mustang coupe is a testimonial to his great skill as a custom painter.

After making sure the body was flawless, Rob covered the vintage coupe with pearl white. The pearl white serves as an excellent base for the multihued candy graphics. He also handled all the detail work such as pinstriping.

PAINT TRICKS MAKE A STOCK BODY A MASTERPIECE

Rob's '72, 351 Cleveland engine received the complete hot rod treatment including Valley Head Service cylinder heads.

The black bucket seats came from a '69 Mach I Mustang. Rob installed a set of Sun gauges to monitor engine conditions.

The graphics on the side of the car give a feeling of motion that isn't just an illusion. The *real* source of motion is a 351-cubic-inch Cleveland engine. It was treated to the full course at the local speed emporium. TRW pistons are connected to Carillo rods and a forged crankshaft. A Schnider camshaft, Isky valve springs, Crane rocker arms, Manley valves, and chromemoly pushrods complete the valvetrain.

The cylinder heads were modified by Valley Head Service in Northridge, California. Accel provides the ignition and Heddman

headers expel the exhaust gases. An Edelbrock manifold sits underneath a Holley 850cfm carb. Just in case the fuel mixture isn't rich enough, there's a nitrous oxide system for high-speed sprints.

The competition look is further enhanced by Center Line wheels, rear slicks, and narrow front tires. A nine-inch Ford rearend absorbs all the power that's transmitted through a Toploader four-speed.

Rob Taylor's '65 Mustang is a perfect example of how far some well-executed paint tricks can go to make a stock-bodied car stand out in any crowd. *M*

Narrow, drag racing-style front tires on skinny Center Line wheels, and a nitrous oxide system on the healthy engine means the performance aspect is more than just looks.

The rearend is a nine-inch Ford unit that's loaded with 5.13 gears.

MUSTANG LETTERING ABCs

AN EASY GUIDE TO CUSTOM LETTERING

BY BRUCE CALDWELL

Making a Mustang distinctive can be accomplished in many different ways, but the easy way to do it is with custom lettering. Adding a car's nickname, engine size, or any other information is one inexpensive way to personalize a Pony.

The '70 Mustang fastback used in this article had a major problem: a dented trunk lid. A long crease ran right by the "M" in the Mustang trim letters. Rather than just replace the factory letter, we decided to fix the dent, remove the stock chrome letters, fill the mounting holes, and apply the Mustang logo in custom lettering.

Bob Cody of Cody Customs (206/847-2325) did the bodywork and custom painting, then Roy Dunn of Dunn Hi-Tech Signs (5426 35th Ave. S.W., Seattle, WA 98126, 206/938-5994) applied the chrome-style custom lettering

to the smooth trunk lid. Bob used several Ditzler products including DX-999 white body filler, Kondar primer surfacer (DZ-7), and Delstar acrylic enamel.

Previously, the supplies for custom lettering and pinstriping were difficult to find, but now the Eastwood Company (147 Pennsylvania Ave., P.O. Box 296, Malvern, PA 19355, 800/345-1178 or 215/644-4412) offers paints, brushes, and instruction books by mail order. Eastwood also stocks Sign Painters' 1-Shot enamel, the primary enamel used by Roy Dunn in all his work. Roy even uses the 1-Shot enamel in his airbrush when he's doing chrome-style lettering, but reduces it with turpentine first.

When using chrome lettering, the idea is to make it seem that the letters are reflecting the sky and ground. Roy's color sequence starts with a white base coat. Yellow is sprayed through the

center of the letters, then orange is applied to the same section. Blue is concentrated along the top part of the letters, then the final color, brown, is applied in a squiggly manner in the center. Highlights and twinkles are done in white using both the airbrush and a No. 00 pinstriping brush. Only two or three twinkles should be placed on a word the size of Mustang, but each receives a small white airbrushed burst which represents the sun shining on the chrome. These bursts should applied on the same side of the letters just as the sun shines from one direction.

Our lettering example was done on a blue car, so the chrome letters were outlined first with purple 1-Shot enamel, then Roy added a stylized outline in a darker shade of blue. The finished product is tasteful and in keeping with the overall look of the car. *M*

1 *The starting point is a '70 Mustang trunk lid with factory emblems. Note the substantial dent by the "M."*

2 Remove the factory chrome letters. Use an electric drill to make holes for the slide hammer.

3 Bob Cody uses a slide hammer to gradually pull out the dented trunk lid. Don't pull the sheetmetal out too far.

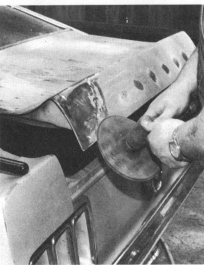

4 Grind away the paint around the damaged area with an air grinder. The body filler has to be applied over bare metal.

5 Use a wire brush in a drill on any low spots in the dented area to remove all traces of paint.

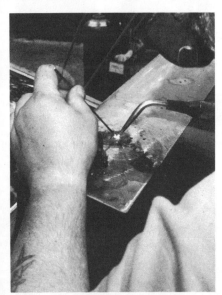

6 The holes from the slide hammer and the original letter mounting holes can be brazed as shown or filled with body filler.

7 When using a torch it is important to control heat buildup to prevent warpage, so Bob cools the weld with a wet rag.

LETTERING

8 *Use the grinder again to smooth the welded areas in preparation for the body filler.*

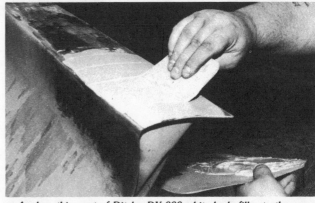

9 *Apply a thin coat of Ditzler DX-999 white body filler to the entire face of the trunk lid.*

11 *Prime and sand the trunk lid, checking for any low spots or areas needing additional work.*

12 *Use Ditzler Red-Cap spot putty (DFL-17) to fill the remaining imperfections. Sand the area to ready for the color coats.*

14 *Use lettering guides for reference, and look at the different styles to find the one that's most suitable.*

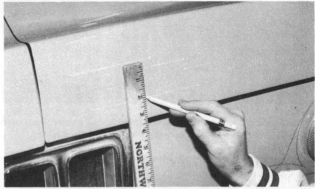

15 *Use a ruler and a white china marker to determine the letters' height and placement. Here the "M" will be 1½ inches tall, the other letters 1¼ inches.*

18 *Use the parallel guide lines and lettering stylebook, then sketch the letters with a No. 2 lead pencil on stencil paper.*

19 *When Roy is satisfied with the letters, he uses an X-acto knife to carefully cut out the stencil. Don't cut the paint underneath.*

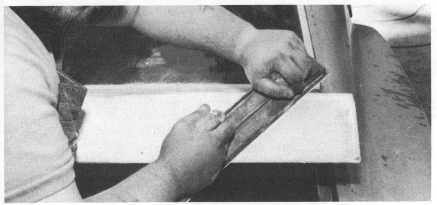

10 *After the filler dries, shape with a cheesegrater file, then sand smooth with a long sanding board until the surface is straight and without any waves.*

13 *Bob Cody used Ditzler's Delstar acrylic enamel in the factory Grabber Blue color. The smooth and straight trunk lid is ready for custom lettering.*

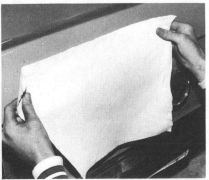

16 *Use Shurtape for a lettering stencil. The mask is adhesive-backed and must be put on wrinkle-free. Adhesive-backed shelf paper can also be used.*

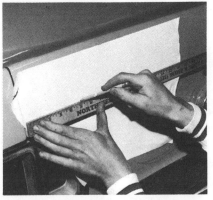

17 *Use a ruler and soft lead pencil to draw guide lines to lay out letters.*

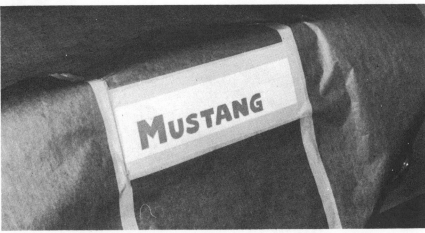

20 *Place masking paper around the stencil to protect the car from any overspray.*

LETTERING

21 *The lettering job can be done with Sign Painters' 1-Shot enamel. The Eastwood Company stocks the entire color range and sells the top-quality enamel by mail.*

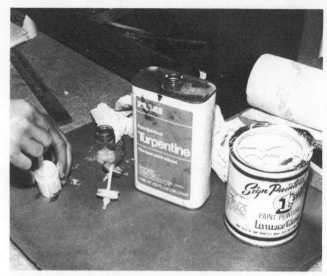

22 *Reduce the 1-Shot enamel with turpentine so it will flow through the airbrush. Use a Popsicle stick to mix the paint and turpentine.*

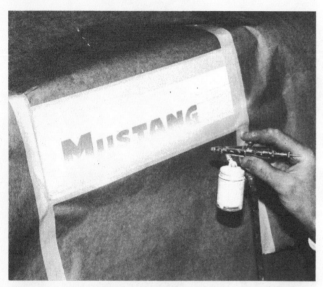

24 *Apply white paint first to act as the base coat, just heavy enough to cover without running.*

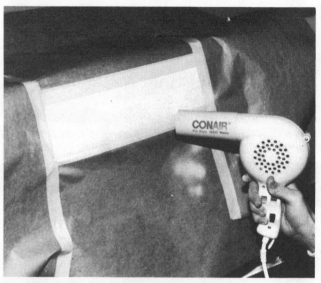

25 *Since enamel is rather slow drying, Roy uses a hair dryer to speed up the time between coats of paint.*

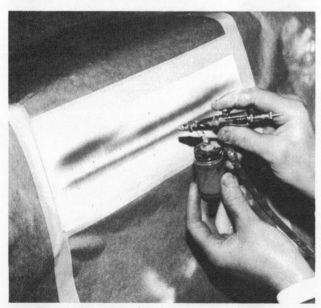

27 *Paint the upper part of the letters blue to represent a reflection of the sky.*

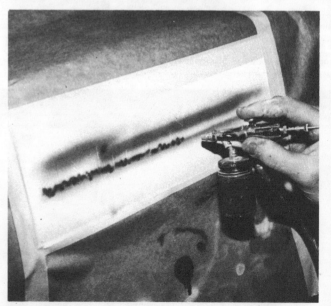

28 *Apply brown paint in the middle of letters in a squiggly manner to represent the ground's reflection.*

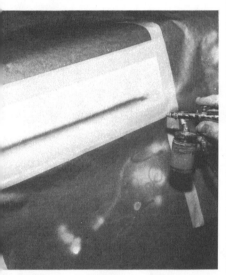

23 *An airbrush doesn't require much air, so Roy uses this portable compressor.*

26 *Fog on yellow paint first, mostly through the center of the letters. Then apply orange in the same general area.*

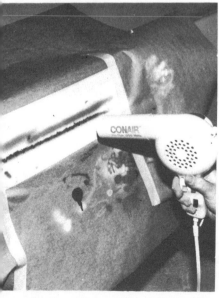

29 *Use the hair dryer to make sure paint is dry before removing the stencil.*

LETTERING

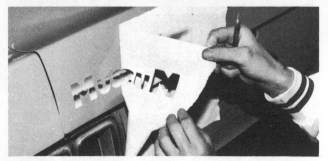

30 *Be careful when removing the stencil. Roy keeps an X-acto knife handy in case any of the paint starts to lift.*

31 *Outline the letters with purple enamel, using a lettering quill. Roy uses his two small fingers to support his hand.*

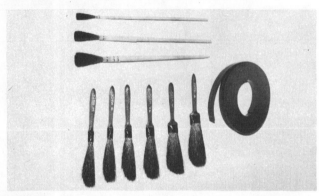

32 *The Eastwood Company stocks quality lettering quills and pinstriping brushes. The round item on the right is their magnetic guide line.*

33 *For a custom touch, apply a second outline with blue paint and the lettering quill.*

34 *Use a No. 00 pinstriping brush and white enamel to make three twinkles on the letters.*

35 *Use the airbrush with white paint to make a burst in the center of each twinkle.*

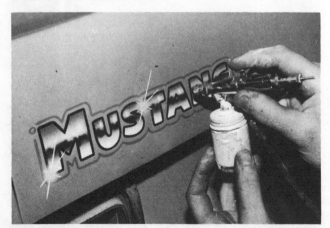

36 *Add a little white burst to each letter to represent the sun shining on the chrome.*

37 *The finished custom Mustang lettering as expertly painted by Roy Dunn.*

INSIDE JOB

MODIFYING YOUR MUSTANG INTERIOR FOR SUPER COMFORT AND LOOKS

By Bruce Caldwell

The funny thing about car interiors is that even though this is where owners spend most of their time, the average owner seldom pays much attention to it. Our Mustang project car is a first-class undertaking, so we wanted an interior to match. Besides, we'd had our fill of uncomfortable interiors. The stock interior restoration covered earlier in this book served as a good basis for our super interior, but we wanted more comfortable seats, better instrumentation, and a super sound system.

The biggest change to our Mustang's interior was the easiest to make. The stock seats (your very basic bucket seat) were removed and replaced with a pair of super-comfortable Recaro Ideal Seat LS models from Recaro USA, Inc. (1152 East Dominguez St., Carson, CA 90746). The original Mustang bucket seat is like a stone wheel compared to the Recaro LS, with its superior support and wide variety of adjustment features. You don't know just how enjoyable driving can be until you have driven in an orthopedically correct seat. When fatigue and discomfort are reduced, driving pleasure is dramatically increased.

Mounting the Recaro LS seats was a snap using Recaro's Mustang adapter brackets. The installation is a short and simple bolt-in operation. Recaro also sells extra upholstery material so that the back seat can match the front. We had our back seat recovered in their Jet pattern (black with brown, red, blue, and green stripes). The finished look is as handsome as the seats are comfortable. Custom séats aren't cheap, but they are one of the best investments you can make because you will get more use and enjoyment from good seats than any other automotive accessory.

To add safety to our Recaro LS seats, we installed a set of Deist competition lap belts and shoulder harnesses. The lap belts are 3 inches wide and the shoulder harnesses 2 inches wide. Normally, shoulder harnesses should be anchored at a point roughly even with

(1) The first step in mounting Recaro LS seats is to bolt on the Mustang adapter frame, which in turn bolts to the floor through the stock mounting holes.

(2) After the brackets were mated to the seat, it was just a matter of four bolts to secure the seats to the car. There are three different types of Recaro head restraints, but we chose the net model because of the superior visibility it provides.

INSIDE JOB

the shoulder height, like to a rollbar or the body of the vehicle. We were able to attach the shoulder harnesses to the floor only because the Recaro seats use a steel back support strong enough to take the type of load that could result from a head-on collision. Shoulder harnesses shouldn't be mounted to the floor when using weak seats because the seat backs could break down, causing the driver to be thrown forward and possibly suffer spinal compression. The people at Deist Safety Equipment are very concerned about your safety and are always glad to answer any safety questions.

Besides the seats, something that you use all the time you drive is the steering wheel. We wanted a comfortable one that looked great, so we installed a Hi-Fi black leather steering wheel from Vilem B. Haan. The Haan wheel is 14 inches in diameter and has four flat black spokes. Haan also supplied the fitted Coco Fiber floor mats to protect our new carpet.

Since our revamped interior was now as comfortable as a fine home, it seemed only fitting to install a sensational sound system. We chose a Motorola system, consisting of an in-dash cassette AM/FM stereo (No. TC894AX), Pow-R-Booster graphic equalizer booster, two D69-29T 6x9-inch three-way speakers, and two D5-20C 5¼-inch speakers. The stereo has a 24-watt power output which, combined with the 40-watt capability of the booster, yields a sound system that will put most home units to shame.

To keep track of all vital engine functions, we installed a dual warning system made up of Auto Meter gauges and Longacre Automotive Racing Products Gagelites. The Longacre Gagelite warning lights are mounted in a pod on the steering column. They signal any trouble, which is then double-checked on the Auto Meter gauges, mounted in flat black individual cups.

(3) The rear seat was recovered in Recaro Jet fabric to match the LS seats. The pattern is a natural with the Mustang rear seat design.

(4) Deist Safety Equipment Company 3-inch lap belts and 2-inch shoulder harnesses were installed for maximum safety.

(5) A super sound system from Motorola makes the Mustang sound like a concert hall. The compact in-dash cassette AM/FM stereo (left) puts out 24 watts, and the Motorola Pow-R-Booster (right) graphic equalizer emits an additional 40 watts. Four speakers are used to spread the sound around.

(6) In order to keep track of all vital engine functions, a complete array of Auto Meter competition series gauges was installed.

The finished interior is one of the trickest parts of the car—as exotic as any sports car's—yet the work was simple enough to do at home. It gets plenty of attention from onlookers and wins rave reviews from passengers. **HR**

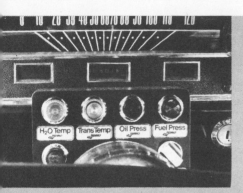

(7) For extra security, a set of Longacre Gagelites was mounted in a pod on the steering column, directly in front of the driver. The knob on the right is a test switch, to avoid the possibility of a burnt-out bulb.

(8) The steering wheel is a very handsome and comfortable Vilem B. Haan Hi-Fi wheel.

(9) The finished interior is as wild as the cockpit of any exotic sports car. Besides their many comfort adjustments, Recaro LS seats also recline. The shifter is a B&M StarShifter, and the floor mats are Vilem B. Haan Coco mats.

CLEANING HOUSE

HOW TO DETAIL A MUSTANG ENGINE COMPARTMENT

By Bruce Caldwell

A lot of care went into ensuring that our dyno-proven 289 engine looked as good as it ran. A beautifully detailed engine is a focal point of any sharp street machine, but the engine alone won't do it. The engine compartment must also be clean and sanitary. Detailing an engine compartment isn't one of the most enjoyable parts of building a car, but the results can make it one of the most rewarding.

Our project Mustang's engine compartment obviously hadn't been cleaned since the day the car rolled off the assembly line. A stop at a high-pressure car wash, along with several cans of spray degreaser, erased some of the grit—but there was still plenty left.

Two things made the engine compartment detailing and the actual engine installation relatively easy: lots of friends and an assortment of Rodac air tools. Gary Harris, Dennis Orlowski, Eddie Paul, and Craig Caldwell made up our pseudo-Woods Brothers pit crew. The Rodac pneumatic tools used included a No. 0606 ½-inch impact wrench, No. 501 air ratchet, No. 0265 right angle grinder, No. 130 die grinder, No. 0310 reciprocating saw, No. 0275 air hammer, No. 203 reversible drill, No. 0633 flutter throttle impact wrench, and No. 0992 spray gun.

Using the impact wrenches and air ratchets, along with an Eagle Specialty Products portable crane (No. 3001980), we had the old engine out in less than an hour. A

(1) A lot of soap, degreaser, and muscle power went into cleaning the engine compartment. The new grille, bumper, and headlight buckets were picked up at our local Ford dealership. The "Hotrod" script on the grille is from the Deuce Factory.

(2) A really sharp engine compartment requires a lot of grinding and sanding, which can be very tedious if done by hand. Luckily, we had a Rodac pneumatic die grinder, right angle grinder/sander, and an orbital sander at our disposal.

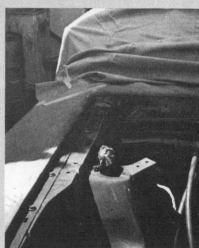

(3) After all the grinding and sanding, the entire engine compartment was wiped down with Ditzler wax and grease remover.

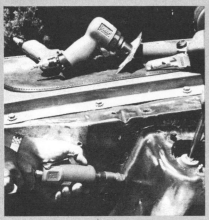

(4) The die grinder is particularly helpful when smoothing rough crevices and along seam areas.

(5) Eddie Paul painted the engine compartment the same shade of red as the body, using a Rodac No. 0992 spray gun. A coat of clear was sprayed over the red to protect the engine compartment and make it easier to keep clean. The stock heater hoses were replaced with braided stainless lines from Earl's Supply.

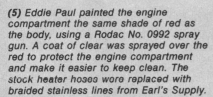

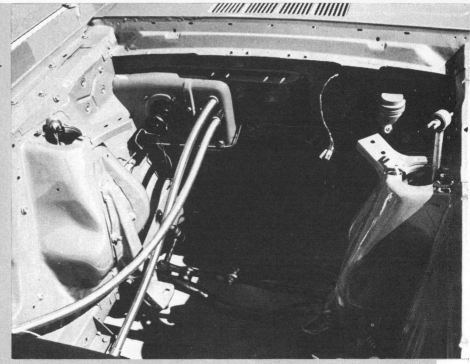

(6) The freshly painted engine compartment. The suspension pieces, heater, and radiator were painted black for contrast. All the fluid lines are braided stainless steel units.

(7) An Eagle Specialty Products portable crane was used to lower the super dyno-proven 289 engine into the sparkling engine compartment.

CLEANING HOUSE

few exhaust parts were rusted solid, but the air hammer and reciprocating saw quickly took care of the problem. The grinders made all the tedious work in the engine compartment (cleaning and smoothing everything in preparation for paint) easy. If you've never had the pleasure of using air tools, you don't know how much unnecessary effort you expend without them and how much time you can save with their help. Modern technology and competition in the marketplace have made air tools easily affordable for the average guy—they are no longer the coveted time-savers of professional mechanics.

After all the grinding, sanding, and priming was done, Eddie Paul painted the engine compartment the same color as the body, Ditzler's Porsche Indian Red. He then covered the color coats with Ditzler Delclear acrylic urethane for added protection.

After the paint was thoroughly dry, the Eagle crane again was called into action, this time to install the new engine. New motor mounts were obtained at the local Ford dealership, and the engine was bolted in place. Here, again, the Rodac pneumatic tools made quick work of the reconnecting chores. All the loose wires were neatly wrapped with Rocket plastic tie wraps, and a Maserati electric air horn from Vilem B. Haan was mounted on the inner fenderwell. Also mounted in the engine compartment was a vital piece of equipment: the motion detector for our Beverly Hills Motoring Accessories SP 777 alarm system. The SP 777 uses sensors for the doors, trunk, and hood, in addition to the motion detector. A hidden transmitter alerts the vehicle owner of any trouble via a Page Alert pocket beeper. For those times when we're out of the beeper's range, we installed the optional siren.

The finished engine compartment of our '65 Mustang fastback project car is now the type that car enthusiasts love so much. It's neat, clean, and super detailed with just the right contrast of paint and polish to highlight a great motor. **HR**

(8) A Beverly Hills Motoring Accessories SP 777 alarm system was installed in the engine compartment. The alarm system utilizes a remote beeper.

(9) The mounting holes for the alarm system and the Vilem B. Haan Maserati air horn were made with a Rodac air drill.

(10) The engine compartment in its final state—all new and ready to run. The entire electrical system—including alternator, distributor, solenoid, voltage regulator, and wires—was refurbished with Accel parts. The air cleaner, fan, and valve cover wing nuts are all blue Chromatized pieces made by Rocket. The engine compartment is really something to see—something that black and white pictures just can not do justice to.

DETAILS, DETAILS...

By Bruce Caldwell

ATTENDING TO LOOSE ENDS BEFORE LETTING IT LOOSE

Project cars never seem completely finished. Some little item always needs additional work. This is especially true when you start with a wrecking-yard reject like we did with our '65 Mustang fastback project car. You never realize how many different components make up an average car until you attempt to replace or rebuild them all. Even though the bodywork, paint, interior, and engine work were completed on our Mustang, there was still a myriad of little details to take care of before the car hit the road.

The first item of business was the exhaust system. The engine sounded great with open headers, but that can get old quickly, especially if you don't enjoy being stopped constantly for equipment violations. In keeping with the performance aspect of our Mustang, we decided to install a high-performance exhaust system from Longacre Automotive Racing Products (15846 Arminta St., Van Nuys, CA 91406). Rather than reduce the exhaust system from 3-inch collectors to 2-inch exhaust tubing, the Longacre system uses 3-inch tubing throughout the system. This makes for a very unrestrictive exhaust system that will take full advantage of the car's headers. Longacre Powertone mufflers are used with the system; they come in different lengths, with the longer ones providing more noise dissipation.

We used a pair of the 36-inch-long Powertone mufflers. The system comes with 3-inch-diameter collectors that bolt up to the headers. The entire system is designed for bolt-on installation. And everything comes off quickly for dragstrip action, although many people find that their cars are just as quick with the Powertone mufflers as without them. This is because the system acts as a collector extension, and most street cars gain bottom end performance through the use of longer collector extensions.

With the exhaust system installed, we started driving the Mustang to shake loose any construction gremlins. After being satisfied that every-

thing was functional, we decided to go to Orange County International Raceway for some performance testing. Before heading for the track we installed one more accessory: a Moroso No. 5115 mechanical tachometer. The Moroso tach has a 4-inch face, telltale needle, and ranges up to 9000 rpm in 100-rpm increments. We mounted the tach in a Moroso No. 5015 gold bracket and connected the tach to our Accel BEI distributor with a 72-inch tach drive cable.

Our first trip to the track resulted in some rather disappointing times. After the first pass, it was obvious the car still had a lot of little bugs to fix. The car ran 15.39 @ 88 mph. We had traction problems, and the car all but stopped before it got to the finish line. It seemed to be running out of fuel.

(1) The exhaust system is a bolt-on, high-performance system from Longacre Automotive Racing Products. The system uses 3-inch-diameter tubing throughout and 36-inch-long Powertone mufflers. The tailpipes are available in a variety of styles and lengths.

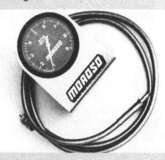

(2) Our Accel distributor is a tach drive model, so we installed a Moroso mechanical drive tach. The big 4-inch-diameter dial is easy to read. The Moroso tach has a telltale needle to record the highest rpm attained on a run at the track.

DETAILS, DETAILS..

We returned to the pits and tried to fix things with the limited equipment on hand. We had a pair of 29-inch-tall slicks that were 10 inches wide. They were too tall for our wheelwells. Next, we tried a pair of 27.5-inch-tall slicks that we borrowed from Tarkus Engineering. Unfortunately, they were too wide, but like Goldilocks and the Three Bears, we had one more set of tires that was just right: a pair of G60-15 M&H Racemaster Street & Strip tires. The M&H tires were mounted on a set of Inglewood steel spoke wheels and easily fit inside our wheelwells.

Steve Banas and Chuck Cox of Tarkus Engineering also loaned us an electric fuel pump that they used for transferring gas from one vehicle to another. Our trackside installation was rather crude, but it worked. Traction was improved and so was our fuel supply, but the car was still having top-end problems. Even so, the time dropped to 15.07 @ 89 mph.

When we returned home, we set out to rectify some of the problems encountered at the strip. A Holley Max-Pressure electric fuel pump (No. 12-802) along with a Holley Max-Pressure regulator (No. 12-803) were installed. The regulator lets us boost the fuel pressure at the track and lower it for street use.

Our carburetor was blueprinted by Edelbrock's Bob Fleckenstein. Bob checked all the passages and carburetor linkage and set the float levels and timing for an initial lead of 18 degrees and a total lead of 36 degrees.

We originally had installed a B&M Holeshot converter, which has a stall speed of about 1800 rpm. Our engine doesn't really start working until almost 3000 rpm, so there was a gap between where the engine and transmission worked best. To remedy this, we went back to B&M for one of their Super Holeshot converters (No. 50432), which put the stall speed right at the 3000-rpm level. The Super Holeshot is still entirely streetable, and it really helped bring our entire drivetrain together as a well-balanced unit.

To fix the octane where we wanted it, we added a can of Performance Lab Octane Booster to our pump gas. When we got to the track we took off the street tires and mounted a set of M&H racing slicks. This time we got the right size tires for the car: 8/26-15s. This may seem rather small for slicks, but they are just great for a street car like ours. They have plenty of traction, easily fit inside our wheelwells, and have the additional advantage of actually lowering the rearend gear ratio. Chuck Cox of Tarkus Engineering did some quick math and figured that

Steve Banas and Chuck Cox loaned us some parts and gave us some technical advice as we tried to dial-in the Mustang at Orange County International Raceway.

We used a variety of tires at the dragstrip including a set of G60-15 M&H Street & Strip tires and a set of 8/26-15 M&H racing slicks.

We had fuel delivery problems, but not after we installed a Holley Max-Pressure electric fuel pump and regulator.

A B&M Super Holeshot converter was installed to make the car leave the starting line harder and better match the transmission to the engine.

the shorter tires effectively dropped our gear ratio from 4.11 to 4.30. We mounted the M&H slicks on a set of rare Motor Wheel Fly wheels.

The weather conditions were unbearable at the track (we were in the midst of a heat and smog wave that was reportedly the worst in 25 years), but the car ran well anyway. Traction, shifting, and fuel delivery were all greatly improved, yielding a best time of 14.08 @ 97 mph. With better weather, more driving practice, and additional fine tuning, our Mustang could dip into the 13s at about 100 miles per hour—which isn't too shabby for a car that wasn't built to be a drag racer.

It took 11 months from the time we started the Mustang Magic project series to the time it was finished. And a great deal of time and effort was put forth by many people. There were moments when we thought the car would never get finished, but it finally made it. The finished car is a real head-turner, attracting lots of attention wherever it goes. It is super comfortable, handles great, and runs strong. Should you decide to build your own Mustang project car we think you will be pleased with the results. The early Mustangs were definitely one of Ford's best ideas, and *modified* ones are even better! **HR**

We had no trouble doing a smokey burnout before a quick run down the ¼-mile. Note that the tire smoke is coming out of the vents in the fender flares.

Bob Fleckenstein of Edelbrock blueprinted our carburetor and checked out the entire car on the Clayton dyno.

Both car and driver need protection from the elements. The car is covered by a Vilem B. Haan car cover, and the driver wears a blue Mustang jacket by Style Auto.

RESTORING AN INTEF

By Bruce Caldwell

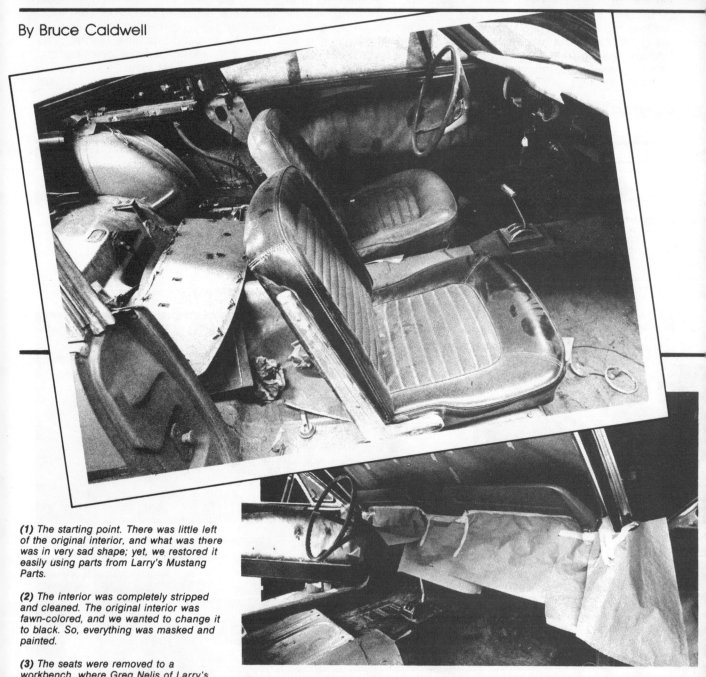

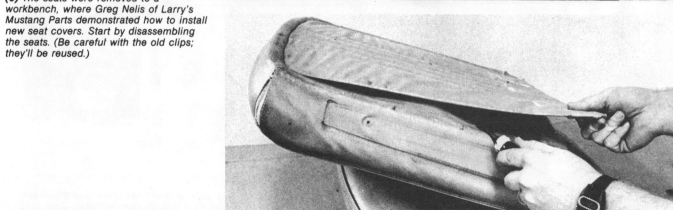

(1) The starting point. There was little left of the original interior, and what was there was in very sad shape; yet, we restored it easily using parts from Larry's Mustang Parts.

(2) The interior was completely stripped and cleaned. The original interior was fawn-colored, and we wanted to change it to black. So, everything was masked and painted.

(3) The seats were removed to a workbench, where Greg Nelis of Larry's Mustang Parts demonstrated how to install new seat covers. Start by disassembling the seats. (Be careful with the old clips; they'll be reused.)

A car with a ravaged interior can be more frightening, from a work standpoint, than a vehicle with wavy sheetmetal or a sputtering powerplant. Damaged body panels can be replaced or repaired, and rebuilding a tired engine is accepted practice; but renewing a battered interior is more than most people care to consider.

In many cases, a person would be wise to avoid a car with a trashed interior because revitalizing can be both difficult and costly. Luckily, such is not the case with early Mustang interiors. A tremendous selection of new, replacement, and very accurate reproduction parts is readily available, enabling the enthusiast to bring even the worst interiors back to like-new condition. And, the nice thing about Mustang interior kits is that the sewing has already been done for you. Outside of making patterns and sewing, interior work is mostly a matter of replacing old parts.

When we acquired our '65 Mustang fastback, the interior was (to put it mildly) the absolute pits. The seats were ripped, filthy, and mismatched, as were the door panels. The carpeting was a mildewed pile in the trunk; the headliner was ripped and sagging; the rear glass and side vents were out of the car; and all the little interior trim pieces and molding panels were dumped in a big box. The back seat, sun visors, door handles, glove box door, instrument panel, and interior lights were all out of the car.

That *we* were able to restore such a wasted interior means that almost anyone can do the same to any other Mustang. What made our interior renovation easy was a copy of the *Larry's Mustang Parts* catalog. This large volume contains everything necessary to restore a Mustang interior (as well as the rest of your Mustang). Larry's Mustang Parts (511 South Raymond Ave., Fullerton, CA 92631, 800/854-0393 or 714/992-4781) is a one-stop source for everything to do with Mustangs from '65 to '73.

So, let's get down to business. Follow along as we show you how to restore a Mustang interior. **HR**

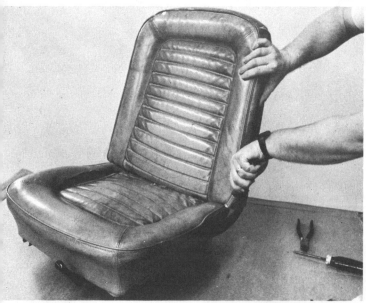

(4) *Separate the backrest from the seat cushion by removing the retainer clip and then, with a screwdriver, forcing the bracket over the pivot post.*

(5) *After the seat halves have been separated, remove the seat adjustment brackets and springs. Note how they go together so you can put them back correctly.*

(6) *After the seat track has been removed, use a pair of side cutters to cut all the hog rings on the bottom of the cushion. (The hog rings are what holds the seat cover to the seat.)*

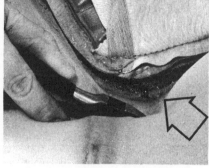

(7) Then, slowly peel the seat cover up over the metal frame and the seat foam.

(8) Another set of hog rings is now exposed in the recessed area (arrow) known as the "horseshoe." Cut these, and the cover will come off.

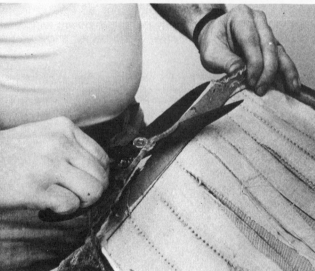

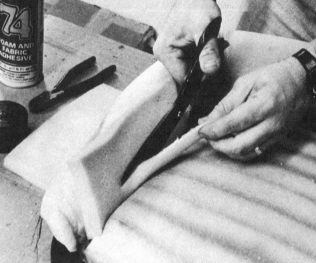

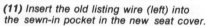

(9) Inside the horseshoe there is a metal wire known as a "listing." It will be reused, so cut it out of the old cover with a scissors.

(10) Parts of the seat cushion will probably be worn out. These can be built up (above) with new 1-inch foam. The foam needs to be cut only to the approximate size because the new seat cover will compress it into shape. Use 3M No. 74 foam and fabric adhesive to secure the foam.

(11) Insert the old listing wire (left) into the sewn-in pocket in the new seat cover.

(12) Use a hog ring pliers to fasten the new cover to the wire that is under the foam in the horseshoe area. Start at the front center of the listing and work around the sides to the back of the cusion.

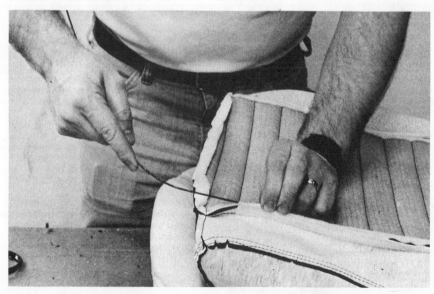

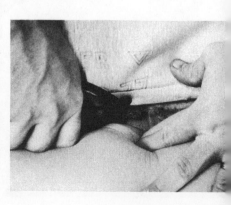

(13) With the center horseshoe secured, stretch the cover over the rest of the seat. Take care not to rip the cover.

(14) Use your hands to smooth any wrinkles. Build up any low spots with foam before fastening the cover to the bottom of the seat.

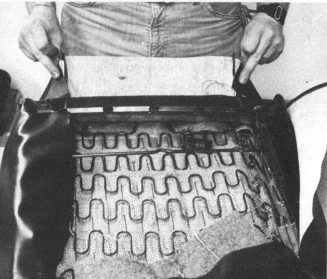

(15) When you are satisfied with the shape of the cushion, fold the cover over the bottom of the seat (left). Pull it tight, and install the hog rings. Trim any excess material with scissors.

(16) The seat back is renewed by first disassembling the old seat back (above). Save the board, as it will be reused.

(17) Lay the backing board on the new material. Line up the seams in the material with the lines on the backing board.

(18) Trim the excess material, and fold it over on the backing board. Staple the fabric to the board using very short (3/16-inch) staples (below left).

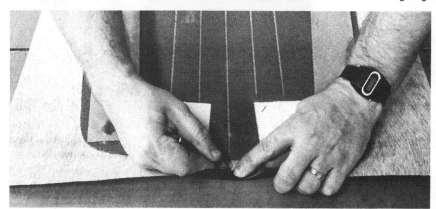

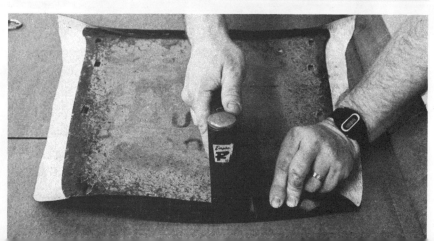

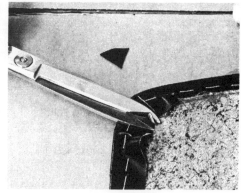

(19) Use scissors to trim the puckers out of the corners so that the back panel will lay flat against the seat.

RESTORING AN INTERIOR

(20) Put the seat back together, and you will have a seat that looks like it just came from the Ford factory.

(21) The techniques for the back seat are the same as for the front. There are hidden hog rings that hold the center hump to the seat frame.

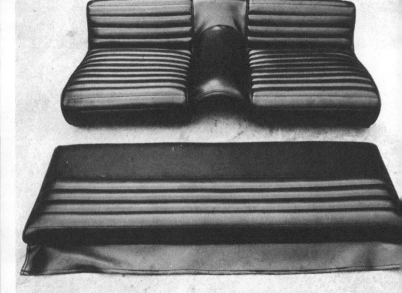

(22) The seat back is removed from the carpeted fold-down plate for the recovering operation.

(23) The recovered rear seat cushions.

(24) The back of the folding seat is recovered with new carpeting, also from Larry's Mustang Parts, that's been trimmed to size and then glued in place.

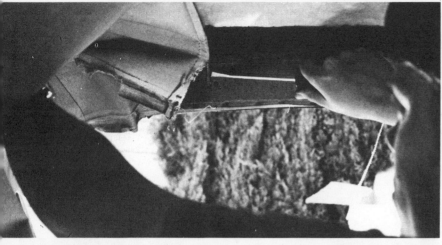

(25) Remove the old headliner by pulling back the glued edges and then removing the top bows with a screwdriver.

(26) The headliner bows are inserted into the new headliner's sewn-in pockets. The whole assembly is then snapped back into the roof.

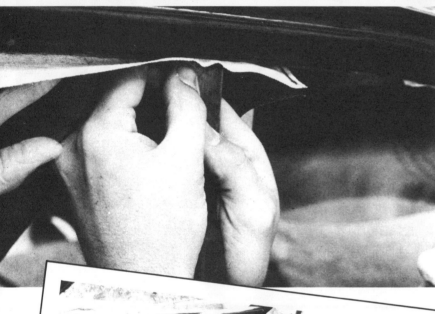

(27) The new headliner must be pulled tight and worked into the channel that runs around the top of the windows; a putty knife works well for tucking in the material (left). Trim the excess with a razor blade.

(28) The headliner edges are held in place with glue and new flexible trim welting (above), which is also available from Larry's.

(29) Besides the seats and headliner, we installed new preformed carpeting, sun visors, armrests, and door panels, all from Larry's Mustang Parts. The finished interior looks great—a far cry from its former state.

SUMMER

MUSTANG SHAPE-UP FOR HOT WEATHER FUN

BY BRUCE CALDWELL

Mustangs are special cars and deserve to be treated as such. A well-kept, super-clean Mustang is the kind of car everyone admires. A dirty, neglected one, however, is a disgrace to the "breed." So if you own a Mustang, keep it sharp, or sell it and get a four-door '61 Comet.

Here are some tips to make car care easier and more enjoyable. If the job is fun and easy, you'll do it often. Frequency is the key to proper car care.

Car care is something that should be performed all year long, but spring and summer seem to be an automotive rebirth time; they naturally make you want to clean up the old pony, get out on the roads, and enjoy your Mustang. If you've been a little lax in the upkeep department, take this opportunity to re-affirm your vows to care for your car.
· If car care turns you off no matter how guilty you feel, look at the subject from a dollars perspective. Mustangs are appreciating in value. Even poor-condition, early models are going

up in price, but the real moneymakers are the beautifully maintained examples. Everyone is looking for a cherry Mustang. While you may have no immediate intentions to sell your car, it's probable you eventually will. By taking good care of it, you're protecting your investment, as well as getting a better-running and better-looking car in the meantime. Considering the very low cost of proper car care, it's one of the best automotive investments around.

MAKE CAR CARE EASY

The secret to making Mustang car care easy and enjoyable is to do it regularly so no one task is insurmountable. If you're already wallowing in car-care red ink, it will take some extra effort. But once your Mustang is in shape, regular maintenance is the easy way to keep everything in top condition.

Develop a schedule that spreads out the tasks. This way you won't be overwhelmed every time you let your car slip too far. A short task that shows

quick results is satisfying and encourages you to repeat it. A well-maintained car is more fun to drive, safer, and the envy of other motorists. All this positive reinforcement makes taking care of your car even easier.

Summer and fall are two obvious times to do more car care tasks: right before the good weather and right before the winter weather season. Doing extra work at these times makes sense because of the changes in your driving needs. It's also a good time for seasonal tasks such as installing fresh antifreeze/coolant, removing or adding winter driving tires, and changing the contents of your tool kit to reflect seasonal needs.

Most owner manuals and factory-shop manuals have maintenance schedules based on time and mileage. These charts are a good starting point for designing your own optimal maintenance schedule. Remember, a collector's Mustang that isn't driven very much doesn't mean it doesn't need regular service.

CAR CARE

1 *The first thing you should attend to when you work on your Mustang is saftey. Sturdy jack stands are a must for safely supporting a car; use a floor or hydraulic jack.*

2 *Use a lot of water when washing your Mustang. Always wash and rinse from the top of the car to the bottom.*

3 *The wheelwells can accumulate a lot of dirt and debris. A pressure washer does an excellent job of cleaning these areas; this is especially important if you drive your car during the winter on salted roads.*

4 *Wash in the shade and dry the car as soon as possible; soft old towels work well for this. Sun and water spots can damage your Mustang's finish.*

KNOW YOUR LIMITS

The best way to make car care fun and easy is to realize your limitations. Know what jobs you can easily and safely perform and which jobs are best left to the professionals. You are your own best judge of skill, but don't jump into a task you feel uncomfortable about. If doing your own tune-ups frightens you, take a night class in auto mechanics. If touching up the paint on your Mustang puts you off, try your luck on an old car, or even an old damaged fender or similar part.

The type of early-model Mustangs owned by enthusiasts has a big advantage over newer cars. Older Mustangs are relatively simple machines that can still be worked on at home. Mustangs don't need all the modern equipment required for new cars with their sealed carburetors and mysterious "black box" engineering.

Areas that involve safety, such as the suspension parts, should be left to professionals or very competent

do-it-yourselfers. Many tasks such as front end alignment are impractical to do at home because of the specialized equipment required.

Many cities have diagnostic centers where for a modest fee you can have your Mustang checked out. Many of these firms will give you an estimate of repair costs. This information can be useful in deciding which tasks to do yourself and which ones to leave to professionals. The diagnosis will also help you avoid being overcharged for work that isn't necessary.

As you perform more and more car-care tasks, your confidence will increase and so will the amount of money you'll save by doing your own work. Start out easy, and gradually increase the jobs you do yourself. Trying to do too much when you're not ready is a sure way to get discouraged from ever working on your own car.

SAFETY FIRST

While maintaining your Mustang doesn't rate as one of the world's most

dangerous jobs, certain precautions should be observed. Cars are very heavy objects, so any time you must elevate one, make sure it will stay put until you're out from underneath it. The factory bumper jack will work, but it's best left for roadside emergencies. A hydraulic floor jack is the best choice for elevating a car, but if you can't afford one, buy a quality, standard hydraulic jack. Buy a jack that's rated at more pounds than you plan to lift; the larger jacks have more lift and larger, more stable bases.

Never rely on just the jack to keep a car up in the air; always use some type of safety stand as well. Jack stands should be placed under a flat part of the subframe. Wiggle the car to test the stability before you remove a wheel or crawl under the car. Remember to set the emergency brake, put the transmission in park or first gear, and block the wheels that are still on the ground. Pick a flat surface to work on your Mustang.

Be especially cautious when doing

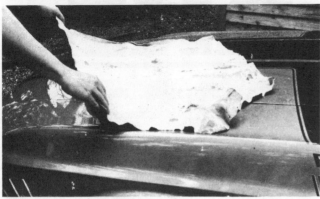

5 *Some enthusiasts prefer a chamois for drying, but that's best for well-waxed cars. Pull the chamois toward you to draw the water off the car.*

6 *There are special, long-bristle brushes that are ideal for cleaning tires and wheels.*

9 *After your tires are thoroughly cleaned, protect them with a liberal application of vinyl-and-rubber protectant.*

10 *Cleaning neglected aluminum wheels can be a tiring and messy job, so it pays to take good care of your custom wheels.*

any adjustments to a running engine. Know where the moving parts are and allow yourself plenty of room around them; don't wear loose clothes that could get caught.

Safety glasses or goggles are always a good idea. They can keep dirt and foreign particles out of your eyes when working under the car or using any chemical substances.

It's a good idea to have a fully charged fire extinguisher handy, especially when working on any part of the fuel system. Watch out for sparks around gasoline and don't allow greasy rags to accumulate.

Common sense is the most important part of safety. Think twice before trying any new task, and always follow instructions and manufacturer's warning labels.

KEEP RECORDS

It's a good idea to keep all receipts associated with car care. A log book noting when each task was performed is a way to know when additional work is needed. Records are also good for tax purposes if you use your car for work. It can help get top dollar when you sell your Mustang. Having all

service records and receipts available is a very impressive selling point.

Future repairs can be anticipated by watching your records. You can take preventative measures before you find yourself stuck on the side of the road. Records can also help pinpoint a problem area. If the car isn't running right but you've just rebuilt the carburetor, you can start your troubleshooting elsewhere.

On collector's cars such as Mustangs, service records and receipts can help document mileage. If the mileage of your Mustang is particularly low, documentation is vital for obtaining top dollar.

THE EXTERIOR

The easiest part of maintaining your Mustang is cleaning and waxing its exterior. Anyone can wash and wax a car, but there are right and wrong ways to do it. A sparkling clean exterior is the most visible sign of a sharp Mustang. A clean car is a psychological boost, too; it makes you feel good to drive it.

WASH IT RIGHT

A super-clean Mustang is a must before proceeding to the waxing and

polishing steps. The main idea behind washing a car is to remove as much dirt and grime as possible without causing any further damage. Improperly removed, dirt acts as an abrasive agent and can scratch the paint. The best method is to flood off as much dirt as possible. Use a lot of water with as much pressure as possible. Start at the roof and work your way down.

Coin-operated car washes are great sources of high-pressure water. There are also high-pressure attachments that hook up to a home compressor and a garden hose. Sears makes a good home pressure washer that can be used with or without a special detergent. These units are especially good for removing all the road grit that gets up inside the wheelwell areas.

Keeping the underside of your car clean is very important if you live in an area where salt is used on the roads during the winter. All that moisture from snow and slush combined with salt is a sure way to start a dreaded case of rust-out, and a badly rusted Mustang is just a step away from the scrap heap. It's also important to check the drain holes in the body to be sure that they aren't plugged.

7 *Raised white-letter tires and white sidewalls can be cleaned with spray-on solutions designed for the job. A stiff-bristle vegetable brush works well for scrubbing the raised letters.*

8 *Curb scars that won't clean up can be covered with a white tire-marking stick.*

11 *It's best to pour liquid wax onto the cloth and then apply it to the car. It's possible for the wax to leave stains if it's applied directly to the surface.*

12 *A different old towel than the one used to dry the car should be used for removing the dried wax. Turn the towel often and shake out the dried wax residue.*

It's best to wash your Mustang in the shade or on an overcast day. The sun shining through water spots can burn little dull spots on the finish. If you must wash in the sunlight, dry the car as soon as possible. If it's really sunny, wash and dry a section of the car at a time.

A Mustang that's cleaned often can probably be washed with very little or no soap at all. The wrong type of soap can dry out the paint and make it look old and faded. If you need to use soap, use one made for car finishes or else the mildest dishwashing detergent.

Only apply the suds after the car has been thoroughly rinsed. Use a washing mitt with a very deep nap. The deep nap helps keep the loosened debris away from the car's finish. Rinse the car and the mitt often.

As soon as you're through washing the car, dry it so water spots don't have a chance to damage the finish. Soft, old terry cloth towels are excellent for drying. If you're really serious about taking care of your Mustang, consider buying a selection of cheap towels just for car-care purposes. Watch for good

deals at a white sale or go to a thrift store and buy used towels. Buy different colors of towels and separate them by function and color. Use different towels for drying, removing wax, and working on chrome trim. Keep the towels as clean as possible so you don't grind old grit over a freshly cleaned area.

A chamois can also be used to dry a car, but that's best for well-waxed finishes. Use the chamois in a pulling motion to wipe the water off the car (it doesn't have the nap of a towel to help keep dirt particles off the finish), and be sure to keep the cloth clean.

WHEELS AND TIRES

A set of high-performance tires and custom wheels, beautiful factory rally wheels, or wire wheel covers is a large investment and should be treated accordingly. The deluxe Mustang wheels are bringing premium prices, so it pays to take good care of them. Also, a sharp set of rally wheels or deluxe wheel covers will make your Mustang stand out.

Wash the rest of the car before

tackling the wheels and tires. Use a large, long-bristle brush designed for washing wheels and tires. The wash mitt will do the job, but the mitt will stay cleaner if you don't use it on the tires and wheels.

Raised white-letter tires and whitewalls require extra attention. There are special chemical cleaners and stiff brushes for this task. If the cleaners leave a few dirty areas or bad scuffs behind, a white tire marker can be used for touch-up work.

After the tires have been thoroughly cleaned, protect them with a vinyl-and-rubber protectant. These protectants are available under a variety of trade names, but they all have a milky white look to them and usually come in a spray-pump container. They'll make the tires look bright and glossy, and help extend their life by protecting against harmful elements such as ozone, oxygen, and ultra-violet rays which can crack and damage the sidewalls.

Wheels can be more difficult to clean, depending on the type you have. If you were fortunate enough to buy clear-coated aluminum wheels, soap and water should be all you need. There are special cleaners made just for clear-coated aluminum wheels. Be sure to use the right cleaner, but not one that contains acid.

Older, non-treated custom wheels can be cleaned by a variety of chemical wheel cleaners which use acids to remove the grime. If your wheels are really dull, you'll probably have to use an aluminum wheel polish. These polishes work well, but require a lot of rubbing. The aluminum polishes create a black residue as they clean, so several rags are needed. Once your wheels are thoroughly polished, clean and polish them often; don't let them deteriorate to the point where the job becomes overwhelming.

Wire wheels or wire wheel covers are types of wheels that should be cleaned often. A really dirty set of wire wheels can be a monumental cleaning task. Chemical cleaners for chrome, and special wire-wheel-spoke brushes will make the job far easier. Painted rally wheels can be treated like any ordinary painted surface. Touch-up paint may be needed from time to time on painted rally wheels. A coat of wax will help protect painted and chrome wheels. There are also special spray products designed to protect chrome-plated wheels.

While cleaning your wheels and tires, take time to check the tread depth. Look at the tires for signs of uneven wear which indicates alignment problems or worn-out suspension parts. Rotate the tires as recommended in your owner's manual.

CAR CARE

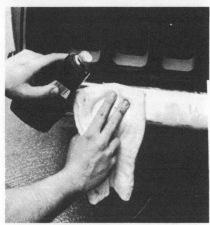

13 *The chrome on this Mustang bumper was in good shape, so we just applied a coat of the same liquid wax used on the paint. Duller chrome will require a stronger chrome polish.*

14 *Clean all the windows inside and out with a household glass cleaner.*

15 *While cleaning the windows, get the headlights too; this will provide better visibility.*

WAXING

A good coat of wax will make your Mustang easier to keep clean. A well-waxed car sheds dirt more easily than an unwaxed one; the car can often just be rinsed rather than washed. As long as the water beads, you know the wax is still present and working to protect your car's finish.

There are as many types and brands of waxes as there are cars. There are liquid, paste, and hard (or carnauba) waxes. Each type has its own supporters, but the most important thing is to use it, regardless of the type. The old adage of the best shine coming from the most difficult waxes isn't necessarily true. Waxing doesn't have to be painful. If you get to the point where your Mustang is entered in concours events, the type of wax may be more critical, but for everyday car care, pick a product that's easy to use.

The condition of your Mustang's finish plays a large part in determining the best wax. An oxidized car needs a cleaner wax which contains mild abrasives to remove the dead paint. A polish doesn't contain abrasives, so it's easier on the finish and should be used on cars in good shape. Only use abrasive products when absolutely necessary; too much use of them can remove all the good paint. The idea is to get as much protection as possible without damaging the existing paint.

As simple as it sounds, be sure to follow the directions no matter what type of wax you use. Some waxes are fine for using in direct sunlight, but the best idea is to wax in the shade, regardless of the type you're using.

Either use the applicator that comes with some waxes or a piece of clean toweling. Apply the wax to the pad or cloth instead of directly to the car. Turn the cloth often to prevent rubbing the already lifted residue back into the paint.

Most people tend to apply too much wax; it doesn't take very much to do a good job. When the directions say "apply sparingly" they mean just that. Allow ample drying time before removing the wax with a clean towel. Turn this towel often and shake out the dried wax.

CHROME CARE

Chrome bumpers and various trim items should be cleaned regularly to avoid rust problems. The time to deal with rust is before it gets started. Once rust has set in on chrome parts you'll never be able to completely get rid of it, so preventative maintenance is the best approach.

Just like waxes, chrome cleaners and polishes come in a variety of strengths. There are products with abrasives for cleaning rusty chrome. Try to use the mildest product that will get the job done; too much abrasion will eventually remove the chrome. Steel wool can be used to remove rust (use the finest grade possible), but it also takes the chrome with it.

Chrome that's in good shape can be protected and cleaned with a liquid car wax or the same wax that you used on the rest of the car. Use chrome cleaners and polishes sparingly around rubber trim because they can leave a white residue that's difficult to remove from the porous rubber.

When waxing around emblems or other small trim parts, it's almost impossible not to leave some residue. An old toothbrush can be used to remove these wax or polish deposits.

VINYL TOP CARE

If your Mustang is equipped with a vinyl top, extra care should be taken to preserve the top and prevent rust from getting started under it. Vinyl tops need to be cleaned often and protected from the elements.

There are many products designed just for cleaning vinyl tops. The tough part is to get out the embedded dirt from the recessed areas of the textured material. A scrub brush is usually needed for this task.

Vinyl-protectant products should be used often and liberally. These products help keep the vinyl supple and prevent aging and cracking.

Beware of any bubbled areas under a vinyl top. This is a sure sign of rust. If any tears develop, repair them as soon as possible to prevent moisture from getting under the vinyl where it can promote rust.

WINDOW WASHING

The glass can be cleaned with the same soap you use on the rest of the exterior, but then use some product designed just for cleaning glass. A standard, household glass cleaner will work just fine.

While you're cleaning the various windows (if you have a '66 Shelby, remember the little quarter windows are plexiglass and require a non-abrasive cleaner), clean the headlights and taillights, too. Clean lights make it easier for you to see and be seen.

Clean all the mirrors, inside and out. When cleaning the rear window, take extra care if an aftermarket, heated-wire rear defroster has been added; you don't want to sever any of the thin wires.

PAINT TOUCHUPS

If you drive your Mustang a lot, rock chips, scratches, and other body scars will accumulate. Major damage will have to be repaired at a bodyshop, but there are several things you can do at home for the minor wounds.

Little chips around the edges of the doors are very common. One solution is plastic or metal door-edge guards. The other solution is to touch up the nicks.

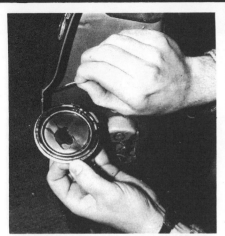

16 *Those annoying little door chips can be touched up with some matching paint applied with a toothpick.*

17 *Parking lot scratches can be removed gently with rubbing compound. Apply pressure gradually so you only remove the other car's paint.*

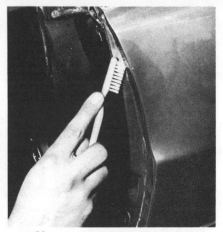

18 *Mustang owners who are detail-conscious use tricks like an old toothbrush to remove the dried wax deposits that accumulate around trim pieces and in the doorjambs.*

Get a small amount of your car's paint and apply it with the end of a toothpick. Dab on the paint so it just fills the tiny crater left by the nick.

Parking lot scratches that leave paint from the offending car can be removed with rubbing compound. Rubbing compounds are abrasive, so rub gently. You only want to remove the other car's paint, not your own. After removing the scratch, wax the area to protect it.

Whenever a scratch or chip occurs, fix it as soon as possible to avoid rust problems. If there's rust in a chip, it must be sanded out or the paint repair won't last. It's much easier to fix a paint chip before rust sets in.

If you use spray cans of factory-match touchup paint, try to control the overspray. A mask can be made out of a file folder so the paint only gets on the desired area. Make the hole in the file folder slightly bigger than the chip. Remember to clean the area before applying the paint, because it won't adhere well to a waxed surface. After the repair has dried for several days, remove the built-up edge with rubbing compound.

MORE EXTERIOR TIPS

After you finish the major exterior-cleaning chores, spend a few minutes checking the little things that many people overlook. Apply rubber-and-vinyl protectant to items such as rubber bumper guards, door and window weatherstripping, and the spare tire.

Wax buildup can occur anywhere there's a seam or crack. Doorjambs are especially prone to wax buildup, and a small toothbrush works well for removing these dried wax deposits.

This is a good time to spend a few minutes walking around your Mustang with a screwdriver and wrench. Check to see that all the fasteners are tight;

this will help prevent losing a mirror or a piece of trim. This is also a good time to see that all lights are in working order. Extend this safety check to include items such as the horn and windshield wipers.

A CLEAN INTERIOR

Few people would choose to ride around all day in the back of a garbage truck, but they often drive a car with an interior that isn't much cleaner. Dirt is an abrasive, and the longer it stays in the interior the more damage it will do. Granted, there are reproduction interior kits for Mustangs, but why spend the extra money when you can keep the original interior in good shape?

SEAT CARE

The seats of your car should receive good care since that's where you spend your time while using the vehicle. Simple cleaning with a vacuum or a wisk broom will do the job if the seats are in good condition.

The type of products used on your seats depends on what they are. Vinyl seats are the most common and easiest to clean; there are a large number of vinyl cleaners and protectants on the market. Test the cleaners on an out-of-the-way part of the seat to be sure it won't discolor. Some cleaners are hard on sewn seams, so don't scrub too much around worn ones. Read the directions carefully to see if the cleaner needs to be rinsed.

Cloth inserts require more care, but there are many good products designed for cleaning interior fabrics. Permanent stains can be avoided by wiping up any spills as soon as they occur. Cruising the local drive-in with your Mustang is fun, but the interior will stay cleaner if you elect to eat inside the restaurant.

CARPET CARE

Automotive carpeting receives the

most dirt and is therefore the most prone to wear. Floormats will help, but frequent vacuuming is the best way to make your carpeting last.

Floormats are best cleaned if they are removed from the car. Vinyl protectant is good for rubber or vinyl floormats. The actual carpeting can be cleaned with a household rug cleaner. When using a stain remover, first test it on an out-of-the-way spot, such as under the seat. Some cleaners are so potent that they discolor the carpeting.

Badly worn carpeting can be replaced with original-quality carpeting from one of the many Mustang carpet companies, or a temporary cure can be had with fabric dyes. There are aerosol products designed just for carpeting, but they usually make the carpet a little stiffer due to the pigment in them.

DOOR PANELS

Since Mustang door panels are vinyl and/or plastic, they are relatively easy to clean. Vinyl cleaners and a small scrub brush will remove ground-in dirt. Professional detail shops often clean door panels with soapy water and a large brush. They lather up the whole panel and then rinse it thoroughly. The doors should be open when cleaning them to keep water off the carpet. The rear panels can be unscrewed and removed from the car for a really thorough cleaning. If you clean the rear panels in the car, place towels on the seats and carpet to absorb the extra moisture. Protect the cleaned door panels with a vinyl protectant spray; this can also be used on the headliner and seats.

DASHBOARDS

Dashboards are real dust collectors. They can be cleaned with a damp cloth or vinyl cleaner. Padded dashboards take a lot of damage from the sun, so they should be kept supple with a vinyl

CAR CARE

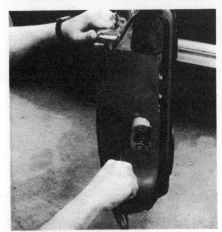

19 *A trip around your Mustang with a couple of screwdrivers can turn up a lot of loose fasteners.*

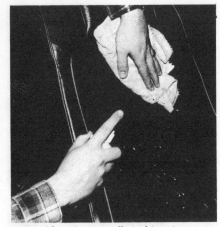

20 *After cleaning, all vinyl interior surfaces should be wiped down with vinyl protectant.*

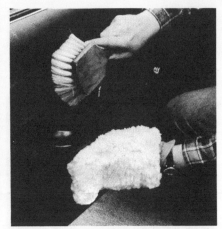

21 *Dirty door panels can be washed with soapy water and a soft-bristle brush. Leave the door open to keep the carpet dry.*

protectant.

A mild glass cleaner, or soap and water can be used on the instrument faces. There are special cleaners for plexiglass and motorcycle face shields. These will work well on the plastic gauge faces.

The painted surfaces of a dashboard and the chrome trim items can be cleaned and polished just like the exterior of the car. Ashtrays can be removed and soaked in soapy water to clean them.

ENGINE TUNE-UP

A car that looks great isn't much good if it doesn't run well. Mustangs aren't mere transportation cars; they're fun to drive—but not if they cough and gasp. Like cosmetic car care, mechanical car care works best if performed at regular intervals. Preventative maintenance is easier and less expensive than waiting until something breaks.

A minor tune-up can be performed by almost anyone, but more complicated tasks should be saved for professionals until you develop the necessary skills. One of the most important skills needed for any tune-up is confidence. Most jobs aren't as difficult as they may seem.

If you fear doing more damage than good to your car when you attempt a tune-up, follow this simple rule: Perform one tune-up function at a time. After each function, start the car and see how it runs. It should run as good or better than before you started. By checking the car often, you can control the number of variables if any problems arise.

SPARK PLUGS

The easiest part of a tune-up and the one that usually shows the most drastic results is changing spark plugs. A fresh set of spark plugs should cost less than

$10 for any Mustang.

It's possible to clean and re-use spark plugs, but for the modest cost, it makes more sense to install new ones. Most spark plugs are close to the correct gap as they come from the box, but you should always check. Use a wire-gapping tool for the best results; a flat feeler gauge isn't as accurate.

Spark plugs can be removed with a common open-end wrench, but the job will be quicker and much easier if you use a spark plug socket and an angle-head ratchet wrench. When re-installing the plugs, put them in finger-tight. Use the plug wrench to tighten standard plugs ¼-½ turn more. Tapered seat plugs should only be tightened 1/16th turn past finger-tight.

While you're changing spark plugs, be sure to check the condition of the spark plug wires. The connectors should be nice and tight. The wires shouldn't be cracked or brittle. If they are, they should be replaced. Spark plug wires should be replaced as whole sets, not individual wires.

ENGINE CLEANING

This step won't make your car run any better, but it will make it easier to work on. It's easier to spot problem areas on a clean engine. Leaks are tough to see on a filthy engine.

You can have the engine of your Mustang professionally steam cleaned or you can do it at the local coin-operated car wash. There are several good aerosol engine-cleaning products that do an excellent job of removing the grime. Remember not to spray the cleaner on the body panels. Anything that's strong enough to clean an engine will also damage paint.

The spray engine cleaners work best on an engine that has been run for a while. Follow the directions on the can and be sure to cover the carburetor and distributor with plastic bags to keep out

moisture. It's a good idea to wear old clothes and safety goggles.

IGNITION TUNE-UP

After replacing spark plugs, the most noticeable performance and economy gains can be seen after an ignition tune-up. This type of tune-up usually consists of replacing worn-out distributor parts and setting the timing to factory specs.

An ignition tune-up for Mustangs with conventional-points-type distributors involves installing new points, rotor, and condensor, plus checking the distributor cap for cracks or deteriorated terminals.

The points should be set to factory specs. A flat feeler gauge will work, but it's much easier to set the points with a dwell meter. Using a dwell meter removes the guesswork associated with trying to get the points right on the pointed part of the distributor cam so they're fully opened. Remember to recheck the dwell after the rotor and distributor cap are back in place.

Proper engine timing is a vital part of an ignition tune-up. Dwell affects timing, so it must always be checked after changing the dwell. A high-quality, inductive pickup timing light is the easiest way to check timing.

A clean engine is easier to time because the timing marks on the harmonic balancer should be easier to see. If the marks aren't readily visible, clean the area (both the balancer and the pointer) and rub some white chalk on them. Consult a factory tune-up manual for the correct timing setting.

FUEL SYSTEM

If your ignition system is in top shape, the engine shouldn't have any problems firing the air/fuel mixture, unless there's a problem in the fuel system. You may not want to do work like a carburetor rebuild, but you can check items such as fuel filters and make sure the fuel pump is working

22 *After washing and drying the door panels, apply a liberal coat of vinyl protectant.*

23 *A clean engine is much easier to work on. Remember to cover the distributor and carburetor with plastic bags during the cleaning process.*

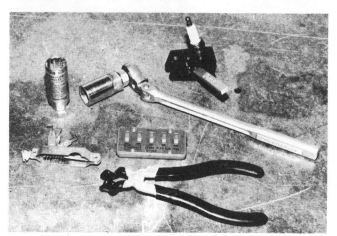

24 *There's a variety of special tools that will make changing spark plugs easier. They include: spark plug sockets, angle-head ratchet wrench, spark plug wire puller, wire-gapping tools, and a special gap-setting tool that holds the spark plug while the gap is set.*

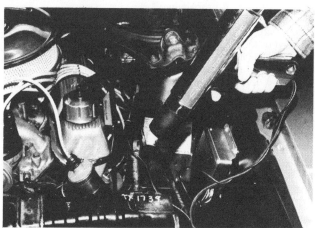

25 *A top-quality, inductive pickup timing light is the best choice for timing an engine. Cheap timing lights are difficult to see in anything but very dark engine compartments.*

properly.

All fuel line and carburetor filters should be cleaned and/or replaced periodically. Fuel filters are meant to get dirty, but one that's saturated with dirt needs to be replaced.

Use care when working on fuel lines; most of the fittings are made out of brass. A set of flare wrenches is best for working on fuel lines because they make contact with a greater part of the fitting than a normal, open-end wrench.

There's a variety of spray carburetor cleaners that can free sticky linkage and help remove tarnish deposits. There are also liquid carburetor products you can pour into a running carburetor.

After checking the condition of the fuel filters, you can check the fuel pump. Factory manuals give specifications for fuel-flow rate. They also give acceptable pressure rates which can be measured by hooking a vacuum gauge to the fuel pump outlet.

A task related to the fuel system is

26 *Spray carburetor products are helpful for removing gum deposits on the carburetor and freeing sticky linkage.*

27 *A way to test the PCV valve on your Mustang is to remove it from the valve cover and place your thumb over the end of the valve. The engine rpm should drop slightly when you do this.*

28 *When installing a new oil filter, apply some fresh oil to the gasket to aid sealing.*

29 *The condition of your Mustang's antifreeze/coolant should be checked with a coolant tester. Weak coolant should be flushed and replaced.*

the PCV valve. It should be checked for proper operation. A properly working PCV should rattle; a clogged one won't. Another way to check the PCV is by putting your thumb over one end of the valve. By listening carefully or using a tachometer, you should notice a slight drop in the engine rpm when the end of the PCV valve is blocked by your thumb.

FLUIDS

Mustangs are full of vital fluids such as gas, oil, and water. These basics, plus others like transmission oil, gear oil, battery electrolyte, and lubricating greases must be in good condition and properly serviced if you expect top performance and long life from your car. A part that runs out of its vital fluid will quickly become a broken one. This can be quite costly when the substance is engine oil, transmission fluid, or engine coolant. Fluids should be checked frequently to avoid these problems.

CHANGING OIL

An internal-combustion engine operates at extremely high temperatures and creates tremendous amounts of friction, so top-quality engine oil is a must. An engine without oil will quickly become a useless mass of seized cast-iron.

Changing the oil in your Mustang is a simple task, but it can be messy unless done correctly. Warm oil drains more quickly than cold oil, so run the engine for a few minutes before draining the oil. Remember that an engine that has been run for any length of time can get warm enough to burn you.

Your Mustang should be elevated for oil changes. Lift the front of the car and support it with jack stands. You'll need a container with at least a six-quart capacity.

Position your drain pan to allow for the arc of the oil when it first comes out of the oil pan. The arc will diminish as the oil drains, so watch it to avoid a messy spill on your garage floor.

The oil filter must be changed every time you change the oil, or you'll be pumping fresh oil through a dirty filter. Use an oil filter wrench to remove the old filter, and be sure that the oil gaske comes off when the filter does. If not, the old filter gasket will cause a leak when the new one is installed.

Smear a light coat of fresh oil on the new filter's gasket to aid sealing. Install the new filter by hand, fill the engine with the correct amount of oil, start the engine, and check for any leaks around the filter or drain plug.

COOLING SYSTEM

Water is another vital fluid in your Mustang. The water should be mixed with coolant/antifreeze in a ratio determined by your climate. The cooling system should be checked at least twice a year. If the system and coolant are in good condition, you only need to change the coolant once a year. Check the condition of the coolant with an antifreeze tester.

If your cooling system is really corroded and the engine runs hot, consider having the whole system professionally back-flushed at a radiator shop. There are kits for doing your own flushing, but the pros can also run tests on the condition of the radiator and find any leaks.

Radiator hoses are a critical part of your cooling system. Check them for leaks or signs of weakness. A bulge means the hose is ready to burst. Squeeze the hoses to feel for soft spots, which indicate that the hose is wearing out. Check the clamps for tightness.

The fan should be checked for tightness, and all fan belts should be checked for proper tension. A fan belt should deflect about ½ inch when you push on it. Look for signs of deterioration and replace belts before they break. It's a good idea to carry a set of spare fan belts in the trunk.

BATTERY

Checking the level of electrolyte in

32 *The condition of the brake system should be checked. Check the pad thickness and look for any signs of scoring.*

your battery is a task that most car owners no longer have to worry about since the advent of sealed batteries. If your Mustang has an original-type battery, the electrolyte level should not be allowed to go below the battery plates. Distilled water is best for topping off a battery.

Regardless of the type of battery in your Mustang, the cables and terminals should be checked and cleaned as necessary. Any corrosion should be eliminated. There are special brushes and terminal tools for making all the contact surfaces shiny clean. Make sure that both ends of the battery cables are secure. The top of the battery can be cleaned with a solution of baking soda and water applied with an old brush. This solution will neutralize any acid on the outside of the battery.

Battery acid is dangerous and corrosive, so keep it away from your skin and clothes.

TRANSMISSION

The level of transmission fluid in an automatic transmission should be checked frequently. The level must be checked with the engine running and the gear selector in park. If additional fluid is needed, use a flexible funnel to

30 *There's a variety of inexpensive battery post and terminal-cleaning tools that can be used to remove any corrosion from the battery and cables.*

31 *While your Mustang is elevated for a grease job, take a flashlight and inspect the underside of it. Look for leaks or any loose parts.*

33 *A way to check the condition of an air filter is to hold a trouble light inside it. A clean filter will pass light, a dirty one won't.*

34 *This is our thoroughly cleaned-and-serviced car. It looks great, drives super, and will maintain its value far longer than a neglected Mustang.*

avoid spilling fluid over the back of the engine. Be sure to use Ford-type fluid in your Mustang; GM-type won't work.

The transmission fluid and filter should be changed approximately every two years. This can be a very messy job if your transmission pan doesn't have a drain plug.

Manual transmissions don't require very much attention outside of periodic clutch adjustment. The transmission-gear oil level should be checked annually and changed every two years.

CHASSIS LUBE

A grease job is a very messy but important part of car care. If you're opposed to getting a little dirty, have the job done at a service station.

If you decide to do the job yourself, elevate the car and place jack stands to securely hold it while you crawl around underneath. A creeper makes it easy to move about, or a big piece of flat cardboard will work. Check your shop manual for the grease-fitting locations, and clean the grease-fitting nipples before injecting new grease. Pump the new grease in until some starts to come out of the seals in the part being lubed.

While you have your Mustang elevated for a grease job, look around under the car with a flashlight. Check fittings, hoses, nuts, and bolts to be sure everything is secure and tight. Look for leaks or signs of damage that could cause trouble later. This is also a good time to check the condition of your exhaust system. Look at the shock absorbers. Fluid on them means they're leaking and should be replaced.

While you're under the car, check the level of axle grease in the rearend. The axle must be parallel to the ground for an accurate check. The fluid should be right at the opening of the filler hole or no more than a ½ inch below. Always use the proper-weight gear lube when adding any fluid.

FLUIDS AND FILTERS

The brake fluid level should be checked when the car is parked on level ground. Always use top-quality brake fluid. Power steering fluid should be checked and topped off if necessary.

Fill the windshield washer with a combination of water and cleaning solution made for windshield washers (some brands are already diluted). If the washers don't work well, check the condition of the hoses and be sure all connections are tight. Check the

nozzles for debris. A straight pin can be used to clean dirt out of the nozzles.

If you didn't already service the fuel filters during the engine part of your maintenance program, do it now. The air filter is vital to the health and operation of your Mustang. Check it frequently (especially if you live in a dusty area) and replace it when dirty. A way to check your air filter is to hold a trouble light inside it: A clean filter will pass light, a dirty one won't.

All Mustangs are great cars to drive and own. They're rolling investments, so it makes economical sense to keep them in top shape. Car care is easy and profitable. The only way you can lose is by not doing it. *M*

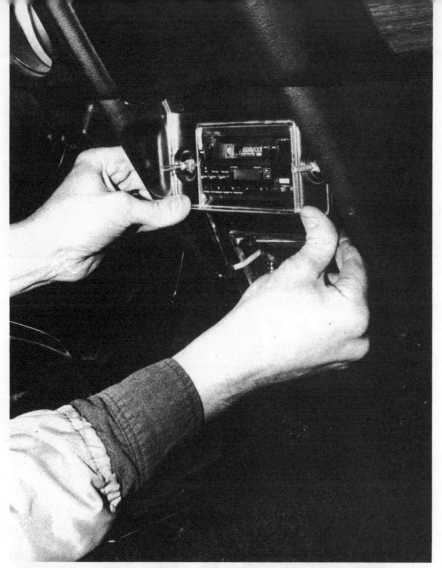

STEREO INSTALLATION FOR THE VIRTUOSO

BY BRUCE CALDWELL

A car without music can be very boring, but if you install a super sound system in your Mustang, even rush-hour traffic can be fun. Well, maybe that's going too far, but listening to your favorite radio station or cassette tapes definitely makes driving more enjoyable.

Unfortunately, most older Mustangs only came with AM radios, or AM/FM eight-track players at best. Tremendous advances have been made in the stereo industry over the past couple of years that make the original Mustang radios and stereos seem positively archaic. Most new equipment uses cassettes instead of eight-tracks, since eight-tracks seem to be headed toward extinction.

There are so many great sound systems from which to choose that, within nearly any price range, the options are unlimited. Good advice to consider when choosing components is to stick with major companies that you know will stand behind their work, and try to pick units that give the most usable features for the money. Some of the market's most sophisticated stereos have many trick features that, unless you happen to have the trained ears of a professional musician, may not be worth the extra expense. There's a

TAKE NOTE

1 *Up front is the Kenwood KRC-3100 cassette receiver and the KAC-801 stereo power amplifier. Behind them is a pair of KSC-1000 bi-modular speakers and a pair of KFC-6910 rear deck speakers.*

2 *The heart of the system is this KRC-3100 digital AM/FM stereo cassette receiver. It fits in the stock Mustang dashboard and features auto-reverse, memory, and signal seeking.*

particularly nice feature that some companies call an amplifier or booster; it can really beef-up the sound of your stereo system. Another handy feature for the tape deck is auto-reverse. This means you don't have to turn the tape over when one side is through, particularly welcome in a car stereo.

New automotive stereos have been getting smaller and better. The stereo companies are stuffing an amazing amount of technology into very small spaces, then adding items such as amplifiers and graphic equalizers.

Speakers are quickly becoming extremely sophisticated, such as the new three-way models. However, these super speakers take up more space, and many early Mustangs don't have a lot of extra space for such items. It was definitely a challenge when we installed a Kenwood system in a '70 Mustang. We managed all right, but anyone thinking about installing the latest megawatt sound system in a Mustang should do some careful measuring first.

The Kenwood components we chose include a KRC-3100 AM/FM cassette receiver, a KAC-801 stereo main amplifier, a pair of KFC-6910 rear deck-mount three-way speakers, and a pair of KSC-1000 bi-modular speakers. The Kenwood model KRC-3100 is an in-dash receiver with features like auto-reverse, digital display, signal seeking, memory, noise reduction, tape advance, and a total output power of 10 watts. The KAC-801 is a high-power, low-distortion 140-watt amplifier. The KFC-6910 rear deck speakers are 6×9-inch oval units with 20-ounce magnets and a maximum input power of 80 watts. The KSC-1000 bi-modular speakers have a woofer and a tweeter. The speaker is

actually two parts that can be separated to make mounting easier, or you can use them in their connected form.

Installing the cassette receiver wasn't a problem, but finding space for the amplifier required a little looking. We've seen Mustang owners put similar amplifiers in the glove compartment after removing the storage box. You then lose the storage, and when the glovebox door is open the amplifier is visible. The rest of the underdash area is pretty crowded with the heater and defroster ductwork. Some people mount amplifiers under the passenger seat, but this tends to be a warm area, and amplifiers are best placed in cooler locations. It helps, therefore, to have airflow around the fins of the amplifier. Kenwood cautions against mounting a stereo power amplifier where there's direct sunlight, excessive heat, or moisture.

The location we chose for our amplifier was the trunk. We mounted it in the innermost corner, above the rear axle and under the rear package tray. This also put the amplifier right under one of the rear deck speakers.

Crawling into the back end of a small Mustang trunk isn't the easiest thing to do, so we unbolted part of the rear seat to gain access. Owners of fastbacks with fold-down rear seats won't have this problem.

The biggest installation problem with Mustangs seems to be door speakers. There's very little room to mount speakers of any size (and size usually relates to performance) in the doors, kick panels, or the panels beside the rear seat. There actually is room in the panels beside the rear seat, but that location doesn't provide much separa-

tion from the rear deck speakers.

The problem with the lower kick panels is interference from the air vents and the emergency brake pedal on the driver's side. There's room in the doors for reasonably sized speakers, but you need to be sure that all the window mechanisms will clear. Our installation was complicated by the fact that the Kenwood KSC-1000 speakers fit in the factory holes just fine, but the problem is they stick out too far to clear the window crank.

We could have moved the new speakers to a different location in the lower door panel, but then we would have a big hole where the old speakers were or two sets of speakers (old and new) in each door, which would also look strange. We're still in the process of reaching a decision about what to do, but add-on power window winders look like a good solution. This shows how important it is to do plenty of measuring before rashly cutting any holes in your Mustang.

Outside of the space problems in the door panels, the installation of the Kenwood stereo and speakers was pretty straightforward. The Kenwood components came complete with mounting hardware, connecting wires, templates for cutting speaker holes, and well-illustrated instructions. The highlight of the day was when the new system was hooked up and ready to go. This proved the only way to listen to the song *Mustang Sally* in your Mustang is on a super sound system.

If you decide to try an installation like ours and want to use Kenwood components, call toll-free for the name of the dealer nearest you, 800/453-9000. In Utah, call 800/662-2500. *M*

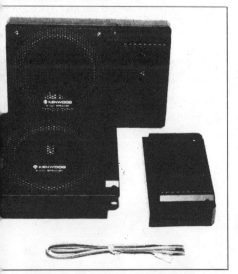

3 *The KSC-1000 is a two-way speaker; the woofer and tweeter can be mounted separately or together. A connecting wire with plug-in ends (foreground) is provided for separating the two parts.*

4 *The back of a KSC-1000 speaker shows how the woofer and tweeter are in separate sections. An Allen-head screw in the front of the speaker holds the two sections together.*

5 *The KFC-6910 is a powerful 6×9-inch speaker with 20-ounce barium ferrite magnets. It's a three-way model that needs to be mounted in the rear deck; it's too deep for Mustang doors.*

TAKE NOTE

6 The KAC-801 stereo main amplifier is a big piece of equipment that helps put out some big sounds when used with speakers like the KFC-6910s.

7 Our original radio was an AM eight-track with one missing selector button. Removal begins with pulling off the control knobs.

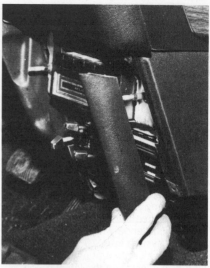

8 On '70 Mustangs, these two plastic sections of the dashboard need to be unscrewed and removed.

12 Use a deep socket to remove the thin nuts on the threaded radio-control shafts.

13 Here's the formed metal plate that secures and positions the radio in the dashboard.

14 With the mounting plate out of the way, slip the old radio out. Remember to disconnect the antenna lead and the power source (disconnect the car's battery before starting the job).

18 Even though there's a small gap between the top of the new stereo and the Mustang's plastic dash plate, the sides of the plate are a tiny bit tight. Use a flat file to trim away the excess plastic.

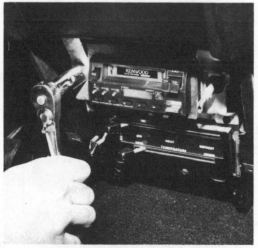

19 The rest of the stereo cassette installation involves reversing the steps taken during removal of the old unit.

20 Install the Kenwood control knobs and the new stereo is ready to go. The stock dashboard isn't damaged in case you ever decide to restore the car to 100-percent stock condition.

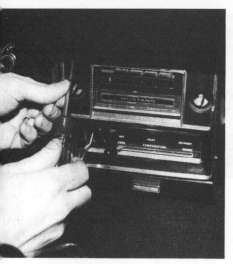

9 *Remove the two screws at the top of the radio faceplate where it meets the dashboard pad.*

10 *Notice that the radio faceplate is also the faceplate for the heater/defroster control panel.*

11 *With the plastic faceplate out of the way, you can see the radio is mounted to a metal plate secured to the top of the heater control panel with two hex-headed screws. The plate is also located by a plastic tab (arrow).*

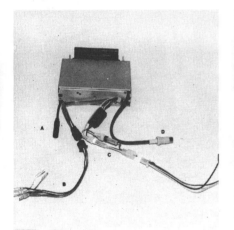

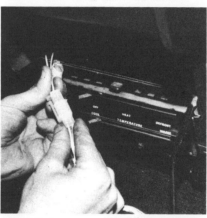

15 *From left to right the plug-in connectors are (a) lead to antenna, (b) speaker leads, (c) power supply and ground wire with two in-line fuses and (d) the pre-amplifier output cable which goes either to the amplifier or graphic equalizer.*

16 *Once the power supply lead, ground lead, memory back-up lead, and power antenna control lead (if used) are wired to the car, connect the stereo by this plug. It has a special clip to keep it from separating accidentally.*

17 *The Kenwood stereo's faceplate is a little smaller than the original Mustang unit, so slip a black rubber adapter over it to fill the gap.*

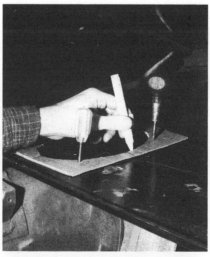

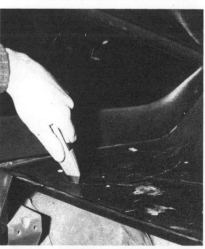

21 *Now for the speakers. Unbolt the top of the back seat so you can reach into the trunk and under the rear deck. Locate the four holes for the speaker and drill with a right-angle drill.*

22 *Place awls in the four holes to locate the cardboard speaker-opening template. Use a yellow grease pencil to trace the opening.*

23 *Use a sharp utility knife to cut the opening in the composition-board rear deck panel. There are openings in the underlying metal framework which are just about the perfect size for speakers.*

95

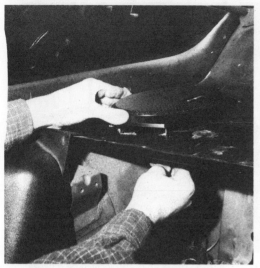

24 *Position the speaker screen on the top side of the rear deck. The four bolts go into the trunk area.*

25 *Put the speakers underneath the rear deck and secure to the speaker screen with the supplied nuts. Having the seat out of the way really helps.*

26 *If your Mustang has the factory door speakers (thin low-performance items), remove them now.*

27 *Notice how much thicker the KSC-1000 speakers are than the stock units.*

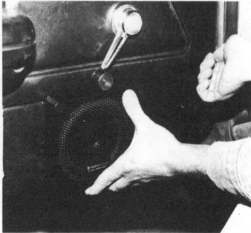

28 *The new speakers will fit the stock hole, but check how the window crank hits the top of the speaker. Either use a shorter window crank or add on power windows.*

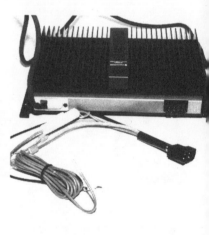

29 *The KAC-801 power amplifier uses a handy plug-in connector which has the leads for the four speakers. The line to the power source has an in-line fuse.*

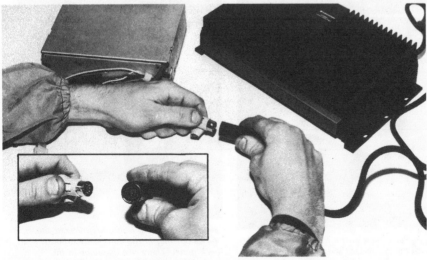

30 *To connect the stereo cassette player to the stereo power amplifier, simply join the male and female ends of the five-pin DIN cables.*

31 *Mount the KAC-801 stereo power amplifier (with sheetmetal screws) in the trunk. Run the wires under the carpet to the stereo cassette player.*

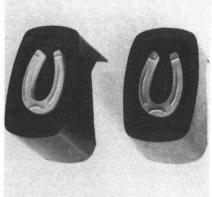

1 *Here are two Bumper-ettes, an original on the left and Don Chambers' reproduction on the right. Both are heavy-duty, solid pieces.*

2 *From the back side, you can see how the Bumper-ettes are installed. A metal bar simply bolts them to the rear bumper.*

REPRO-TECTION

HOW TO INSTALL "LUCKY" BUMPER-ETTES

BY JERRY HEASLEY

Adding extras to the interior or exterior of some cars, (if it's done to any great degree) can detract from its looks, and lessen its market value. Not so with the original '65-'66 Mustang, though, if you add the right things. The Mustang was built for "personalization," which is a major reason the car was so popular back in the Sixties, and more popular today.

Among the nicest aftermarket additions ever made for the Mustang are the "Bumper-ettes," which protect the fragile Mustang rear bumper, the rear trunk deck lid, and the taillights.

But these attractive, rugged, and functional dealer-installed accessories were discontinued many years ago, and the supply of NOS and excellent used Bumper-ettes ran out more than a

decade ago.

Our Mustang supplier (Don Chambers of Mustang Country) has come to the rescue with an accurate reproduction of the original that's just right for your early Mustang.

The installation is fairly simple, and you'll see how with a little ingenuity, the Bumper-ettes can be added without removing the rear bumper. Young Laura Gilbert, a real Mustang fan, demonstrates how on a '66 coupe.

These faithful reproductions are made by Don & Ailene Chambers of Mustang Country. Retail price is $59.95 per set, and if you're interested in this handsome addition to your Mustang, contact Mustang Country, 14625 Lakewood Blvd., Paramount, CA 90723, 213/633-2393. *M*

3 *First, place an eyelet of the metal strap through the top stud of the Bumper-ette. Screw the nut down, but keep it loose so the metal strap will swing back and forth with the force of gravity.*

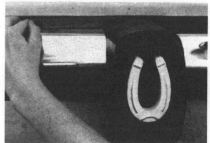

4 *Slip the eyelet of the metal strap over the bottom stud and screw on the nut. The installation is so easy a child can do it, with results that add a custom touch to your vintage Mustang.*

By Bruce Caldwell

The 289 Ford is a great little engine. It can easily give 100,000 miles of relatively trouble-free service before needing an overhaul. The engine in our '65 Mustang fastback project car was just such a high-mileage 289, and although it was way out of tune, it still ran okay. We wanted more than just an okay engine; we wanted a strong street and occasional strip motor that would be up to the level of the rest of our Mustang revitalization.

Since the engine in our Mustang still ran well enough to get the car to and from the various shops it frequented during its rebuilding process, we decided to leave it alone and build another one. This method is especially good if the car you are rebuilding is your only source of transportation. Used 289s are inexpensive, so you should be able to pick up a core engine for under $200 in running condition and even less if it doesn't run. Our core engine was free (all we had to do was pull it out of a wrecked Mustang sitting in a friend's backyard), but it didn't run. Our bargain engine's demise was thought to be due to lack of oil pressure, but judging by the shape of the car it came out of, death could have been caused by a terminal case of sludge.

Jim McFarland of Edelbrock generously offered the services of Edelbrock's engine dyno, but when "the engine that ate Cleveland" showed up at their sanitary El Segundo, California, facility, everyone shielded their eyes and left the room. Luckily, noble development engineer Curt Hooker stepped forward and volunteered to work on it.

Disassembly of an engine is pretty straightforward: simply remove everything until you are down to the bare block. Along the way, inspect all the parts for wear and damage, mark and keep track of where every part goes for reassembly, and try not to damage anything through use of excessive force. Use a lot of coffee cans, boxes, or bags to segregate parts. Mark the containers, or draw diagrams of how things came apart. At the time you

tear down the engine, everything is fresh in your mind, but later you might forget where that strange part goes. If at all possible, steam-clean the engine before disassembly.

The basic sequence of disassem-

bling a 289 Ford is just that—basic. Mount the engine on an engine stand for working ease; drain the oil; remove front-of-the-engine accessories like air conditioning, alternator, and power steering pump;

(1) This once-noble Mustang coupe gave its motor for our Project Mustang. The engine was free for the taking, and by rebuilding this engine, we were still able to drive our Mustang.

(2) Our free engine as delivered to Edelbrock's sparkling dyno facility. Not a pretty engine, but not unlike what most people start with, either.

(3) The engine was definitely not a cherry, as witnessed by the water pump leak that was repaired with body filler.

(4) Upon disassembly, we discovered many things about our motor, including the reason for its death—a broken oil pump shaft (arrow).

(5) Curt Hooker of Edelbrock checked the crank with a micrometer to see if the crankshaft needed to be reground. The crank was slightly off, so a regrind was ordered.

(6) All the machine work was done at Valley Head Service. Before the engine could be cleaned, all plugs had to be removed. Here the cam bearings are being driven out of the block.

remove the exhaust manifolds and carburetor; with the valve covers out of the way, loosen and remove the rocker arms and the pushrods; and take off the cylinder heads. That takes care of the top of the engine.

Now, remove the oil pan and turn the engine over on the engine stand. Next, remove the oil pump. (The oil pump shaft was broken on our engine, which explained the loss of oil pressure.) Continue disassembly by removing the rod caps and bearings; removing the pistons; using a puller, removing the harmonic balancer from the front of the engine, which will make the timing chain and cover accessible; removing the main bearing caps and lifting out the crankshaft; and removing the camshaft and lifters. What you have left is a bare block.

Besides a bad oil pump, Curt's inspection revealed that our freebie engine also had bad bearings, clogged oil rings, a loose timing chain, and a crankshaft that was slightly out of round. The engine appeared basically sound and fine for rebuilding. It was a typical 100,000-mile-plus, used engine: tired out, gummed up, but plenty good for another 100,000 miles after a rebuild.

Next on the agenda was the all-important visit to the machine shop. We took our project Mustang engine to Valley Head Service's huge machine shop and engine-building facility at 19340 Londelius, Northridge, CA 91324, (213) 993-7000. Valley Head Service is equipped to handle everything from cleaning and machining to engine assembly and dyno-testing. Besides doing a tremendous amount of local business, Valley Head Service also provides mail-order service.

Valley Head Service's owner, Larry Ofria, explained what needed to be done to our engine. Rather than use a lot of exotic speed equipment, we decided to build a strong, reliable, balanced-and-blueprinted engine. This type of engine works beautifully with common aftermarket speed equipment, and if we later get the urge for more horsepower, the basic engine will be able to handle the extra load. Too many people build an engine backward; they add all the trick eyewash items but ignore the basic powerplant. All the camshaft and carburetion in the world won't do you any good if the bottom falls out of the motor.

The goals for our engine were as follows: power in the 275 to 300-horsepower range, plenty of bottom-end torque, quarter-mile

BLUE-PRINTING THE 289

(7) Our slimey block was subjected to a long stay in the hot tank. A hot tank is like an oven which cleans with heat and a caustic solvent.

times in the high 13s to low 14s, 15 to 20-mile-per-gallon economy under everyday conditions on standard pump gasoline, smooth around-town operation, and good emissions levels. Both Jim and Larry felt the 289 Ford was easily capable of the above parameters.

Very few people can do their own machine work, so we'll just present an overview of what is involved in blueprinting an engine. The basic premise of blueprinting is to build a perfectly matched and balanced engine. Tolerances are closely adhered to, and cleanliness is paramount. Every part is inspected for weaknesses, and only perfect parts are used.

Before any machine work could be performed, our crusty engine needed a thorough cleaning. All freeze plugs and cam bearings had to be removed because they will dissolve during the hot-tanking process. All the parts were placed in the hot tank, which cleans by means of a heated and very caustic solvent. After the engine was through in the hot tank, it was rinsed, followed by additional cleaning of small passages with solvent

and small bristle brushes. After everything was clean, it was "Magnafluxed." Magnafluxing is the cheapest engine insurance you can get, for you find weak parts before they are reinstalled in your engine, not when you make your first high-speed pass.

The main bearing bores were checked to see if it would be necessary to align-bore the engine. Larry said small-block Fords very seldom need align-boring (the odds are about 20 to 1). Our engine was within acceptable tolerances, so there was no need to align-bore. Before checking the main bearing bores, it is a good idea to use a flat honing stone dipped in solvent on the cap surfaces of the block and the mating surfaces of the bearing caps. This assures the contact areas are flat and clean. Also, chase and clean the main cap threads with a tap so torque wrench readings will be accurate.

Our cylinder walls needed more than a touch-up hone, so we decided to bore the block .030-inch over and use .030-inch over Speed-Pro forged pistons. The boring is done in two steps. First, the block is set up on a boring bar that locates the block off the main saddles so the bores are perpendicular to the crankshaft. Each bore is enlarged .025-inch on the boring bar. The last .005-inch will be done on a Sunnen CK-10 honing machine. Each piston is checked with a micrometer before honing. This way the same piston-to-wall clearance (.0035-inch in our case) can be maintained in all cylinders. The honing was done with a torque plate in order to simulate the loads imposed on the cylinders by the cylinder heads.

The block was then decked to make sure that the distance between the centerline of the crankshaft and the head surface (deck) was the same at all corners of the block. The tolerance was held to .001-inch. After the machine work was performed on the block, the block was again hot-tanked to remove honing oils and any accumulated debris.

With the block out of the way, Larry's crew moved on to the internal pieces. The crankshaft was checked with a micrometer and found to be .0005-inch out of round, so it was reground. Before being reground, the oil holes were chamfered with a hand-held grinder to improve oiling. Then the crank was reground and micropolished to

(8) All mating surfaces for the crank saddles should be touched up with a honing stone. This ensures good metal-to-metal contact and accurate torque readings.

(9) With the main saddles torqued in place, the bore of the crank bearings is checked. If they are not within tolerance, align-boring is necessary to correct the problem. Our block, like most 289 blocks, didn't need to be align-bored.

(10) A boring bar was used to enlarge each cylinder .025-inch. The boring bar locates the block so that all bores are perpendicular to the crankshaft.

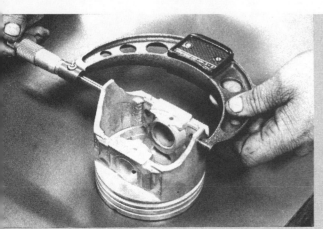

(11) Each Speed-Pro piston is miked before the final honing operation. This way the same piston-to-wall clearance can be maintained throughout the engine.

(12) The last .005-inch of the boring operation is performed on a Sunnen CK-10 honing machine. A torque plate is bolted to the block to simulate the cylinder head.

(13) Before the crank was reground, the oil holes were chamfered (right) with a hand-held grinder to improve oiling.

make sure there were no burrs sticking up above the bearing surfaces. Micropolishing gives the crankshaft a mirror-like finish.

The next step was to rebuild the rods. First, the rods are Magnafluxed and bead-blasted clean. Then, the rods are disassembled in a rod vise, which has smooth surfaces designed not to damage rods. A honing stone is used on all mating surfaces, and the rods and caps are put in a Sunnen cap and rod grinder to make the contact areas perfect. The rods are reassembled and put on a rod hone to hone the bearing area. Then the rods are put in a rod heater that heats the small end of the rod to 500 degrees F., and the pins are pushed into the pin boss bores on a pin fixture so that the pins are centered. The rods are put in an alignment fixture so that the pins are perpendicular to the center of the bore. This ensures the piston will travel straight up and down the cylinder bore.

The rods are balanced by weighing both ends and finding the lightest rods for each end. All big ends are matched to the lightest one, as are all the small ends. The excess weight is removed from the pads at each end of the rods.

The crankshaft is balanced with the flywheel and the harmonic balancer attached because the 289 Ford is externally balanced. The crank is balanced on a Stewart-Warner balancer, which uses bob-weights to simulate motion. A formula involving rotating mass (big end of rods, bearings, and a few grams of oil) and reciprocating mass (weight of rings, the small end of the rod, the wrist pin, and piston) is used to determine where to add or subtract weight on the

(14) All the rods are Magnafluxed and rebuilt prior to balancing. Rod assembly and disassembly is done in a rod vise to keep from damaging the rod.

(15) Each end of the rod (below) is weighed separately to find the lightest ones. All the rods are matched to the lightest ends.

(16) To match the rod weights, the pads on the ends of the rods are ground on a belt grinder.

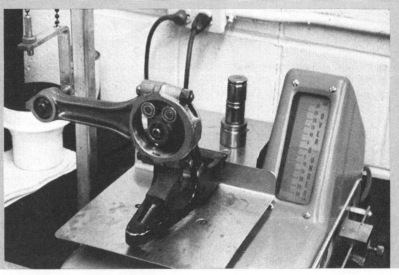

BLUE-PRINTING THE 289

crank counterweights.

That just about covers the machine work on the block except checking the cam bearings. New cam bearings were installed and checked for fit with our new Crane cam. It is a rare case when alignboring is needed, but it should always be inspected anyway.

ENGINE ASSEMBLY

After all the machine work was completed, we gathered up our freshly balanced parts from Valley Head Service and took them to Edelbrock's dyno room. We also brought along a big goodie box of new aftermarket parts that Jim Mc Farland picked as the best matched components for our needs.

The first order of business was to mount the bare block on an Eagle Specialty Products heavy-duty engine stand (part No. 3001991). We converted the three-wheeled engine stand to a sturdier four-wheel model with Eagle's No. 3001992 conversion kit, which fits all three-wheeled Eagle stands. Then the engine was rolled outside and thoroughly cleaned with solvent to remove any contaminants left during the machining operations. After the solvent, the block was washed with soapy water, rinsed, and air-dried. It may seem like we are overdoing this cleaning business, but cleanliness is vital to a properly blueprinted engine.

With the block cleaned and dried, it is a good time to apply paint to the lifter galley if you feel so inclined. The main purpose of the paint is that metal fragments will show up more readily when you inspect the engine later. Also, the paint aids oil return. Curt uses Rust-Oleum Damp-Proof red primer No. 769 and lets it dry 24 hours.

. The first part of the assembly process was fitting the rings. Speed-Pro R-9343, .035-inch-over rings were used so they could be individually ground to fit our .030-

over bores. The rings were fitted to their respective cylinders by inserting each ring in the bore, measuring the end gap, removing the necessary amount by filing, and re-inserting for a final measurement. The rings were correctly positioned in the bores by pushing them with a piece of round aluminum stock that Curt uses just for fitting rings. The top of a piston will also work for this purpose. The rings were filed down on a ring grinder, but they can also be ground with a hand-held file. The gap on the top ring was .014-inch and the middle ring gap was .012-inch. Curt makes the top ring gap larger than that of the second ring because the top rings absorb more heat, which causes them to expand more than the second rings. The ring gaps are always measured with a flat feeler gauge.

Before installing the rings on the Speed-Pro .030-inch-over forged pistons (part No. 8-7006P), we cleaned the pistons, rods, and caps in solvent and dried them with an air hose. The rings can be installed by hand, but a ring expander is inexpensive insurance against

(17) Before the engine was assembled, it was thoroughly cleaned—first with a degreaser, then soapy water, and then clear water. The engine was mounted on an Eagle engine stand.

(18) All bearing surfaces were lubricated before final assembly. First apply assembly lube; then, cover the area with motor oil and work it into the bearing with your finger.

(19) Curt makes constant use of a torque wrench when blueprinting an engine. An engine stand greatly simplifies all assembly work.

breaking a ring. Put the oil rings on the piston with the expansion ring's break pointing at the center of the wrist pin. Offset the two retainer rings for the expansion ring 45 degrees to each side of the wrist pin. The second ring's break should face 180 degrees away from the oil

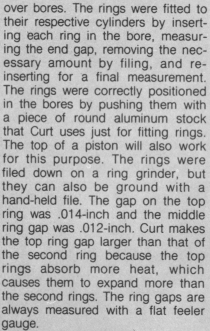

ring, and the top ring's gap should be on the same side as the oil expansion ring.

Curt always double-checks all work done by the machine shop, just in case there ever happens to be an error. Never take anything for granted when blueprinting an engine. Check and double-check every measurement and facet of the engine-building operation. It is much easier to remedy mistakes before the engine is assembled than after. Everything on our engine was as it was supposed to be.

The main seals from a Rocket gasket set (part No. R1410) were installed, and then the crankshaft bearings (Sealed Power .010-inch-undersize) were lubricated and installed. Curt puts a light coat of assembly lube on the bearings and then covers them with 30-weight motor oil, working the lube into the bearings with his fingers. This lubrication helps protect the engine when it is first started. Then the crankshaft end play was checked with a dial indicator and found to be .005-inch, which falls right within the .004 to .008-inch range of acceptability.

The rod bearings were lubricated in the same manner as the main bearings, and then the pistons were checked to ensure they were correctly installed on the rods. The number on the rod and on the piston should face toward the outside of the engine. The rod bearings were Sealed Power .010-inch-undersize (technically oversize) units because the crank was ground .010-inch under. Before in-

(20) Crankshaft end play is checked with a dial indicator and screwdriver. A dial indicator and micrometer set are vital to proper blueprinting.

(21) This is a ring-locater made by Edelbrock's Murray Jensen. A smaller disc of aluminum fits inside the bore to position the ring squarely for gap measurement.

(22) Use a flat feeler gauge to measure ring end gap. A piston will work well to locate the ring for measuring. Each ring should be matched to a particular cylinder bore.

(23) A ring grinder is the easy way to enlarge the amount of end gap. Speed-Pro .035-over rings were used and fitted to our .030-over block.

(24) A ring expander is the safest way to install rings without breaking any, but the rings can be installed by hand. Spiral the ring around the piston as shown. The piston is a Speed-Pro forged unit.

(25) A ring compressor sleeve should be used to install the pistons. Gently tap the pistons into the bores, being careful not to scratch the crankshaft.

BLUE-PRINTING THE 289

(26) To be sure we had the desired compression ratio, Curt measured the combustion chambers' displacement with a burette.

stalling the piston/rod assemblies, Curt made sure the crank spun freely and then put a generous coating of 30-weight oil on the pistons and cylinder walls. A ring compressor was used to fit the pistons, which were carefully tapped in place with a rag-covered mallet handle. The rod caps were torqued to 24 ft.-lbs.

To be sure the compression ratio was where we wanted it, Curt measured the piston and cylinder head displacement. Even though the Speed-Pro pistons were 10.5:1 units, the Valley Head Service porting job increased the cylinder head capacity, and we ended up with a 9.4:1 compression ratio. This was perfect since carbon buildup should raise the ratio after the engine is driven a while. If we wanted the 9.6:1 ratio right away, we could use a slightly thinner head gasket.

Next, the cam was installed, and the cam that perfectly matched our parameters turned out to be a Crane Blazer 288-2H grind (part No. 36380), designed for smooth idle and good low to mid-range horsepower and torque. The Crane Blazer cam's specs are: *intake,* 218-degree duration, .480-inch valve lift; *exhaust,* 230-degree duration, .496-inch valve lift; and a 114-degree *centerline.* We selected the Cam-Ponent Kit (part No. 36301), which included the complete cam and kit consisting of hydraulic lifters (part No. 99280), inner and outer valve springs (part No. 99858 and 99836), steel spring retainers (part No. 99944), and Crane valve seals.

Like all other parts, the cam was cleaned before being installed. The cam lobes were coated with Crane Assembly Lube (part No. 99000) to protect the cam during initial fire-up. The cam was gently worked into the block, using a screwdriver to support the outer end of the camshaft. A Crane timing gear and chain (part No. 36999) were also installed.

After installation, the cam was degreed off the lifters using a dial indicator and degree wheel. A solid lifter must be used to obtain accurate readings. Curt set our cam 2 degrees ahead of the recommended specs because the cam will retard as the timing chain stretches. With everything checked out on the cam, the front engine cover was installed. Since our original water pump had a large crack that had been filled with plastic body filler, we installed a new Sealed Power water pump (part No. PC-315). All-new freeze plugs were also installed, using a Sealed Power

freeze plug kit (part No. SH-510 S). A little Loctite was applied to the freeze plugs before inserting them into the block. Remember, the cam blocks access to some of the plugs, so be sure to install them before installing the camshaft.

The last part of the short-block assembly was to install the oiling system. Since this is one of the weakest links in the 289 Ford, everything was replaced with superior aftermarket parts. A heavy-duty Sealed Power oil pump (part No. 224-411Z8) was installed with a Milodon oil pump shaft (part No. 22500). The Milodon shaft is made out of 4130 chrom-moly and features heat-treated ends for maximum strength. We installed a Milodon Super Street oil pan, which has a seven-quart capacity but a low profile for good ground clearance. A Milodon oil pickup (part No. 18375) must be used with the Super Street oil pan. We also used a set of Milodon's trick pan bolts (part No. 85010) to hold the beautiful gold-irridited pan in place and eliminate oil leaks. Normally, this would have been a good time to install the fuel pump (in our case, a Carter Super Pump, part No. M6904), but since Edelbrock's dyno has its own fuel system, we didn't install the Carter pump until after the dyno tests.

THE CYLINDER HEADS

With the short-block assembled, we turned our attention to the cylinder heads. The valve job and head porting were also handled by Valley Head Service. Ford fanatics will be interested to know that Valley Head Service did all the competition headwork for Carroll Shelby. Our engine received a "Marathon" valve job and a "Streetmaster" porting treatment.

First, the heads were hot-tanked

and Magnafluxed. Then the stock valve guides were bored out and replacement guides were pressed in place and spot-faced to the stock valve guide height. Sealed Power stock-size replacement valves were used, and each was matched to its guide after the stem was checked to guide clearance.

The next step was the Streetmaster porting job, basically a competition porting job for the street. The difference between a full competition job and the Streetmaster is that the Streetmaster doesn't place as much emphasis on the intake ports. After 1000 miles or so, the intakes get loaded up with carbon, so a lot of porting here is wasted money. Templates are used as a guide to how much metal to remove, and then the final touches are done by polishing the ports.

The Marathon valve job is a competition-type valve job for street applications. The exhaust seats are ground to an exact width of .080-inch, and the intake seats are ground to .060-inch. All seats are located .0015-inch from the edge of the valves. The intake valves receive a three-angle grinding of 45, 35, and 25 degrees. The exhaust valves receive a two-angle grinding of 45 degrees with a 25-degree backcut. Then the valves are hand-lapped to ensure a positive seal and verify proper valve location.

Following the valve job and porting, the heads were assembled using new Sealed Power rocker arms (stock-type replacement units) and Crane double springs, retainers, and seals. Spring shims were used to ensure installed heights within ±.005-inch. All springs were checked for binding.

The Rocket head gaskets were installed and the heads torqued in

(28) There are several ways to degree a cam. This is the lifter method. Be sure to use a solid lifter for accurate readings, even though you may have a hydraulic-lifter cam.

(29) The oiling system needed a little help (above right), so we installed a new Sealed Power pump, Milodon heavy-duty shaft, and Milodon pickup.

(30) Take time and care when inserting the camshaft. A screwdriver works well to support the end of our Crane Blazer cam. Lubricate the cam thoroughly with Crane Assembly Lube.

(31) The special Milodon oil pickup is necessary for use with a Milodon Super Street seven-quart gold-irridited pan. The pan features a low-profile for street use.

BLUE-PRINTING THE 289

place, using the pattern specified by Ford, to 70 ft.-lbs. The Crane hydraulic lifters were slipped in place after being thoroughly covered with assembly lube while the lifter bores were covered with oil before the lifters were installed. The pushrods were also oiled, and the pushrod ends were covered with assembly lube before being in-

(32) A Streetmaster porting job starts with a template to scribe the rough shape where material will be removed from the head. The ports are then ground and finally polished.

(33) All areas of the head that are worked over are carefully polished before the job is finished. Old valves (not the new ones) are used during the grinding and polishing procedures.

(34) A Valley Head Service Marathon valve job includes a three-angle grinding on the intakes and a two-angle grinding on the exhausts.

(35) After the machine grinding, the valves are hand-lapped to their final fit.

(36) The factory valve guiders are drilled out and replaced with new pressed-in guides. The new guides are honed to fit each valve stem.

(37) All the valvetrain pieces are laid out and checked prior to assembly.

(38) The Crane springs were checked with a caliper and spring tester prior to being installed on the engine. Spring shims were used to keep installed heights within ± .005-inch.

(39) The Crane hydraulic lifters were thoroughly lubricated before being installed in the lifter bores. The pushrods and rocker arms were also generously covered with oil and assembly lube.

stalled. Stock Ford pushrods were used in conjunction with Sealed Power rocker arms (part No. 2R-836). All contact areas were coated with assembly lube. Curt likes to put plenty of oil in the center of the rocker arms so they have oil when the engine is first fired. Valve lash was set at zero because of the hydraulic cam.

The final touch was to cover the valvetrain with a pair of polished Edelbrock valve covers (part No. 4160). Curt painted the area between the fins with Rust-Oleum National Blue paint to match the block. The intake manifold best suited for our needs turned out to be an Edelbrock Torker (part No. 2755). The Torker is a high-performance street manifold designed for midrange rpm, which is exactly where our engine will operate best.

The recommended carburetor is a Carter 9627 Super Quad AFB, which is rated at 625 cfm and has an electric choke for easy starting.

The entire ignition system is comprised of Accel parts, including a BEI-II breakerless ignition (part No. 39201), 9mm "Fat Stuff II" yellow silicone supression-core spark plug wires, Yellow Jacket spark plugs, and a Super Coil (part No. 140001). If someone wanted to use mechanical points, a good choice would be one of Accel's dual-point distributors. Dual-point distributors were used successfully on the Shelby 289 engines. The rest of the electrical system—alternator (part No. 190201), regulator (part No. 200201), and starter solenoid (part No. 40200)—is also from Accel. The starter is a Weber Ultra-Tork unit (part No. 397102).

The headers are Eagle Gold Label headers (part No. 2101) from Eagle Specialty Products, Inc. The Gold Label headers are made of extra-strong, 14-gauge .075-inch steel and coated with baked-on gold paint. To keep the engine properly lubricated, a Pennzoil PZ-1 oil filter was installed and the oil pan filled with seven quarts of Pennzoil 20W-40 oil. The engine was removed from the engine stand and installed on Edelbrock's dyno with a McLeod flywheel and bellhousing.

The engine sounded great during the break-in cycle, and everything checked out fine; so Curt and Edelbrock's Murray Jensen proceeded with the power runs. The total lead was set at 36 degrees, the carburetor was left in its out-of-the-box state, and H&H racing gas was used. The engine ran strong all the way to 6000 rpm, our imposed limit. With the stock rods, caps, and bolts, we were hesitant to push the engine any farther, although the power curve was still going up at 6000 rpm. Our final figure at 6000 rpm was 276 horsepower with 242 ft.-lbs. of torque.

DYNO RESULTS

RPM	HORSEPOWER	TORQUE (ft.-lbs.)
2000	79	207
2500	103	217
3000	131	229
3500	168	252
4000	197	258
4500	226	264
5000	252	264
5500	275	262
6000	276	242

BLUE-PRINTING THE 289

The final figure was short of our original goal of 300 horsepower, but the results still indicate that we will have a great street engine. The torque curve was amazingly flat, which means that all the engine pieces are well-integrated and the engine is very efficient. According to Edelbrock's Jim McFarland, a flat, broad torque curve is the sign of a strong street engine. The closeness of the torque figures indicates that very little additional effort is needed when the engine moves up to a higher rpm range. This also means that the engine is very fuel-efficient and should easily provide 15 to 20-mile-per-gallon economy. Jim said we probably could have experimented with tuning techniques on the dyno run and squeezed another 15 horsepower out of the engine, but our tight time schedule precluded that.

Jim also pointed out that our 276 horsepower was *honest* horsepower, whereas many factory ratings are optimistically unrealistic. As a case in point, he stated that the Mustang high-performance 289, which was rated at 271 horsepower, probably put out 230 horsepower at best, and without the efficiency of our blueprinted engine. So, all things considered, we were very pleased with the results of our 289 Ford engine blueprinting operation. **HR**

(40) The finished engine as hooked up to Edelbrock's dyno. A McLeod flywheel and bellhousing were used to mate the 289 Ford to the dyno. The engine ran like a champ during the tests.

(41) The induction system consists of a Carter 625-cfm carburetor and an Edelbrock Torker manifold. Also visible in the picture are the Accel BEI-II breakerless ignition and the Edelbrock polished valve covers.

(42) The finished engine waiting to be installed in our '65 Mustang. With all the blue paint, gold Milodon oil pan, gold Eagle headers, yellow Accel ignition pieces, polished Edelbrock valve covers, blue Chromatized Rocket air cleaner, fan, and valve cover wing-nuts, and stainless steel braided hoses and Econo-Seal hose ends from Earl's Supply, the small-block Ford looks as good as it runs.

Mustang Magic

SHAKE, RATTLE & ROLL

SUPER-TUNING THE SUSPENSION AND TRICKING UP THE TRANSMISSION

By Bruce Caldwell

Building a project car or undertaking a major restoration isn't all glamour and wax. For every hour spent bolting on some shiny new part, three or four more hours must be spent immersed in greasy, rusty drudgery. And that's just the way it was when we decided to tackle our '65 Mustang fastback's worn-out suspension and transmission. After 100,000-plus miles, the suspension, brakes, transmission, and rearend were pretty tired, so a complete update was in order.

The first item to be reworked was the transmission. The 3-speed C-4 transmission had become a 2-speed; high was no longer a part of the program. The problem was handled easily by treating every transmission component to the B&M performance program.

Normally, the B&M parts would be obtained at a local high-performance shop, but since B&M's Chatsworth, California, factory is close to HOT ROD's offices, we went to the source to see what is involved in building a high-performance automatic transmission. Our project Mustang received a B&M Street & Strip C-4 transmission (part No. 50110). These complete transmissions are usually sold on an outright or exchange basis, but since we took our old transmission to the factory, B&M used our core. The core transmission had the usual hardened seals (hence, no high gear) and worn-out sprigs. The transmission was completely disassembled, cleaned, and rebuilt with new, high-performance parts. All the new parts are as good or better than stock pieces for improved performance and reliability.

After the transmission was built, it was tested on B&M's transmission dyno (as are all B&M transmissions). Besides the standard Street & Strip C-4, we added a deep, finned transmission pan for increased oil capacity and better cooling. It also looks trick. The transmission was matched to a B&M Holeshot converter (No. 50412), which is an 11-inch converter that increases stall speed about 800 rpm over stock. A B&M Super Cooler (No. 80260) was se-

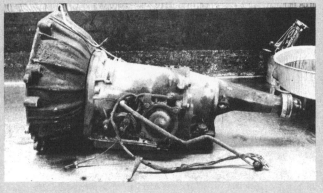

Our tired out, original C-4 transmission as it came out of the car. Only two of the three speeds were in working order.

lected to keep things cool, and a B&M StarShifter (No. 80675) was chosen to make shifting easy.

Admittedly, we opted for the quick cure to our transmission ailments. But the same results could have been obtained at home using a B&M Transpack (valve body kit) or TransKit (complete transmission kit) because B&M includes very thorough instruction booklets that take the mystery out of doing your own transmission work. The best thing about using a complete B&M transmission is that it is a quick and easy operation that just bolts in; and you know everything was

done right.

The suspension was totally thrashed, so we decided to completely update all chassis parts. Stock pieces are still available from Ford, but we wanted to go a step further for super handling. So, we picked up a Maier Racing Enterprises catalog and ordered a well-rounded suspension package. Maier Racing Enterprises (235 Laurel Ave., Hayward, CA 94541) is the country's leading source of high-performance Mustang parts, and their catalog is loaded with tuning and handling information.

We obtained their heavy-duty

SHAKE RATTLE & ROLL

mation on rearends is available in *Petersen's Big Book of Auto Repair.*

We removed the entire third member from the car to make work easier and facilitate cleaning and painting the housing. After a trip to the local car wash, we took the rearend to Customs By Eddie Paul, where Eddie applied Ditzler DU-9001 Durethane black enamel with a Binks Model 15 spray gun. Ditzler Durethane is a very tough, high-gloss paint that uses a catalyst to achieve a super-hard finish. The Binks Model 15 is a touch-up gun that is just the right size for spraying small quantities of paint, like that needed for rearend painting.

The final area of our chassis that needed work was the brakes. All the old parts were replaced with new Deccel parts. The master cylinder was replaced with a new Deccel unit, as were all the wheel cylinders. Deccel premium brake shoes were installed; Deccel heavy-duty brake fluid was added; and the

front and rear springs, which minimize body roll, improve handling, and lower the car one inch. For quicker steering, we got a Quick Steering Package (No. 236), which includes a pitman arm and idler arm. The package duplicates the quick steering kit that was offered with the '65 to '66 Shelby GT 350s. The lower A-arms, rod ends, upper and lower ball joints, and strut rod bushings were all replaced with heavy-duty Maier parts. For shock absorbers, Carroll Shelby knew what he was doing, so we went with the tried-and-true Koni adjustables. These super shocks are a simple bolt-in operation for any '65 to '70 Mustang. Keeping with the Shelby theme, we stiffened the front end (which aids handling on a subframe car like the Mustang) with a Maier front fender support bar and an export brace. Both parts are simple bolt-on jobs. To top off our suspension overhaul, we installed Addco Industries' front and rear handling kits, which consist of front and rear anti-sway bars and all the necessary hardware. We used bars No. 1214 and 14032 to replace the stock front bar and add a rear anti-sway bar, respectively.

One of the quickest and most cost-effective ways to improve performance is to change rearend gears. We discarded the anemic 2.80 stock gears and replaced them with Perfection American Zoom 4.11 gears (No. 180040). We also used Zoom gaskets, shims, bearings, and 90-weight gear oil. Changing gears is an exacting operation, one that can't be accomplished without the use of precision tools. The way to make gear changes much easier is to use Perfection American's ring and pinion gear setter kit (No. 220000), which comes in its own wooden carrying case and contains a micrometer, dial indicator, instruction manual, and all necessary clamps, extensions, and locators. Additional infor-

(4) All B&M Street & Strip trannys are tested on a transmission dyno before leaving the factory.

(5) A B&M deep pan was used, which requires an adapter to properly locate the filter.

(2) The transmission was quickly and expertly disassembled by the experts at B&M. Nothing was overlooked in this total rebuild.

(3) All the old parts are replaced with new B&M parts, which are as good or better than factory pieces. Here is the new heavy-duty clutch pack.

(6) Our finished B&M Street & Strip transmission along with a Holeshot converter, Super Cooler, StarShifter, and Trick Shift transmission fluid.

brakes are now better than new.

Two annoying problems always crop up while you're doing chassis work: grease and seemingly immovable fasteners. We easily conquered those problems by using a Super Speed Equipment (1550 Clark St., Arcadia, CA 91006) parts solvent bath and a Sears Craftsman air impact wrench (No. 18944). The Super Speed parts washer can be operated on either household current or a 12-volt battery. The Craftsman air impact wrench delivers more than 300 ft.-lbs. of torque, so removing rusty suspension fasteners was no problem.

Reworking the chassis of an early Mustang is not particularly fun work. Few observers know how much effort you put into areas of the car that are both unseen and unglamorous. But you'll know it was worth it when you drive the car, and your friends will know when they try to follow you on a winding mountain road. **HR**

(7) The entire suspension was updated with new, heavy-duty parts. The springs, control arms, rod ends, bushings, and a quick steering kit are all from Maier Racing Enterprises.

(8) Addco front and rear anti-sway bars were installed (below right). The Addco bars come with the necessary mounting hardware.

(9) Both front and rear shock absorbers were replaced with Koni adjustable shock absorbers (below). These are the same shocks used in Shelby Mustangs.

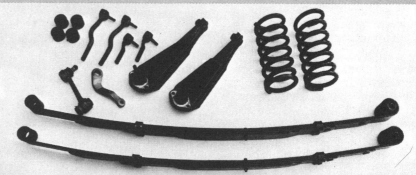

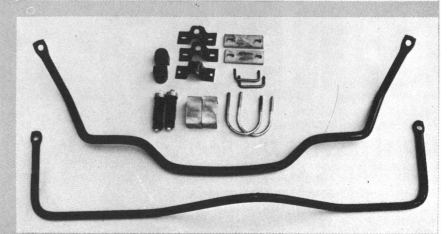

(10) A lot of dirty parts were encountered during the chassis work. A Super Speed parts washer cleaned them all easily.

(11) The entire third member (above right) was removed for ease in working and taking photos. Eddie Paul sprayed the rearend with black Ditzler Durethane using a Binks Model 15 touch-up gun.

(12) There are a lot of stubborn fasteners in a rearend, but a heavy-duty air impact gun like this Sears model (No. 18944) handles even the toughest nuts.

(13) The stock gears were replaced with 4.11 gears from Zoom (right). American Perfection's ring and pinion setting kit was used to accurately set up the gears. The kit includes all necessary instruments, instructions, and hardware.

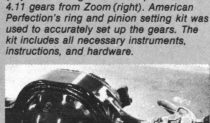

(14) The brake system was completely redone with Deccel parts, including new shoes, wheel cylinders, and a new master cylinder.

BOUNCE BACK

HOW TO PUT THE SPRING BACK IN YOUR REAR SUSPENSION

TEXT AND PHOTOGRAPHY BY ERIC RICKMAN

ALTHOUGH, AS A MUSTANG OWNER you may want to deny the inevitable, sooner or later you'll find that your car is not an exception to an immutable law of nature—the rear springs will begin to weaken and lose their temper. At the same time, the rubber bushings will become increasingly worn and softened, resulting in a lowered rear end that shifts from side to side very disconcertingly when cornering.

A quick-fix solution is to install longer rear shackles, which has also become a common method of raising the body to clear larger tires. This is definitely not recommended, for at least two reasons. First is the fact that once the spring begins to lose its temper and de-arch, it's a progressive situation; you'll have to install longer and longer shackles with increasing frequency to stay ahead, and eventually you'll have to fix the problem anyway. Second, longer shackles, combined with soft rubber bushings, allow increased lateral motion, adding to the car's instability when cornering—not only very annoying, but also quite dangerous.

Two alternatives are possible when faced with remedying this situation correctly. The first and most obvious is to buy new springs. Doug Norrdin, owner

of Global West Alignment Specialties (5660 Arrow Hwy., Montclair, CA 91763, 714/946-7828), can supply new custom-made springs (with a much lower-than-stock spring rate) to use with his new, virtually frictionless Del-

1 *Safety is the first consideration on this job. Use stands to support the car body solidly, then use a floor jack to support the axle housing after unbolting the U-bolt shackles.*

Alum bushings. Depending on how high-performance you want to go, Doug's springs range in price from $160 to $270 per matched pair. The top-of-the-line HyPro set is made from a higher grade steel and has leaves

BOUNCE BACK

designed to reduce wrap-up, in addition to having their spring rates very closely matched, and calibrated to your car's weight.

The second, and probably the less expensive route, if you just want a nice ride and aren't a HyPro fanatic, is to take your springs to a spring shop and have them re-arched. This requires the services of a well-qualified shop, as the springs must be disassembled and subjected to a very exact heating and tempering process. A good job will last through several years of driving, and indefinitely on a show car. Locally, we

got a quote of $80 if we brought the springs in—a very reasonable figure.

Once the springs are ready, they still need to be reinstalled—the second part of the process.

Doug has spent a great deal of time researching this problem as it relates to most vehicles, and has discovered a new material made by Du Pont, "Delrin," that has proven ideal as a replacement for the stock soft rubber bushings when remounting your springs.

Delrin is Du Pont's copyrighted name for this acetyl homopolymer, a crystalline polymer of formaldehyde that's classed as the world's toughest acetyl resin. This stuff is so good it has been approved by the FDA and USDA for use in food processing and hospital

blood-pumping machines. A short list of its properties, taken from a technical bulletin, will give some idea of how good it really is. Delrin has a high modulus of elasticity, high strength, stiffness, a low coefficient of friction, good abrasion and impact resistance, low moisture absorption, and excellent machinability. You can't go wrong with credentials like that! Solid Teflon is probably the closest thing it can be compared with; Delrin has the appearance and slick feel of Teflon, but is many orders tougher and denser.

Doug has designed a bushing of this material and manufactures a replacement kit under his trade name "Del-Alum," consisting of a combination of Delrin and aluminum bushings and washers, with much sturdier rear

2 Upper spring and shackle are old and tired, and the spring has lost its temper. New (lower) spring, supplied by Global West, is available in various spring rates. Custom high-performance springs made from ultra high-quality steel can be produced for special orders.

3 Global West's Del-Alum bushing kit utilizes anodized aluminum bushings in the spring eyes and shackles, pivoting on Du Pont's friction-free Delrin inner bushings and spacer washers. Note use of Zerk lube fittings and extra-heavy shackles.

4 New shackles have ³⁄₁₆-inch side plates, with full-length ½-inch-diameter Grade 8 bolts for increased shear resistance.

5 Delrin washers retain spring alignment; note use of Zerk fittings. Shackles have a lifetime guarantee; if lubed properly, they won't wear out.

6 After removing the shackle side plates, use a screwdriver to pry out the old rubber bushings.

7 Pry off spring and outboard bushing from the lower shackle bolt. Use a hammer to drive the upper shackle bolt and rubber bushing out of the frame.

BOUNCE BACK

shackles. This kit produces a virtually frictionless mounting, and restrains the lateral movement so well that the Shelby's rear panhard bar can be eliminated. Kits are for sale for '64½-'66, '67-'70, and '71-'73 Mustangs at a cost of $210. In addition, Del-Alum upper bushings are also available for Mustang IIs.

Installation of the kit is a straightforward R&R (remove and replace) procedure as far as the springs are concerned. The kit's aluminum bushings must be pressed into the spring eyes with an hydraulic press, being careful to ensure the Zerk lube fittings will be accessible after the spring is installed in the car.

To remove the old springs, first be sure the car is supported properly on stands, with the rear wheels off the floor. After loosening the spring retaining axle housing U-bolts and shock mounts, use a floor jack under the differential to lift the axle housing off the spring saddles and support it during the swap. Be careful not to damage the brakelines while doing this. Remove the nuts securing the rear shackle's inboard plates, and pry the plates off. Using a long screwdriver, pry the inner half of the rubber bushing out of the spring eye, then pry the inner half of the upper bushing out of the frame mount. With the inner halves of the bushings removed, the spring eye can now be pried off the lower outboard half of the shackle, and the shackle driven out of the frame mounting hole.

Clean the hole carefully with a scraper and sandpaper to ensure that the new aluminum bushing will press into the frame without interference. The front spring eye is secured by a long bolt that passes through the frame and the spring's rubber bushings. This bolt must be loosened and driven out of the spring eye to release the front of the spring. Clean the bolt carefully on a wire wheel, or with sandpaper, and inspect the threads, as this bolt will be reused.

After the Del-Alum bushings are pressed into the spring eyes, the rear upper shackle bushing must be installed in the frame hole that you cleaned so carefully. The aluminum bushing can be gently tapped into

8 *An air gun is handy, but you can remove the front spring eye bolt with a box wrench and socket. Inboard end of the bolt is reached through an access hole in the frame.*

9 *Lube spring eyes with Neo-Grease, or a graphite grease, before installing the aluminum outer bushings.*

10 *Use an hydraulic press to press the front bushing into the spring eye. Zerk fitting determines depth. Position fitting so it's accessible from under the car when spring is in place.*

11 *Delrin washers are of different thicknesses. Kit instructions show proper location to align spring with car frame.*

12 *If you're lucky, the frame-mounted upper shackle aluminum bushing will tap into place after thoroughly cleaning the opening. Do not force the bushing into the frame—soft aluminum will deform.*

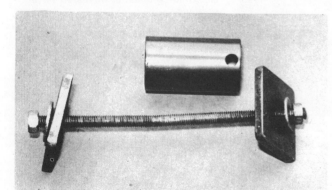

13 *If upper shackle bushing is a tight fit, this trick homemade tool can be used to draw the bushing into place. Tool is made from ¼-inch steel plate and ⅜-inch threaded steel rod.*

14 *Install aluminum bushings with lube hole outboard and downward for accessibility. Mark location and drill frame flange with a No. 3 drill, then tap with a ¼x28 tap to accept the Zerk.*

BOUNCE BACK

place with a hammer if it isn't too tight a fit. Never try to drive the bushing into place; instead, you may have to resort to a special tool made from an eight-inch length of ⅜-inch threaded rod, a pair of ⅜-inch nuts, and a couple of drilled squares of ¼-inch plate. This tool will draw the bushings into the frame. The Del-Alum bushing has a lubricating hole at one end; this must be positioned outboard (and at the bottom when mounting in the frame) to be accessible for lubing. Mark the hole location on the flange of the frame opening, as this must be drilled and tapped to accept a Zerk fitting aligned with the hole in the bushing. Use a No. 3 drill

and ¼x28 tap for this job.

If you encounter a bushing that fits too loosely, it must be pinned in place to prevent its rotation in the frame. A small hole is drilled in the inboard end of the frame's bushing opening flange, and into the aluminum bushing. A roll pin is driven into the hole to lock the bushing in the frame; be careful not to drive it into the Delrin inner bushing. Cut the outer end of the pin off flush with the frame flange.

Several thicknesses of Delrin washers are supplied with the kit to ensure proper spring and frame alignment. The proper location of these washers is described in the complete directions supplied with the kit. To install the spring, lube the Delrin bushings and washers thoroughly with Neo-Grease (Doug can supply this) or a graphite grease—*do*

not use a lithium-based grease. The front eye is secured with the freshly cleaned stock bolt.

You'll note that the rear shackles provided in the kit are much sturdier than the stock shackles, having full ³⁄₁₆-inch side plates. The Grade 8 bolts are the full diameter over their entire length (not necked down at the threaded portion as are the stock bolts), which greatly increases their shear strength. Here again, carefully lube the Delrin bushings and washers and refer to the instructions for proper washer location.

With this new, softer, yet more stable ride, you may want to consider some new shock absorbers to match the new spring rate, making a complete and properly matched rear suspension system. *M*

15 Zerk fitting in frame flange must align with hole provided in the aluminum bushing, and be accessible after the shackle is installed.

16 If aluminum bushing fits too loosely and rotates in the frame, drill through the inboard frame flange and bushing, and drive a roll pin into the bushing to pin it in place. Pin must not extend into bushing opening, so cut pin flush with flange.

17 With upper bushings in place, install the shackles. Follow kit directions for washer location according to thickness.

18 Proper location of the Delrin washers ensures spring alignment with the frame. Note accessible positioning of Zerk fittings.

19 Solid Delrin washers and bushings restrict spring movement to the vertical plane, preventing lateral movement when cornering.

LESS IS BETTER

A SUSPENSION SWAP THAT LIGHTENS THE LOAD

TEXT AND PHOTOGRAPHY BY DON EMMONS

ANY MUSTANG OWNER WHO DOES his or her own maintenance work knows what a hassle it is to change plugs or do any other work around the sides of the engine. And drag racers know what a chore it is to try to do any fast pit repairs with the engine compartment totally filled up by the engine. The spring towers and inner fender panels make for a tight fit. So any time you can make things work better and shave weight, it can't be too bad a deal.

Manny Ramirez, owner of Prestige Auto Body in Anaheim, California, campaigns a '70 Mustang drag car and is forever on the lookout for something to make his car a little more efficient and

his workload a little easier. Weight shaving has always been the name of the drag car builder's game. In addition, a steering swap eliminated the original factory power steering; he was never totally satisfied with the handling anyway.

Manny and his friend, Dave Belski, owner of Dave's Brake and Alignment Service in La Habra, California, tossed around ideas for changing the steering and front suspension to rid the inner panels of those large spring towers. After a lot of checking and measuring various front end units, they decided that a '76 Pinto front end assembly was almost too good to be true—it was tailor-made to fit the Mustang front end

and filled their requirements to the letter. It's much smaller and more compact than the original assembly, with short coil springs and shocks mounted inside the coils. Plus, it was the right width between the framerails, making it an easy interchangeable installation. They picked up a '76 Pinto front frame section from Clark's Auto Salvage in Placentia, California, and took it to Dave's shop. There, the Mustang's engine was removed and the cutting got under way.

After the removal of the Mustang suspension, the first step was to box in the front fenders for support when the inner fender panels were removed. One-inch-square pieces of tubing were

attached to the framerails and firewall. Another piece was added below the area where the fender lip and the inner panel bolt together. This framework was installed first to give support to the front sheetmetal.

With the inner panels removed and the fenders supported by the square tubing, the Mustang was ready for the new suspension.

As noted earlier, the Pinto unit came from the salvage yard. Usually, that means more frame structure than is necessary is still attached. Only the crossmember, suspension pieces, brakes, and rack and pinion steering unit are really needed. The framerail portion of the Pinto structure must be cut away, leaving only the crossmember and upper and lower control arm assemblies.

The Pinto assembly is installed on the Mustang frame by cutting open the outside portion of the framerails and peeling open the side section. The next step is to slip the Pinto unit up from below into the framerails so the upper control arm mounting area is even with the top surface of the Mustang framerails.

Dave suggests taking measurements and checking for squareness of the crossmember from the lower radiator core support. The unit should be checked to make sure it sits on a parallel plane with the framerails. The outside portion of the frame can now be brought back and wrapped over the sides of the new crossmember, and it's ready to be welded together.

Although the Pinto front end comes with disc brakes, Manny wanted to retain the stock Mustang drum brakes. The upper and lower ball joints are interchangeable, so it was a simple swap, requiring only a spindle change. Others doing this swap might want to use the stock Pinto setup.

This front end swap is relatively easy and eliminates all of the spring tower area. It probably makes for a stronger front end as well, with the coil springs and shocks housed between the control arms, rather than held in place by sheetmetal panels. Plus, it leaves lots of work space in the engine compartment. Now a good set of headers can be built that will work properly.

This setup was a trick swap that noticeably cleaned up the front end of Manny's car. And with the elimination of the Mustang power steering when it became a drag car, it also gained the pluses of a rack and pinion unit.

Manny says the steering is much better than before, and cutting down the coils allowed the car to be lowered to less than four inches of ground clearance. We realize that this swap is not for all of you out there, but a lot of Mustang drag cars still campaign around the country. And those racers want the best machine they can build. *M*

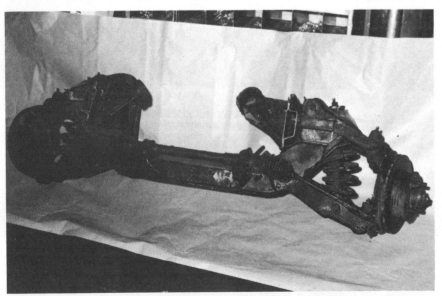

1 *Here's what you need to accomplish this front end swap. Make sure you get the rack and pinion steering unit, too—it's the best part of this swap.*

2 *Cut away framerails—only the crossmember portion is used.*

LESS IS BETTER

3 Install the Pinto unit with the spindle upper control arm removed. Retain the Mustang strut rod and bolt to lower control arm.

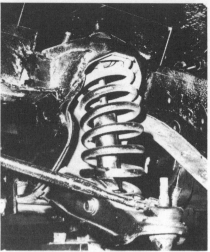

4 Another view of the Pinto unit welded into place. Note how the Mustang frame metal was formed to the side of the Pinto spring cup and welded to it.

5&6 Pinto and Mustang ball joints are the same, so swapping the spindle and brakes can be done without making changes on the system.

7 Swap has been completed. Brakes are in place and ready for the steering to be fitted.

8 The stock motor mount and mounting area were not changed. Top portion had to be cut and boxed in (arrow).

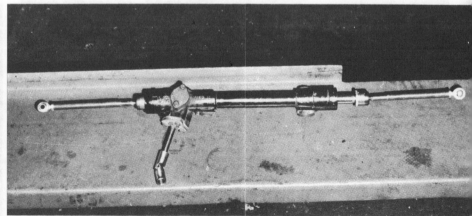

9 Dave Belski reworked the steering unit a little. Tie rods were changed in favor of a stiffer unit from Alston Race Car Engineering in Sacramento, California. The chromemoly tubing (part No. 2616) comes threaded and has Heim joints.

LESS IS BETTER

10 *Finished setup shows the Pinto suspension mounted and the steering bolted into place. Use the stock Pinto disc brakes or change over to stock Mustang drums, as shown here.*

11 *Bolt the rack and pinion steering to the Pinto crossmember. Attach new tie rod and Heim joints to the stock Mustang arms.*

12 *Hook steering to Mustang column with new U-joint. Fender support tubing can be seen below top edge of fender and box above upper control arm.*

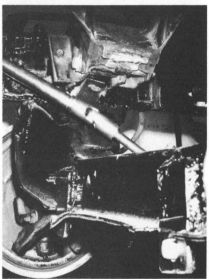

13 *Notch the crossmember slightly to allow the steering to pass by.*

14 *Installation is complete, engine is in place, and headers added. Unit provides a good compact suspension and an excellent steering setup.*

15 *With engine reinstalled, space saved by the removal of the towers is obvious.*

HANDLE WITH CARE

T his is a test—if asked to define the expression "optimum handling," would you answer: A) Being able to negotiate very sharp turns; B) The greatest reduction in body lean; C) Perfect traction for acceleration; D) Stability at high speed; E) Fantastic braking power; F) Neutral steering in corners; or G) All of the above. If you answered "G," all of the above, you're on your way to understanding that handling is a blend of several qualities, not just increased roll resistance and spring stiffness.

If you've ever been lucky enough to drive or ride in a fully-prepped road-racing car around a tight track, you may recall being amazed at what the car could do. Just when you think the car has reached the limits of road adhesion, it surpasses that point of seemingly-no-return like a tach on a racing engine that's been decked coming out of a corner.

Regardless of whether we're talking about chassis preparation for drag racing, slaloms, or high-performance street driving, Mustangs are the perfect production cars to use in this discussion. As the originator of the sporty "pony" car era, the Mustang has been subjected to more kinds of competition and performance work than probably any other American car outside of the Corvette. The horse cars have been up Pike's Peak, down drag strips, first across the finish line at the SCCA Trans-Am championships two years in a row (1966 and 1967), tested by every automotive magazine, and street-raced by thousands of drive-in cruisers across the nation.

Going back to the early performance years, all the techniques used by Shelby American back in 1965 and 1966 (wider wheels, high-performance Goodyear tires, Koni shocks, stiffer anti-sway bars, heavy-duty ball joints, quicker steering, engine compartment tube stiffeners, disc brakes up front, proportioning valve, and metallic big-

car brakes on a 9-inch rearend, which also featured a Detroit Locker differential and traction bars) are applicable to just about any year Mustang. Some of the parts used on the Shelbys can still be purchased from Ford, and many of them can be used on later Mustangs. Other parts no longer in production by Ford can still be obtained at a number of Mustang specialty houses which have limited supplies of original Shelby parts, and what isn't available from these sources is made up now by new manufacturers of Mustang and Shelby reproduction parts.

The 1974-1978 Mustang II, being

Adding the over-ride traction bars like the early Shelbys were equipped with means cutting some slots in the sheetmetal flooring and welding in the mounts under the rear seat. The rubber piece is for covering the slot.

One of the biggest improvements you can make to any year Mustang is to add a stiffer front anti-sway bar. This 1-inch bar from Maier Racing fits Mustangs from 1965-1973.

more of an economy car than a performance machine, has considerably less aftermarket equipment available for it, though you can find the anti-sway bars and shocks you'll need from a few sources. It's still a little early to tell how much aftermarket equipment is going to be made available for the new 1979-'80 Mustangs. If the response by enthusiasts to the overall car is any indication, however, the "Mustang III" could be the rebirth of the Mustang as one of the leading "supercars."

Rims and Rubber

Whatever your performance interests in Mustangs may be, your first modification from stock is probably going to be wheels and tires. Most enthusiasts change to custom wheels and tires immediately after purchasing a vehicle for looks if for no other reason—and in most cases, any other reasons may only be vaguely understood.

EVERYTHING YOU'VE EVER WANTED TO KNOW ABOUT MUSTANG HANDLING —AND THEN SOME

By Jay Storer

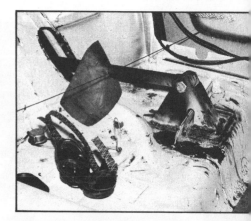

The biggest reason for switching to other tires is to gain *traction*. This is the overall key to handling for any form of driving because it all boils down to staying stuck to the ground. No matter what modifications you make to a vehicle's engine or chassis, the final contact between that vehicle and the pavement is the most important link in the chain. Some people think of traction only as it applies to drag strip starts, where rear wheel traction is certainly important, but it's just as important for developing cornering force and controllability—and for all four wheels, not just the rear two.

Many factors enter into the selection of drag slicks—tire pressure to be run, rim width, horsepower, automatic or stick transmission, car weight—so for a serious strip effort, you should contact the drag slick makers or dealers for just the right

Real handling makes the difference between just managing a corner and taking a corner, and Mustangs are the perfect raw material for building up a Porsche-swallowing road car.

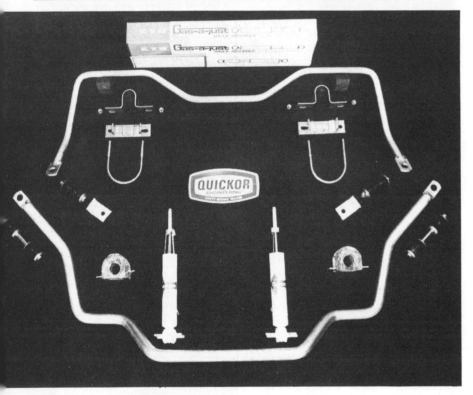

Quickor Engineering offers this complete set for early Mustangs with 1⅛-inch front bar, 3/4-inch rear bar, and four KYB gas-pressure shocks. A complete set is also available for the 1974-1978 Mustang IIs.

size and rubber compound. Too small a tire, too hard a compound, or too much air pressure, and the tires will spin excessively; too much in the opposite direction, and the engine will bog off the line. At the front, you need to run as narrow a tire as possible for the least amount of rolling resistance, and such light-weight, low-resistance tires are made for the front of stock-bodied drag cars.

Back to our quest for more traction on a street, or road-race, type Mustang, and we're back to getting as much rubber on the ground as possible front and rear. Check the rules for most sports car clubs that run slalom or gymkhana events, and you'll see how important tires are. Tire size is one of the main differences in rules between the classes in slalom events. With most street-type cars, you're limited in the amount of tire you can add by the shape and size of your wheelwells and the type of wheels you choose.

You should always choose your tires and wheels as a "package,"

also taking into consideration the suspension modifications you may be making later on. For instance, if you plan on lowering the car later, the wheelwell-to-tire clearance problem may become exaggerated, and you may be forced to go to a smaller tire.

Without going to the expense of custom steel fenderwells (done by a custom bodyshop at an average cost of $100-$200 per wheelwell) or hassle of "blend-on" fiberglass panels, some clearance can usually be gained in the stock opening. The outer fender panel usually has a lip facing the inside that contacts the tire first; this can be trimmed off with tinsnips or cut and folded up inside for more clearance. If you go the cut-and-fold route, make the cuts no more than ½-inch apart, otherwise the outside of the lip will look wrinkled after the folding operation. When you have a wheel and tire mounted on the car for a clearance check, don't forget to turn the front wheels lock-to-lock and bounce the car at each extreme to see if anything rubs.

Choosing the proper wheels will have a lot to do with how much rubber you can safely use. Wheels with too much positive offset will make even small tires interfere. Offset is the most important facet of wheel-buying, and refers to whether the bulk of the rim is to the inside or the outside of the mounting flange. More rim to the outside means positive offset, to the inside means negative. To fit the widest possible tires, find the tire manufacturer's recommendations for wheel width versus tire width.

If you're buying wheels for better performance rather than looks alone, your second consideration should be weight. The original purpose of "mag" and aluminum wheels was to reduce unsprung weight. Unsprung weight includes all the components that move up and down with the wheel, including the wheel and tire. Those components that are attached to the wheel/spindle or rear axle at one end and to the chassis at the other end make up both sprung *and* unsprung weight, so chassis engineers usually figure half of their

HANDLE WITH CARE

weight as unsprung. These half-and-half components include such items as traction bars, sway bars, strut rods, A-arms, and shocks. Unfortunately, there isn't much the street enthusiast can do about reducing this weight, so keeping the tire and wheel weight down is very important. Generally, you try to at least compensate for the extra weight of the larger tires by a reduction in wheel weight. Shop for the lightest street-legal wheels you can find (bring a bathroom scale to the store and freak out the salesman); you'll be surprised at how much some popular aluminum wheels weigh.

The type of tire construction you choose is another subject on which an entire article can, and has been, written. Most of the Mustang modifiers we've talked with expressed a variety of reasons for preferring radials for street-style Mustangs. Much has been said about the benefits of radials, but to make it as simple as possible, we can say the more-flexible sidewalls contribute to lower rolling resistance and more sideways traction. By developing higher side forces at smaller slip angles, your steering is effectively quickened. You will also realize a better road feel, and, of course, tire manufacturers' advertising campaigns won't let us forget that radials' lower rolling resistance is a proven aid to fuel economy, an important factor to offset their higher initial cost. High-performance radials, such as the popular B.F. Goodrich T/A Radials, are offered in the low-profile category of 50 and 60 series, making them as low as they are wide—also advantageous to handling.

Weight Distribution

A problem with various models of the Mustang is weight bias. Despite a relatively good, low overall weight—compared to other muscle cars and Detroit barges—Mustangs have a typically-American frontward weight bias. The average early Mustang had an overall weight of from 2800 to 3200 pounds, depending on what options it was equipped with, and an average weight bias of 56 percent (front)

and 44 percent (rear). The later Mustangs, with the big-block engines and heavier bodies, had as-delivered weights 500-600 pounds heavier and with more of it up front due to the heavier engines.

In addition to the importance of reducing unsprung weight as much as possible, it's important for any performance car to reduce *overall* weight, which has the effect of adding horsepower without any of the negative effects of gaining horsepower through engine mods. And for a vehicle to be used effectively in a handling sense, it's also important to bring the front/rear weight bias to as close to a 50/50 distribution as possible. Such "ideal" distribution (for handling, not drag racing where more rearward bias is important for rear wheel traction) is not achieved easily on most American cars with V8s up front.

Just to show you how easily changes can be made in a Mustang's weight distribution, check this trick out. In a '65 Mustang fastback weighing 2800 pounds, add-

Three modifications seen at the rear of this Mustang are the Koni shocks, 1-inch lowering blocks, and the five and one-half-leaf heavy-duty rear springs, which reduce spring wrap-up.

ing an 80-pound sandbag to the trunk will change front/rear weight distribution from 56/44 to 53/47! When you can shift weight from the front of the car to the rear, improvements are quite dramatic for the weights involved, and one of the modifications Shelby made to the original '65s for his GT 350s was to move the battery from the engine compartment to the trunk. In a 2800-pound car, every shift of 28 pounds from front to rear is a full one percent improvement! This is a simple modification anyone can

make using a long, heavy-duty battery cable (an old length of arc-welder cable is perfect) and a plastic marine battery box. Chrysler's Direct Connection parts program offers a whole battery-transfer kit.

Naturally, removing weight *from* the whole car is also important, particularly up front. You can do this most easily by replacing steel body parts with fiberglass ones. The hood, lower splash apron, and even the front fenders can be replaced with rustless fiberglass parts. Maier Racing offers front fenders in 'glass that are already flared for

Semi-metallic brake pads will add fade-resistance to any disc-brake-equipped Mustang. They are shown here with the anti-squeak pads and the Kelsey-Hayes proportioning valve used on disc-ed Mustangs with rear drums.

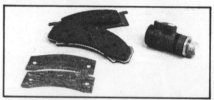

This '66 GT 350 features several modifications applicable to Mustangs up to 1970, such as the ball-bearing idler arm conversion (arrow), lowered A-arm pivot point, heavy-duty A-arm bushings with grease fittings, Koni shocks, and 620-pound cut-down springs.

wider tires, too. The total weight for a 'glass hood, two front fenders, and gravel shield is only 69 pounds, obviously a considerable savings over the steel parts.

Front Suspension

As most handling enthusiasts already know, the average American car leaves Detroit with soft springing to appeal to the bulk of the buying public who want that old boulevard ride and maximum isolation from the road beneath them. This is fine until an enthusiast gets behind the wheel and starts hanging corners. The soft springing and large amount of wheel travel designed in for a good ride result in a lot of lean in tight corners, lean that comes in *very* quickly. When you hit a bump or something during cornering, the suspension is already so close to its limits that it quickly bottoms out, and the tires

Maier Racing sells this complete set of new 2½-inch rear drum brakes with the segmented metallic linings.

If you get into serious racing, where fade is a problem even with the metallic brakes, duct some cool air from outside to the rear fenderwell. This is the stock ducting on a 1966 GT 350. Outside is a scoop. Both scoops and ducts are available from Maier Racing and others.

slide to the outside of the turn.

When the rear end of the car slides out first, this is referred to as *oversteer;* when the front end slides first it's *understeer.* The ideal situation, of course, is when neither end slides out and you have *neutral steer,* which means the car goes where you point it! Unfortunately, unless you have a computer and a few other sophisticated tools at your disposal, you're not going to achieve great handling without some sacrifice in ride quality. Increasing cornering power means stiffening the suspension to limit body lean and keep the components from bottoming out.

If you are limited as to how much suspension work you can do, and we hope you're not, change your shocks if you do nothing else.

There is a wide variety of aftermarket shock absorbers available today, ranging from heavy-duty units, with larger-than-stock pistons and rods; to three-way adjustable types, with a range of soft-firm-extra firm; to gas-filled types; to fully-adjustable shocks.

While there are a lot of shocks on the market, talk to members of the Shelby American Automobile Club and other modified Mustang enthusiasts, and you'll find one name mentioned continually, Koni. These Dutch-made shock absorbers are fully adjustable through a wide range, and the consensus among Mustang modifiers seems to be that

Maier Racing, Street Customs, and C&J Racing all offer fiberglass parts for Mustangs that contribute to lower weight and greater tire clearance.

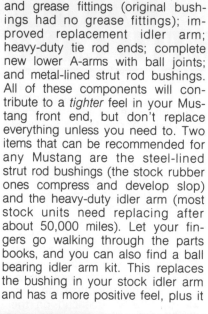

they flat *work.* They were Shelby's number one choice of shocks for his production GT 350s, which says a lot right there.

The initial expense is high for Konis because of their precision construction, but they have 'been known to last for more than 100,000 miles, outlasting several sets of regular shocks. And, they *can* be rebuilt, unlike almost every other shock. They're available for every year of Mustang except the new ones, although the original Shelby shock fits only the '65-'70 models; that shock can be made to fit the '71-'73 Mustangs with commercially-available adapters, and there are separate Koni part numbers for '74-'78 Mustang IIs.

There are quite a few other modifications that can be made to the front suspension, depending on how serious you are and how much you have to spend. Moog and TRW both offer a complete line of heavy-duty replacement parts that include: heavy-duty upper control arm kits, which include a new bar, bushings,

and grease fittings (original bushings had no grease fittings); improved replacement idler arm; heavy-duty tie rod ends; complete new lower A-arms with ball joints; and metal-lined strut rod bushings. All of these components will contribute to a *tighter* feel in your Mustang front end, but don't replace everything unless you need to. Two items that can be recommended for any Mustang are the steel-lined strut rod bushings (the stock rubber ones compress and develop slop) and the heavy-duty idler arm (most stock units need replacing after about 50,000 miles). Let your fingers go walking through the parts books, and you can also find a ball bearing idler arm kit. This replaces the bushing in your stock idler arm and has a more positive feel, plus it

has the added feature of a grease fitting.

After shocks, the biggest improvement in handling will come from a stiffer front anti-sway bar. The Shelby GT 350s used a 1-inch-diameter front bar, and you won't believe how differently your Mustang will handle with one of these! It will also ride more stiffly, too stiffly for some drivers' tastes. All Mustang aftermarket suppliers list these bars for '65-'73 Mustangs, but bars for the Mustang II aren't as common. If the 1-incher is too stiff for you on an early Mustang, Addco Industries has both .750-inch and .875-inch bars that are bigger than stock, yet not as firm as the Shelby's.

Thickness is not always a guide when discussing non-Ford-made bars since aftermarket manufacturers may use different types of steel in their bars. Quickor Engineering, for example, markets a high-quality line of anti-sway bar kits that are computer-chosen for each application; their front bar for early Mus-

HANDLE WITH CARE

tangs is 1⅛-inch, and the rear bar is ¾-inch. They also offer KYB Gas-A-Just shocks for all years of Mustangs, and have just come out with an anti-sway bar package for the new '79-'80 Mustang.

Special shocks and anti-sway bars are common handling improvements with any car, but there are some front suspension modifications that are peculiar to Mustangs. One that has proven popular with many Mustang builders is lowering the upper A-arm pivot points. This is another modification first made by Shelby American on the early GT 350s. You must strip the front suspension components and remove the upper A-arms, scribe a straight line between the two stock pivot bar holes, and drill two new holes exactly 1 inch below them on a line parallel to the stock holes. When the A-arm pivot bar is bolted back up in the new location, caster change during a turn is quickened, reducing the front end's tendency to "plow." This modification applies to all Mustangs up to 1970 since the spring towers are the same from '65-'70. You need to use new pivot bar bolts, grade 8 quality and ½-inch longer than stock to allow for more adjustment, and the bolt heads should be tack-welded in place. Use new Ford mounting nuts torqued to 75 ft.-lbs.

Once you've achieved an increase in front roll stiffness, there's only so much handling improvement you can make without adding a rear bar, too. This is Maier Racing's rear bar kit with three adjustments. Minor welding is required for this installation.

While you're making the above change and have the suspension apart, it might be wise to think about springing. Standard Mustang front springs range from 380 pounds (per inch travel) to 460 (heavy-duty) pounds. For limiting lean for performance driving or racing, something on the order of 620 pounds is about right. Such a spring rate is easiest to achieve by using Boss 302 front springs (C90Z-5310-L). Cutting one and one-half coils from these springs and regrinding the ends to fit the spring socket will give your Mustang a stock ride height with a 620-pound rate. If you want to lower the front end 1 inch for a lower center of gravity, then cut two and one-half coils instead of one and one-half. Naturally, you'll need to have the front end realigned after the above modifications.

Most early Mustangs (with manual steering) don't seem to need much help in the steering department, which is quite responsive when the box is properly adjusted and the slop is eliminated from the other components. Stock steering is usually around three and one-half turns lock-to-lock, but if you want it quicker, several companies make reproductions of the Shelby "quick-

This Shelby features the Monte Carlo bar (just above the distributor) and the "export" brace at the firewall, both worthwhile additions to stiffen the spring towers for hard driving.
The export brace replaces the two separate braces found on stock Mustangs. It's available from Ford and fits all 1965-1970 Mustangs.

steering kit," which include longer pitman and idler arms and result in two and one-half-turn steering. Be advised that adding wider tires and wheels will increase steering effort, and so will the quick-steering kit.

Now that you've considerably improved the cornering power of your Mustang's front end, you're going to want to drive harder and faster (when prudent, of course). This may call for some extra stiffening of the engine compartment bay itself. The unibody structure is stiff enough for normal driving, but the extra loads of wider tires and stiffer suspension have been known to flex the sheetmetal spring towers.

There are two bolt-on items that handily solve the problem. All Mustangs have some sort of brace going from the top of each shock tower to the firewall, which resists bending in a fore-and-aft plane but doesn't do much for side forces. The Shelbys were equipped with a one-piece part that tied both towers into the firewall flange and resisted forces in two directions. This "export brace" is still available from Ford and many aftermarket Mus-

A rear anti-sway bar with five adjustments is available from Quickor Engineering for early Mustangs

EXISTING UPPER ARM MOUNTING HOLES

FRONT OF CAR

1.00"

17/32" DIAM. DRILL — 2 HOLES

Relocating the upper A-arms is a popular trick borrowed from Shelby's GT 350. After centerpunching the new locations, scribe a ½-inch circle around each spot as a guide to tell if your drill bit is "walking."

tang companies, and fits Mustangs from '65-'70. Tying the spring towers together in a direct, side-to-side plane is the job of another brace referred to as the "Monte Carlo bar" (the bar was developed for the Falcons that ran in the '63 Monte Carlo rally). This bolts to the top of each inner fender panel just ahead of the spring towers. Reproductions of those used on the Shelbys are available for '65-'70 Mustangs through the aftermarket, and you can easily build one yourself. Just make up two brackets that bolt to the sides of the tub, and bolt a length of 1-inch tubing to them. The Monte Carlo bar requires using a smaller-than-stock air cleaner, and somewhat restricts distributor work unless removed.

Rear Suspension

Shocks are the first order of busi-

On Lee Fulton's racer, notice the aluminum blocks used to raise the front shocks' upper mounting points. This is to keep the front shocks from bottoming out with their radically-lowered suspension. With street cars only lowered an inch, it's not needed.

ness here, too. Choose either the Gabriel "E," Bilstein, KYB gas-pressure type, or the Konis. A rear anti-sway bar is a fantastic addition well worth the expense, especially if you have added a stiffer-than-stock bar up front. With front bars up to 1-inch in diameter, the rear bar should be from ½-inch to ⅝-inch in diameter. If you used a 1⅛-inch bar up front, then the rear bar should be ¾-inch in diameter. For more flexibility, if you plan to often switch from street driving to racing, an *adjustable* rear anti-sway bar would be the hot setup. These have several sets of holes in the ends of the bar so the same thickness of bar can be set for several stiffness rates. Ford made two adjustable rear bars (⅝-inch diameter DOZX-5A772-B and 11/16-inch-diameter DOZX-5A772-A), and Mai-

er Racing and Quickor offer adjustable bars also.

Springs are an area for considerable experimentation. Stock Mustangs usually have rear springs with rates of from 120-140 pounds, with four leaves each. The leading Shelby supplier today, Maier Racing, offers replacement rear springs with four leaves at 180 and 200 pounds, the latter recommended just for racing. These springs are just for '65 to '70 Mustangs. Ford lists three optional rear springs: a 180-pound model (DOZX-5556-C), a 200-pound model (DOZX-5556-B), and a super heavy-duty 220-pound model (DOZX-5556-D). Ford also listed a special Boss 302 racing rear spring package (DOZX-5A816-A) which consisted of two 200-pound springs with five and one-half leaves each and a rear track bar, or Panhard rod (which limits sideways rear axle movement in relation to the chassis). The extra half-leaf is on the forward part of each spring, to provide extra resistance to spring wrap-up under acceleration. These springs also come with aluminum eye bushings instead of rubber and steel sleeves for the bolts. The Panhard rod requires welding to install and probably isn't necessary for a street Mustang unless you're dead serious about your slaloming.

If you've changed your front springs and lowered the nose while you were at it, you'll also want to lower the rear of the car a similar amount. Maier and others sell lowering blocks that go between the springs and the rear axle pads for a lowering of 1-2 inches. Longer U-bolts are also included with the blocks. You can also lower the car by having your springs rebuilt at a spring shop; simply tell the shop just what spring rate you want. If you're autocrossing and want to lower the car more than an inch or two without using long lowering blocks, have a new main leaf made

up with the eyes reversed; this will lower the car 2-3 inches.

If you've ever tried a drag strip start with your Mustang, you already know that they have a rear traction problem. The springs tend to wrap-up under torque causing the rear tires to hop and chatter. There are two types of traction bars that can solve the problem, depending on whether you're more interested in drags or road racing. For drag racing, the standard bolt-on-at-the-spring-pad type work well enough, especially in conjunction with an extended pinion snubber. These bolt-on bars, and the under-the-chassis weld-on types, all have one drawback in common for handling purposes—they cause *chassis lift.* This is great for drag strip traction in a straight line, but you don't want your rear end to lift while cornering!

Again, referring to the good work done by the Shelby American team, the type of bar needed for road racing is the "over-ride," which was fitted to the GT 350s. The over-ride bars mount to a bracket welded to the top of the rear axle tube and extend forward through the floor sheetmetal under the rear seat, where they fit into brackets welded to the flooring. Cutting and welding are required to install them, and you'll need to install rubber boots (like shift boots) over the bars where they come through the floor to keep dirt and water out; but the over-rides really work. Instead of lifting the chassis, they induce squat. Properly installed, they won't stiffen your ride noticeably, and keeping the axle located means you won't be ruining your springs.

Braking Power

Chances are your Mustang already has excellent front disc brakes, in which case you might feel confident in your braking power. However, if you've never tried repeated braking such as that encountered in a slalom or road race, you may find the stock brakes have a tendency to fade. This is easily rectified by switching to metallic-type heavy-duty pads. Such pads were used on the GT 350s and are available for all Mustangs up to 1973. If your car has drum brakes all around and you don't want to go to the trouble and expense of adding discs, you can achieve almost equal braking by installing segmented metallic shoes on all four wheels. Your local brake relining shop should be able to in-

HANDLE WITH CARE

stall the Velvetouch-brand linings for you.

If you're *really* serious about braking power, there are three more modifications you can make. The Shelbys used big-car Ford rearends, which were fitted with 2½-inch-wide drum brakes with metallic linings. You can adapt these yourself with parts from a Ford dealer or wrecking yard, or you can get a complete kit from Maier with segmented shoes, backing plates, drums, and cylinders for '65-'73 Mustangs.

axle housing, and mounting the set-up while checking for runout. Building the adapters is the hardest part. You also have to switch to a 1-ton-truck master cylinder (C9TZ-2140-F), which has a 1⅜-inch diameter piston from which you remove the outlet port check valves. Naturally, you must use a proportioning valve (C5ZZ-2B091-B) and adjust it so that the front brakes lock up just ahead of the rears. Adjust the screw outward to make the fronts lock up sooner, inward to make the rears lock up sooner. Pedal effort is higher with metallic linings anyway, but with four discs, these linings, and no power assist, braking effort with cold pads is high, which is one reason this is more of a race-only setup.

Mike Wescott's shop performs a lot of Mustang suspension modifications. One of the favorites is adding '65-'67 Lincoln or big Ford discs complete with the bigger spindles, using a set of tapered shims to adapt the lower ball joint since the Mustang ball joint is smaller than those of the big cars.

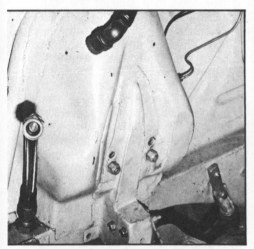

With the engine out of Richards' Solo Automotive race car, you can see the relocated A-arm bolts and the various places where the chassis has been rewelded, those areas where the factory only made spot-welds. His towers are notched for a Cleveland.

Those who race Mustangs often replace the small front disc brakes with the bigger calipers and rotors from a '65-'67 Galaxy or Thunderbird. These can be used spindle-and-all by using tapered shims to adapt the ball-joint studs and '63 Thunderbird tie rod ends. The benefit of using the larger spindles is greater strength and bigger bearings, which are more suitable for wide rubber. The ultimate in Mustang braking is four-wheel discs, usually accomplished by installing the big-car discs up front and adapting the original Mustang front discs to the rear. This is not an easy job, and the kit that Ford once offered is no longer available.

The swap consists of spot-facing the rear axles for minimum runout, building a set of caliper-mounting brackets to go on the ends of your

George Doty's race-style GT 350 features the stock Mustang front discs adapted to the rear axle, flattened rear springs with aluminum bushings, air ducts to the wheelwell, steel cable straps to limit axle travel, and healthy lowering blocks. Fenders are definitely flared on this lowboy.

Mustang IIs and IIIs

So far we've been discussing modifications and parts that apply only to the '65-'73 Mustangs; this has been for two reasons. These are the cars that have the lion's (or horse's) share of interest in them from the high-performance crowd, and the special parts are available for them. The Mustang II, introduced in 1974, was a scaled-down economy car with little thought of going after the performance market. Despite the low interest in these models on the street, there are a few companies making parts for them for improved handling. Addco and Quickor both offer sets of anti-sway bars, and Koni and KYB both have special shocks. We don't know of anyone offering special brakes for these cars over the

Early Mustang discs go for a premium in wrecking yards, but with these Kelsey-Hayes caliper mounting brackets (54313-RH and 54313-LH) you can take advantage of any of the Ford four-piston calipers and bolt them onto your drum-type early spindles.

counter, but a brake reliner could set you up with some metallic Velvetouch linings for more-than-adequate braking. The standard heavy-duty suspension or Cobra II optional suspension, with the very nice TRW rack-and-pinion, makes for a fun car to drive—even when down on horsepower compared to the previous models. They offer reasonable fuel economy (an important enough consideration today) and aren't expensive. With a few bolt-ons, and some good radial tires you can build yourself a mean macho mini!

The latest in the Ford Mustang family may never be the car that the GT 350 was, but it shows promise of being the most fun-driving car of the present. The basic design of the new car is one of the finest chassis ever to come out of Detroit. The front end features a modified MacPherson strut design, standard disc brakes, and a very-responsive-feeling rack-and-pinion. An anti-sway bar is standard, and the new rear suspension

On the esoteric/racing side, this is the front suspension used on Wayne Richards' B Production racer. The discs are unavailable Holman-Moody parts with homemade cooling ducts and stock calipers. The anti-sway bar is an adjustable Halibrand sprint car unit, partly because the regular type bar will hit the chassis with a car lowered this much. Seat belt straps are used to keep the A-arm in place when the car is jacked up. That's how much the springs are shortened! Shocks are double-adjustable Koni units.

features coil springs and a four-bar link setup for good axle location and stability.

The car handles well in standard form, but for the enthusiast there are two optional levels of suspension tightness. The Handling Suspension option includes different spring rates and stiffer shock valving, a special rear anti-sway bar, and stiffer front and rear suspension bushings. It's not exactly a slalom package, but then again it won't jar your teeth out going over railroad tracks, either. The second option is, in our estimation, the premium deal—the TRX suspension.

The '79 Mustang was the first American car to offer the all-new metric-sized Michelin TRX tires, and they only come mounted on Ford's forged-aluminum metric-sized wheels. These ultra-low-aspect-ratio tires were thoroughly tested on the European Ford Granada with great success, and promise exceptional stability and steering control To take full advantage of these unique tires, the Ford computer worked overtime to come up with a complete suspension package for use with the TRX wheel/tire setup. Unique shock valving, increased spring rates, and thicker front and rear anti-sway bars make up the package, which is standard with the

dianapolis race, the suspension required the least modification of any part of the car. All the engineers did was slightly stiffen the shock valving and add semi-metallic brake linings. The semi-metallic linings are part of the 2.3 liter Turbo engine option (along with aluminum rear drums with iron liners), and can be added to any 2.3 or 2.8 liter '79-'80 Mustang. (For those Mustangs made before Jan. 2, 1979, the part number for these linings is D9ZZ-2001-B, and D9ZZ-2001-D after that build-date.) The 5.0 liter (302 V8) Mustangs have larger front disc brakes that are interchangeable with the Fairmont brakes. The semi-metallic linings used on the V8 pace car were from the Fairmont Police Package (D9BZ-2001-C before Dec. 8, 1978, and D9BZ-2001-E after). An additional note to those modifying the new Mustang is to keep the front/rear ride height in a stock relationship. If you raise or lower the car, do it by the same amount at each end or you'll upset the precisely-designed brake proportioning by affecting the weight transfer.

The new Mustang represents the

MUSTANG SUSPENSION SUPPLIERS

Kensington Products
150 Green St.
Hackensack, NJ 07601
Importers of Koni Shocks

Quickor Engineering
6710 S.W. 111th
Beaverton, OR 97005
Anti-sway Bars and Shocks

Addco Industries
Watertown Road
Lake Park, FL 33403
Anti-sway Bars

Maier Racing Inc.
235 Laurel Ave.
Hayward, CA. 94541
Original and Repro Shelby Parts

C&J Racing Enterprises
29559 Ruus Road
Hayward, CA 94544
Fiberglass Body Panels

Street Customs Limited
11737 Cardinal Circle
Garden Grove, CA 92643
Fiberglass Body Panels

Shelby American Automobile Club
24-C April Lane
Norwalk, CT 06850
Information

Michael Wescott's Performance Unlimited
21160 Foothill Blvd.
Hayward, CA 94544
Mustang Chassis Work,
Big Front Disc and
Rear Disc Kits

Stam-Bar Stabilizers
2609 Janna Ave.
Modesto, CA 95350
Bolt-on Rear Anti-sway Bars

Seeking to lighten your '69-'70 fastback Mustang? C&J Racing offers this complete set of fiberglass parts that includes, ram-air hood, gravel shield, front fenders and headlight buckets, rear quarters, rear quarter extensions, and trunk lid. Quarters and front fenders are flared enough to use 8.5-inch rims on a lowered car.

Cobra option group. It's a fine-handling machine that still rides luxuriously even with the optional stiffer suspension.

It's a testament to the engineering in the new Mustang's suspension that when it came time to modify a production Mustang to serve as pace car for the 1980 In-

beginning of another era of cars. There may never be another Carroll Shelby to come along and build us the car of our dreams from a production model; the cost of gasoline and the efforts of legislators, insurance companies, and safety lobbyists have seen to that. But if we've learned anything from the past decade and a half of enjoying the Mustang in its several metamorphic stages, it's that the car responds well to modifications, and the Mustang that Ford and Shelby never built can be ours if we're willing to turn a few wrenches—no matter what the year and model of the raw material. **HR**

INCREASE YOUR HORSEPOWER BY AT LEAST 50 PERCENT AND GET . . .

CHARGED UP

BY MARLAN DAVIS

Almost everyone, at one time or another, has swapped intake manifolds or changed belts and pulleys. Well, gang, if you've mastered those two operations and have a low-compression motor (7 to 8:1 preferred), there's no reason why you can't install a GMC 4-71 or 6-71 super-charger on your car. Blower Drive Service (12140 East Washington Blvd., Whittier, CA 90606, 213/693-4302) offers everything needed to do the job right, from complete blower assemblies and manifolds to specially recalibrated Holley carbs and blower camshafts. Even if you have an oddball combination not covered in BDS' regular line-up, owner Craig Railsback can make up a custom kit on a special-order basis.

The heart of the BDS system is, of course, a GMC supercharger. The smaller 4-71 provides adequate boost for mild street motors through 400 inches, but most BDS customers prefer the larger 6-71's "Top Fuel" esthetics. The 3-71s are available to fit many small sixes and fours, while the huge 8-71 can be special-ordered, although it's definitely not needed for the street.

All BDS blowers are disassembled and inspected for wear and cracks. Bad components are replaced with good new ones. The rotors are triple-pinned for strength on the shaft driving ends. Oversize seals and shaft-saver surfaces are installed on the rotors as well, since they're usually too worn to accept standard-size seals. A heavy-duty aluminum rear bearing plate replaces the stock plate. Up front, street blowers retain the stock plate, reinforced with a 4130 chrom-moly steel ring manufactured by BDS. For racing use, a special heavy-duty front plate is used. All blowers are "show polished," with the street assemblies clearanced to run on gas from 25-30 percent underdriven to around 25 percent over.

If you use a blower, the engine should be in good condition, with the valves and pistons sealing properly. A forged bottom end is not mandatory in mild street use under 5000 rpm with an underdriven blower. If you're rebuilding for high-performance, a stainless steel compression piston ring with chrome

The BDS blower kit for Ford 289/302 engines, like all their other packages, comes complete with blower, manifold, drive assembly, 2 or 3-inch (on 6-71) drive pulleys and belts, and all necessary nuts, bolts, and gaskets. Instructions are also included.

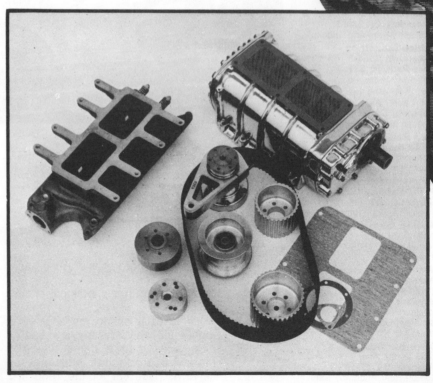

128

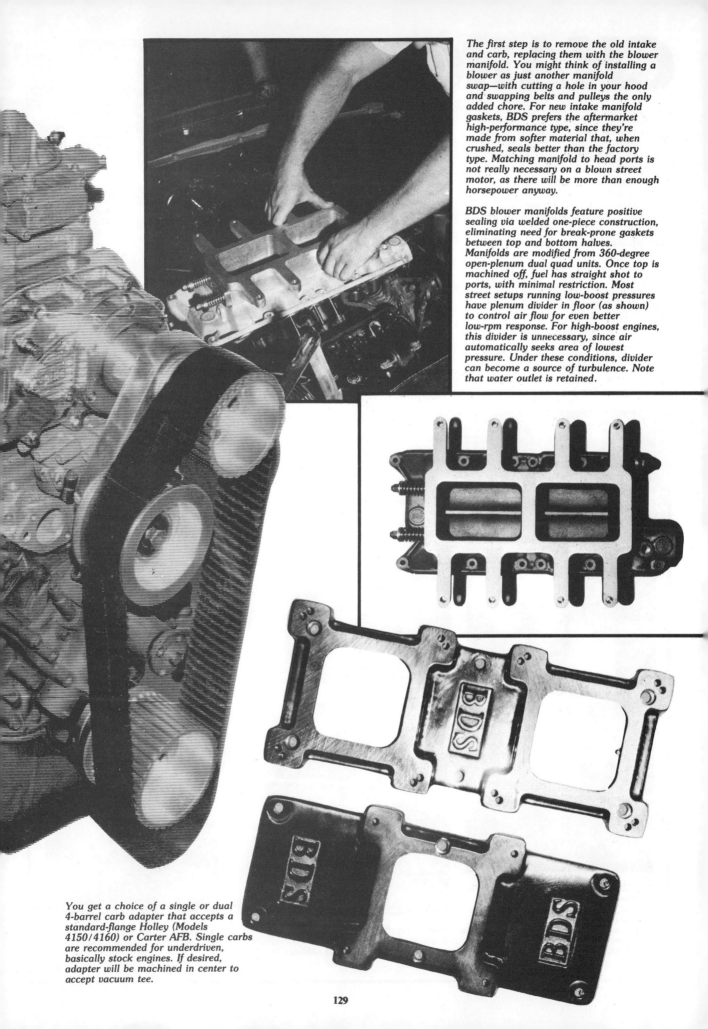

The first step is to remove the old intake and carb, replacing them with the blower manifold. You might think of installing a blower as just another manifold swap—with cutting a hole in your hood and swapping belts and pulleys the only added chore. For new intake manifold gaskets, BDS prefers the aftermarket high-performance type, since they're made from softer material that, when crushed, seals better than the factory type. Matching manifold to head ports is not really necessary on a blown street motor, as there will be more than enough horsepower anyway.

BDS blower manifolds feature positive sealing via welded one-piece construction, eliminating need for break-prone gaskets between top and bottom halves. Manifolds are modified from 360-degree open-plenum dual quad units. Once top is machined off, fuel has straight shot to ports, with minimal restriction. Most street setups running low-boost pressures have plenum divider in floor (as shown) to control air flow for even better low-rpm response. For high-boost engines, this divider is unnecessary, since air automatically seeks area of lowest pressure. Under these conditions, divider can become a source of turbulence. Note that water outlet is retained.

You get a choice of a single or dual 4-barrel carb adapter that accepts a standard-flange Holley (Models 4150/4160) or Carter AFB. Single carbs are recommended for underdriven, basically stock engines. If desired, adapter will be machined in center to accept vacuum tee.

CHARGED UP

A

facing seems to work best. Blowers respond just as well as a normally aspirated engine to such typical hot rod tricks as headers, a cam, or steeper rearend gears, but will run okay without them. One area where major changes are necessary is carburetion, which must be specially modified. The complete supercharger assembly adds from 100 to 125 pounds on the front end, and sometimes requires stiffer springs, especially when combined with a heavier-than-stock engine. Depending on the specific vehicle, most street blowers seem to run between 180 and 200 degrees in the summertime.

To prove how simple a blower installation really is, Craig bolted one on a shop Ford 302 motor. Naturally, doing it in-car will be harder—you'll need a friend to help position the blower properly and pass the brew. *M*

B

BDS Ford 289/302 setup demands use of shorter-than-stock flat-top Mallory YL Marine-style distributor (part No. 2544501), available as a dual point or with electronic triggering, to clear blower case bottom. Design allows BDS to cut height of complete assembly considerably. YL series sparksorter comes with "do-it-yourself" full-centrifugal advance curve; Craig recommends 32-34 degrees total advance at 2500 rpm on pump gas for most engines, with 10-12 degrees initial lead.

Next, drive assembly should be installed on blower case. You may find it easier to do this before it's placed on motor, especially if the blower is being installed on an in-car engine. Gear coupler goes on first (A), before snout assembly and upper front pulley are installed (B). Front case should be filled with 90W rearend lube at this time.

Most factory cast-iron harmonic balancers have tendency to fracture in severe use, so Craig manufactures 4140 chrom-moly, heat-treated, heavy-duty steel hub to replace it. Since Ford small-block is externally balanced, a counterweighted hub like this one is required.

Not all combinations are exactly parallel to crank, so belt may tend to "crawl" toward high side of installation, were it not for crown machined on idler pulley. Drive pulleys, on the other hand, must be flat to achieve maximum contact with belt teeth.

Unit is installed just like normal harmonic balancer, followed by aluminum spacer, V-drive pulley, and Gilmore belt

drive pulley, all machined to standard six-bolt pattern.

Belts are next item to go on after pulley installation. After checking for proper alignment and clearance, carefully adjust tension so that, when fully tightened, belt can be deflected with finger ½-inch in center between drive pulleys on pull (passenger) side of system. Replacement Gilmore belts can usually be purchased from bearing or industrial shops, as well as from blower rebuilders.

During blower operation, pressure from air that has escaped by front seals builds up in front gear case. Some manufacturers vent the front case, which normally results in oil and grease being pushed out all over blower front. BDS likes to see some positive pressure in the case; they believe sealing is enhanced because the seals adhere more tightly to the driveshafts, reducing further leakage to a minimum. However, tension on seals should be relieved when engine is not in operation, so pressure release button is provided. It should be pushed when engine is shut down.

Two backfire valves are built into rear of intake. Should there be a lean fuel condition, resulting in backfire, these valves will open momentarily and relieve backpressure, saving blower from damage.

Screened carb adapter-plate-to-blower gasket prevents foreign objects from falling into housing and damaging rotors.

Out-of-the-box carbs don't work well with supercharged engine; they must be totally recalibrated in order to respond properly. BDS blueprints carbs on request for each individual's specific requirements. Idle, intermediate, and high-speed circuits are modified to eliminate acceleration stumble and backfiring. Craig has found Holleys easiest to rework, thanks to good parts availability. The 600-cfm carbs in photo (list No. 0-1850) are recommended for street engines and are installed backwards to simplify throttle linkage. Competition-oriented motors with wild cams require carbs with mechanical secondaries. Chokes are removed to smooth airflow on street carbs, unless customer plans to operate car in winter. Airhorn is also machined off for all-out competition.

GREAT LINES

HOW TO INSTALL BRAIDED STAINLESS STEEL LINES

BY BRUCE CALDWELL

There are the automotive parts that work well, and the ones that look good, but the best possible ones are those that look as good as they work. Braided lines and high-performance hose ends fall into that dual-purpose category; they're high on form and function, as well as having high-tech and high-status looks.

Most owners of street Mustangs will admit that the good looks and race car image are prime reasons for plumbing a car with braided lines, but a real benefit is the superior strength of properly installed lines and hose ends. A broken fuel line can be a problem, regardless of whether your car is used on the street or the track.

We called on Earl's Performance Products (825 E. Sepulveda, Carson, CA 90745, 213/830-1620), which is recognized as a leader in the braided line industry. The Earl's Performance Products' catalog (available for $4.00) is jammed full of vital information, and includes listings of their extensive line.

There are several grades of hose. Perform-O-Flex is the premium-quality racing hose; it has an inner braid surrounded by another layer of rubber, and finally the stainless braid outer covering Econ-O-Braid hose is less expensive; it has only one layer of rubber hose, and Econ-O-Flex hose has a bright yellow outer cover instead of braided steel. Tu-Braid is the stainless braided outer cover alone, which is ideal for covering large, hard-to-form radiator hoses.

Earl's selection of hose ends is extensive. They offer straight, 45-degree forged, 90-degree forged, 45-degree bent tube, 90-degree bent tube, 120-degree bent tube, 150-degree bent tube, and 180-degree bent tube hose ends. There are special male-end pipe threads, male AN threads, and a huge selection of adapter fittings, as well as a great number of fittings just for brake systems. There's also the whole line of Econ-O-Fit fittings, which look like the Swivel Seal hose ends, but are less expensive because they use a worm-gear clamp inside the hose end. These are available in red, blue, chrome, and gold to afford many ways of making your engine compartment distinctive.

Earl's Performance Products are available in bulk quantities and precut kits. Many of the more popular applications such as heater hoses, oil lines, fuel-pressure gauges, and Holley carburetor lines come in kits which include the proper length of hose and the necessary hose ends. Earl's Performance Products are also stocked by quality speed shops all around the country.

Speed shops usually have a radial saw so they can make quick, precise cuts on the braided lines. You can cut your hoses at home with a hacksaw, but if you know the exact measurements, it's far easier to let the speed shop do it. Earl's stocks a special hand-operated cutting tool called a "Beverly Shear," which gives a smooth clean cut for easy installation. If you do a lot of work with braided lines, you might consider purchasing one.

The Earl's hoses and hose ends used here are installed on a 302-cubic-inch Ford engine, slated for a Mustang fastback. The engine is black, so he chose the blue hose ends for a handsome contrast. The braided lines stand out nicely against the black block and cylinder heads.

Braided lines and high-performance hose ends are those easy-to-add touches that will set your Mustang apart from the rest of the herd. *M*

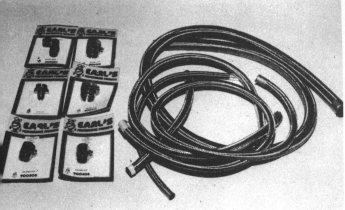

1 *Earl's Performance Products makes everything you need in the way of high-performance braided lines and hose ends.*

2 *Here's a sampling of hose ends, from left to right: 180-degree bent tube, 90-degree bent tube, 90-degree forged, and straight.*

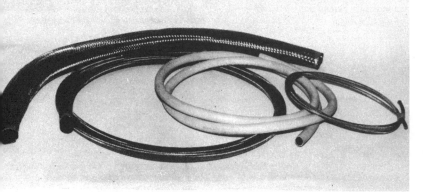

3 *Braided lines come in many styles, too. From left to right: Tu-Braid stainless braided cover, Econ-O-Braid hose, yellow Econ-O-Flex hose, and Fluor-O-Flex pressure-gauge line hose.*

4 *Econ-O-Fit hose ends look like the real thing, but they're actually a worm-gear clamp inside a hose end. These chrome models complement any engine color.*

5 *Earl's offers several precut kits, such as this heater hose one, which comes with everything you need to plumb a heater.*

6 *The Beverly Shear has a lot of leverage, thanks to its long handle. Mount it to a workbench for best results, and always wrap the end of the hose with duct tape before cutting.*

7 *Most do-it-yourselfers use a hacksaw (use a 32-teeth/inch blade) to cut braided line. Cut through the duct tape; this avoids frayed ends.*

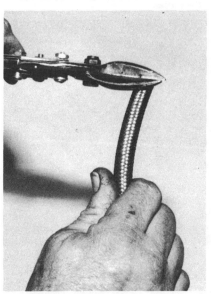

8 *If you encounter any stray strands of the braid, use a tin snip to trim them. Be careful; the little pieces of braid can cut you.*

LINES

9 *Hose ends are easy to scratch or damage if roughly treated. The trick setup is to use Earl's special hose end wrenches, which are color-coded for quick size identification.*

10 *Earl's hose end wrenches are made short so you can't exert undue pressure on the aluminum fittings. The short length also makes it easier to work in tight spaces.*

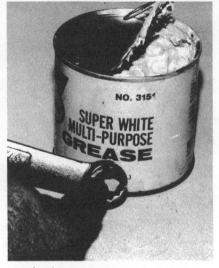

11 *Another way to protect the hose ends when using a regular wrench is to coat the inside of the wrench with white grease.*

12 *Most of the white grease will squeeze out as the fitting is tightened; just wipe off the excess.*

13 *Fittings like this fuel line should receive Teflon tape for sealing purposes. Permatex No. 14A thread sealant with Teflon comes in a tube and is an easy way to prevent leaks.*

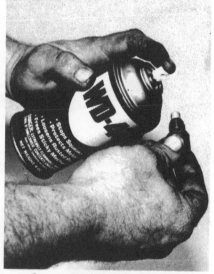

14 *Spray a light coat of silicone to help put two threaded fittings together.*

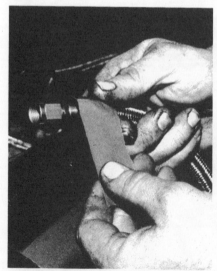

15 *Wrap duct tape around the anodized hose end that's already attached to the braided line.*

16 *Clamp the wrapped end in a vise, so it won't get scratched while you install the threaded fitting with a hose end wrench.*

17 *The braided line should butt right against the lip on the inside of the hose end.*

LINES

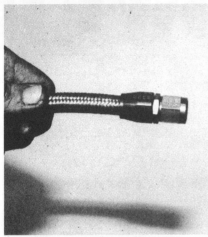

18 A typical braided line and hose end. The fit should be tight, without any wiggle.

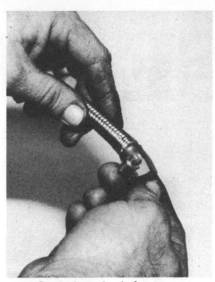

19 Cut the hose cleanly for easy installation of hose ends. Notice how this Econ-O-Fit hose end is tipped slightly as it's pressed on to the braided line.

20 Secure the Econ-O-Fit ends with a screwdriver. The trick finned-aluminum fuel filter is from O'Brien Truckers (5 Perry Hill, North Grafton, MA 01536).

21 Use a 90-degree forged hose end to keep the braided line close to the engine block during the fuel pump installation.

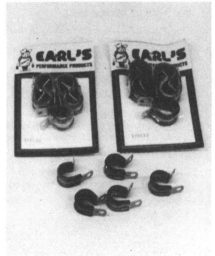

22 Earl's makes a large selection of cushioned tubing clamps which keep braided lines neat and organized.

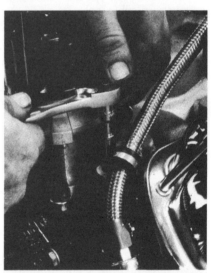

23 Bolt a cushioned clamp to the intake manifold to keep this braided fuel line in place.

24 Route the line for the PCV hose along the edge of the valve cover and use the wing nut to secure the clamp, hose, and valve cover.

25 Using Econ-O-Fit hose ends, secure the rest of the PCV hose to the PCV valve and the back of the intake manifold.

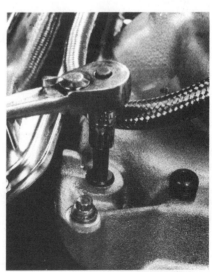

26 For a completely detailed engine, try Earl's blue-anodized Allen-head pipe plugs to fill the unused intake manifold holes.

HORSE POWER

By Al Kirschenbaum

Have you ever noticed that the more some things change, the more they seem to remain the same? Take Ford's Mustang engine line-up, for example. When the Dearborn autoworks presented their little prototype pony (then called the Mustang I) in the early Sixties, it was powered by a foreign-built 4-cylinder Ford powerplant. Now, nearly two decades later, the freshest factory Mustangs feature 4-bangers as standard, and their one-time 260-inch, then 289, then 302, then 255-cube base eight has been opened back up to 302 muscular cubic inches.

What *has* changed forever, however, is nearly everything powerful in between. In the 20-year period, the Ford ponycar line has seen all manner of motors—from muscular to minuscule—and nearly all have made their own scorched rubber marks on modern motoring.

For the purposes of this top-option review we're condensing history and looking only at the line's highlights. Granted there are a few notable pony motors that we're flat-out ignoring (the 390 and 427-inchers in particular and all Shelby engines in general), but the subject of an era's supermotors is entirely too broad for *the* final word on all the ultimate Fords. So for the moment, at least, we'll touch only on the highest of the Mustang's mechanical high points and look to future issues of HOT ROD for all of Ford's old-but-better ideas.

289 HIGH PERFORMANCE

The Mustang's very first taste of high-output breeding came late in 1964 when Ford fitted their popular ponycar with a solid-lifter model of their 289-cube small-block V8. The little engine featured longer camshaft timing, free-breathing exhaust manifolds, a high-strength crankshaft and connecting rods, threaded rocker arm studs, dual-point ignition, and a low-restriction air cleaner. Check out our spec chart for the HiPo motor's internal details and see HOT ROD, December 1980 for additional information on the complete Mustang/motor combination.

BOSS 302

In many ways, Ford's Boss 302 engine was a hot rodder's fantasy executed in iron. But far from being an all-too-typical home-brewed exercise in excess, the factory package was built on time-tested hardware with a solid engineering edge. In other words, what the motor folks in Dearborn did

was simply to refine—hot rod style—their already proven 289.

A high-strength "stroker" crank bumped the cubes to 302 while an extra pair of bolts at each center main added structural support to the forged steel shaft. New cylinder heads, Cleveland-style, were also included, and their arc-shaped combustion chamber roofs permitted the fitting of extra-large valves which, in turn, fed through even larger ports and passages.

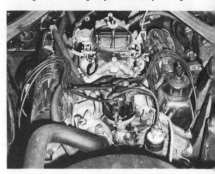

MUSTANG MUSCLE MOTORS

ENGINE	YEAR(S)	HORSE-POWER	TORQUE	COMPRESSION RATIO	BORE	STROKE	INTAKE SYSTEM					CAMSHAFT			VALVE SIZES	
							MANIFOLD		CARBURETOR							
							TYPE	MATERIAL	MFG'R	FLOW RATING		DURATION	LIFT	TYPE	INTAKE	EXHAUST
289 High Performance	1964-1968	271@ 6000 rpm	312@ 3400 rpm	10.5:1	4.00	2.87	1x4 180° dual-plane	cast-iron	Autolite	480 cfm		310°/310°	.460	mechanical	1.78	1.45
Boss 302	1969-1970	290@ 5800 rpm	290@ 4300 rpm	10.5:1	4.00	3.00	1x4 180° dual-plane	aluminum	Holley	780 cfm		290°/290°	.477	mechanical	2.23 (1969) 2.19 (1970)	1.71
Boss 351	1971	330@ 5400 rpm	370@ 4000 rpm	11.7:1	4.00	3.50	1x4 180° dual-plane	aluminum	Autolite	(1)		290°/290°	477	mechanical	2.19	1.71
428 Cobra Jet	1968-1970	'68: 335 @ 5600 '69-'70:335 @ 5200	'68: 445 @ 3400 '69-'70:440 @ 3400	10.7:1	4.13	3.98	1x4 180° dual-plane	cast-iron	Holley	735 cfm		270°/290°	481/.490	hydraulic	2.09	1.66
Boss 429	1969-1970	375 @ 5200 rpm	No data	10.5:1	4.36	3.59	1x4 180° dual-plane	aluminum (low-profile)	Holley	735 cfm		'69 (all S, early T) 288°/292° .493/.501 hydraulic (3) '69-'70 (later T) 300°/300° .509 mechanical			2.28	1.90

The '69 Boss intake valves actually proved to be too large for suitable street response, and they were later downsized for the following model year.) Free-breathing was further promoted through a generously proportioned inlet manifold and a high-volume Holley carb. And on top of this, the entire intake works could be even further enhanced through the use of the factory's optional over-hood Ram Air. Details on the Boss motor's internals are included in the Muscle Motor chart.

BOSS 351

Unlike the other Boss Mustang models, the '71 351 wasn't built to satisfy a race sanctioning body's minimum production demands, but rather to suit a variety of

"new age" marketing conditions. "Tamer" is probably the best word to describe the 1800 or so Boss factory fastbacks that rolled out during the single year's run, and all were designed for smoother, more streetable response.

The cars' performance level was maintained through the use of the same camshaft specs and the same style cylinder

heads as the Boss 302 along with similarly engineered internals. Ram Air was again installed while oiling and cooling improvements (including the power steering fluid cooler seen just forward of the driver's side valve cover) helped the relatively short-lived "middle" Boss to close out Ford's muscle generation in very street-wise style.

428 COBRA JET

Civilized muscles sprouted under Mustang bonnets when Ford upgraded their 428-cube Police Interceptor FE-series engines around 427 race-style cylinder heads in late '68. The resulting Cobra Jet powerplants packed more torque than the Mustang's street rubber could handle, but a lack of initial traction was hardly enough to keep a good option down. In fact, the 'Stangs that were so equipped became one of the most popular street machine assemblies ever offered.

The big wedge fed on fresh air pulled in from above the hood through a "Shaker" scoop/air cleaner that was optional on the

'69 and '70 Mach I models. There's little doubt that this neat Ram Air arrangement was what helped the CJ package to put Ford right up there again with the street fleet's big-inchers from Chrysler and GM.

Details on this Mustang's under-hood mechanicals can be found in the chart, while additional data on the 428CJ is provided in HOT ROD, December 1979.

BOSS 429

Of the five engines reviewed here, only the Boss 429 was really a new piece for the street rather than an outgrowth of another motor. At least it didn't **look** like any V8 that came before it. Ford decided to shoehorn 852 of these Blue Crescent-based engines into '69 Mustangs (505 were assembled for 1970) when a minimum of 500 production models equipped with the engine were required in order to qualify it for competition in NASCAR's Grand National stocker ranks. Fortunately for enthusiasts, the company decided to have their Kar Kraft subsidiary fit the staggered-valve monster motors to the sportier Mustang models rather than to the full-size Galaxies as they'd initially intended.

Equipped with exotic aluminum cylinder heads that were really considered the life-breath, heart, and soul of the "Boss Nine" package, the few 429 Mustangs that did find their way streetside were actually down on both bottom-end torque and top-end carburetion. Huge intake ports and extra generous oval-shaped exhausts made the Mustang better-suited to the high-banks than to the highways, but as the rules would have it, only Ford's larger cars ever saw big-time roundy-round competition with the Boss 429 aboard.

CKER RM TIO	IGNITION SYSTEM	CRANKSHAFT		CONNECTING RODS			FRESH AIR INTAKE SYSTEM
		MATERIAL	MAIN BEARING JOURNAL DIAMETER	MATERIAL	LENGTH	JOURNAL DIAMETER	
0:1	dual-point w/o vacuum advance	high-nodular cast iron	2.2486	forged steel	5.155	2.1232	not available
'3:1	dual-point w/ dual vacuum advance (2)	forged steel (4)	2.2486	forged steel	5.150	2.1232	optional "Shaker" hood w/scoop attached to air cleaner
3:1	dual-point w/ dual vacuum advance	high-nodular cast-iron (specially selected)	2.749	forged steel	5.78	2.311	optional ducting between dual hood scoops and air cleaner
'3:1	dual-point w/ dual vacuum advance	high-nodular cast-iron	2.749	forged steel	6.488	2.438	hood scoop on late 1968 models, optional "Shaker" hood in 1969-'70
5:1 ake 5:1 aust	dual point w/ dual vacuum advance (2)	forged steel	3.00	forged steel (3)	6.549 ('69 S) 6.605 (late '69-'70 T)	2.50	manually controlled hood scoop ducted to air cleaner

Notes:

(1) Ford's Autolite carburetors were not rated by official flow figures. Estimates for the Boss 351's model 4300-D spread-bore carb fall into the 600-750 cfm range.

(2) Both the Boss 302 and the Boss 429 Mustangs built for 1970 were equipped with rev limiters. These units were individually calibrated for each engine and were designed to limit and then cut voltage to the coil at predetermined points. Fortunately, Ford retained the standard under-hood wiring harness even when a limiter was fitted, and all that was required for "unlimited" off-road operation was some minor plug-in rewiring.

(3) Two street versions of the Boss 429 were built. The first few hundred were designed for heavy-duty use and were designated "820-S." They use a super tough crank, rod, and piston combo. Later "street" versions are called "820-T" and use a different crank, rod, and piston. All "S" engines and early "T" engines came with a hydraulic cam. Late '69 "T" engines and all '70 "T" motors use a mechanical cam, the same one as used in 429-SCJ engines. There was also a race-only NASCAR 429 with different heads, rocker arms, and reciprocating assembly.

(4) The Boss 302's steel crankshaft was forged with hollow throws in 1969 while the 1970 versions were solid shafts which, unlike the earlier models, weren't cross-drilled for oil flow

Give DIFFERENTIAL BLUES The Slip

HOW TO REBUILD A FORD NINE-INCH REAREND

TEXT AND PHOTOGRAPHY BY ERIC RICKMAN

IF YOU OWN AN OLDER MUSTANG, and you drive it from show to show, sooner or later you're going to have to do some work on the differential. The problem will arise even sooner if you're an habitual lead foot, or urban racer. To find out just what's involved in rebuilding a Ford nine-inch differential we went to our local gear guru, Tom Watt, owner of Tom's Differentials (15551 Paramount Blvd., Paramount, CA 90723, 213/634-8431).

Early Mustangs were built with three differentials; the nine-inch ring gear was an option from 1965-'67, at which time it became standard equipment. Basically, the nine-inch gear is found in the 302-cubic-inch and larger engines, used up to 1973.

As engine size increased from 1965-'73, Ford changed from cast iron differential housings to the stronger nodular iron housings, increasing the size of the carrier bear-

ings at the same time. The ideal differential is a nodular iron case with the larger carrier bearings, identified by the casting code CA4WA-B molded in the case, and the letter "N" molded in the crown of the bearing caps. The use of the following rebuilding techniques is recommended for all rearends.

Ford also made another change in the evolution of this rearend, so you may find either a solid-cover ring gear carrier, or one with four lightening holes. The solid is the more desirable, as the four-holer's webs have been known to crack, allowing the hub to tear out. Inspect your four-holer for stress cracks; if none show up, you can use it after carefully radiusing the edges of the holes with a small high-speed grinder. Sand the edges smooth with wet 180 wet/dry emery paper to remove any nicks or dings; these act as stress risers, allowing cracks to start. Remove both

the ring gear and carrier from the housing, and separate them.

You'll find a pair of Phillips-head screws countersunk in the gear mounting flange. Remove these screws to get the case apart. Older cases may require some gentle persuasion with a soft hammer. Ford assembles these units with a 1500psi clutch plate loading. If you're working on a newer unit, or there's any doubt about the remaining pre-load, it's advisable to install a couple of safety bolts through the flange so the case can't pop open unexpectedly. With the case open, you'll find the pinion (spider) gears in one half, and the clutch pack in the other. Remove and discard the square pre-load spring plate and the four springs.

The use of a pre-loaded clutch pack between the rear axles ensures equal power is delivered to both rear wheels, regardless of the amount of traction available at either wheel.

DIFFERENTIAL

When cornering, the clutch pack permits a degree of slippage (differential action) to allow for the different distances traveled by the inner and outer wheels.

By discarding the pre-loading springs and slightly increasing side gear thrust washer thickness, Tom has found that clutch loading and wear will be greatly reduced. The clutch "lock-up under load" feature is retained by side gear thrust loading that occurs under heavy acceleration. This moves the gears apart slightly under heavy loading, causing them to apply pressure to the clutch pack to lock the axles; under light loading and cornering there will be little clutch pack drag (wear). This trick also reduces rearend cornering chatter and ratcheting.

Getting back to the task at hand, you'll find that the spider gear shafts are held in the carrier by roll pins. Use a drift punch to drive the pins out, then remove the long shaft first, using a brass punch and driving on the solid end of the shaft. Be careful not to score the shaft holes. Keep the shafts, pins, gears, and thrust washers in proper relationship, as they must be reassembled exactly as they were removed.

The first step in rebuilding this unit is the proper preparation of the carrier case after removal of the clutch pack, spider gear assembly, and all the various thrust washers. These, too, must be kept in proper relationship. Tom cleans and inspects the carrier case carefully; if reusable, he works over all the edges and corners with a small high-speed grinder to radius and chamfer everything. After grinding, he smooths the surfaces with wet 180-grit wet/dry emery paper to prevent the formation of stress cracks. He then smooths all the mating surfaces with a small, flat, fine-grit stone. The case halves must be washed in solvent and blown dry to remove all abrasive residue.

Reassemble the empty case halves, secure them with the Phillips screws, and place them in a lathe between centers to make a fine truing cut across the ring gear mounting flange. New cases have shown as much as .010-inch runout. Be sure to stone the freshly machined flange, and rewash the case.

Before assembly, inspect everything for wear and replace the tired parts with new components. There are two side (axle) gear thrust washers; discard the clutch pack side. The other should measure at least .030-inch thick, and the steel clutch pack plates should be not less than .005-inch thick; they should be replaced if worn. Check the fiber-faced plates; they wear first, and are often the only ones to be replaced.

1 Traction-Lok ring gear carriers were made in two configurations. Earlier unit is on the right; later unit at left is the more desirable, particularly if you have added horsepower.

2 Too many horses and too much traction result in case breakage around the lightening holes. Unit still works, but cast iron debris wears off and contaminates gears and bearings.

3 The ring gear mounting side of the desired case reveals a pair of Phillips-head screws that must be removed to part the case halves.

4 A soft hammer may be needed to part the case. Heavy clutch pre-loading in new cases requires the use of safety bolts, as cases may spring apart dangerously.

5 Clutch pack and axle side gear are on right, with spider gears, pre-loading hub, and springs at left.

6 Remove the pre-load plate and springs, which will be deleted on assembly. Mark everything to ensure the correct relationship of parts on assembly. Use chalk, paint, crayon, or whatever you have on hand.

7 With a drift punch, remove the three roll pins used to secure the pinion shafts. Be sure the punch is the same size as the pin being removed. Remove long shaft first.

8 After the retaining roll pin is punched out, use a larger drift punch to drive the shaft out of the carrier. Be careful not to create any gouges or burrs in the case.

9 Next, remove the short shaft retaining roll pins. Tap the pins out gently—force is not the way to go.

10 Start short shafts out of the case with the drift punch at an angle. A roll pin punch can be inserted in the shaft and used to pull it the rest of the way out of the case.

11 Use a small high-speed grinder to relieve all sharp edges. Also radius edges to remove sources of stress cracks.

12 Use a cone-shaped stone to relieve the sharp edges of each bolt hole. Be sure to do both ends of each hole.

13 Carefully sand all previously ground radii smooth with 180-grit wet/dry emery paper—use it wet.

14 Surface the mating flanges of the carrier halves with a fine-grit flat stone; also do the ring gear mounting face after it has been trued.

15 Before final assembly, bolt the carrier together and mount between centers in a lathe. Make a very fine clean-up cut across the face of the ring gear flange. New carriers have been known to have as much as .010-inch runout.

16 Before reassembly, wash everything in detergent and hot water, then solvent, and blow dry. Thrust washer between case and side gear should measure at least .030-inch. If questionable, replace it—they don't cost much.

17 Apply a generous coating of Tom's special Posi-Lube on everything during assembly. Install the thrust washer on the side gear before installing gear in the carrier case.

18 Install long shaft pinions after the side gear is in place. The wider sides of the center block should face the long shaft pinion gears. Be sure all gears, shafts, and thrust washers go back in the same order they were removed.

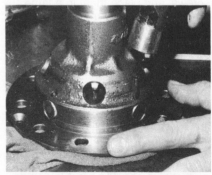

19 Use a drift punch to align roll pin holes, then carefully drive pins into place. Pins should be a snug drive fit, not too loose. Use new pins if in doubt about fit.

DIFFERENTIAL

To assemble the spider gear half of the case, lube and install the side gear thrust washer and gear, then install the spider gears, thrust washers, and shafts in their original locations. The long sides of the center block should face the long shaft-mounted spider gears. Roll pins must be a snug drive fit, or be replaced. In assembling the clutch pack half of the case, don't forget to leave out the thrust washer. You'll find a large clutch pack shim, or shims, between the clutch pack and carrier housing, which should measure at least .030-inch. Tom adds another .010-inch shim at this point for trial assembly.

Soak the fiber-faced clutch plates in Tom's 140 gear oil for one-half hour before assembly. There's one composite plate, with both a steel and fiber face, which is installed on the clutch hub first, fiber face toward the hub's steel face. After that the plates are stacked alternately: fiber, steel, fiber, steel, etc. After the pack is assembled and the small ears lined up, drop the pack into the case without the thrust washer. Small half-circle steel clutch plate ear guides are installed to prevent the steel ears from abrading the iron case.

After placing the side gear in the clutch pack hub, you're ready to put the carrier halves back together. Don't invert the clutch side, and keep it on the bottom. Tom does the assembly on a short length of axle held vertically in a vice. The case halves are aligned with the Phillips screws and drawn together with temporary Allen bolts and wing nuts, using a crisscross torquing pattern. With the case halves solidly bolted together, the assembly should be able to be turned on the axle stub, using both hands, against a fair amount of drag. If the assembly is too loose or too tight, disassemble it and correct the problem by adding or removing shims from the .040-inch trial shimming stack. Shims are available as thin as .005-inch, providing plenty of adjustment latitude.

With the carrier assembled, you're ready to install the ring gear. Clean out the bolt holes in the ring gear and wire brush the bolt threads. Wash with acetone and blow dry. Install the ring gear on the carrier, aligning the bolt holes, and put a drop or two of BLUE Loctite in each bolt hole. Install the bolts loosely, making sure the thin steel washers are in place on each bolt. Draw the gear down square on the flange, and torque the bolts to 50 ft.-lbs. in a crisscross pattern, then, in the same pattern, take them to 75 ft.-lbs. of torque and double-check the reading.

Be sure the carrier bearing mounting bosses and shoulders are smooth and clean. Wipe both the boss and the inner face of each

bearing race with acetone, then wipe a drop or two of RED Loctite over the cleaned areas. Next, it's time to install the carrier bearings in an hydraulic press; be sure to start the bearings square and avoid cocking them as they're being pressed into place. Keep the outer races mated to their matching bearings.

With the ring gear and assembly completed, turn your attention to the differential's ring gear housing. Tom prepares the housing by grinding away all casting flash inside and out, radiusing all corners and edges, and finishing the job with 180-grit emery paper. If it's a nodular iron case, or a C7AW-G cast iron case with the large carrier bearings, Tom drills and taps the ½-inch bearing cap bolt holes deeper to accept ½x3-inch Grade 8 Allen-head cap screws, which he recommends using with all nodular iron bearing caps. After the case is prepared, press the pinion shaft nose support bearing into the case with a drop of RED Loctite to hold the bearing and its lock ring in place.

Now you're ready for the pinion gearshaft and bearing assembly. After the pinion shaft bearing races are pressed into the carrier housing with a bit of RED Loctite insurance, the inner bearing is pressed onto the pinion gearshaft, keeping the bearings and races paired. If it goes on too easily, include RED Loctite in the assembly. Tom has found that the use of a crush sleeve in setting the pinion shaft pre-load is not necessary; he prefers to use RED Loctite to secure the outer bearing. All mating surfaces must be cleaned with acetone to ensure Loctite's adherence. Apply a drop of RED Loctite to the inner race of the outer bearing, then lube both bearings generously with Tom's gear lube and drop the outer bearing into the nose of the case.

Permatex the outer flange of the grease seal using Permatex No. 2 and coat the inner lip with white grease, then install the seal over the outer bearing. Seals can be tapped into place with a hammer, but a press is recommended to get a solid and square fit in the housing. Apply a bit of RED Loctite to the pinion shaft at the front bearing location, then slip the pinion gearshaft and bearing into the housing and through the front bearing and seal. Install the universal yoke over the shaft splines, securing everything with a *new* nut and GREEN Loctite on the threads.

Tom holds the nut with a socket and flex-handle braced against the vice and rotates the yoke with a pin-face spanner wrench. Tighten the nut until things are snug; now you're ready to check the bearing pre-load. Tom uses a small in.-lb. wrench to rotate the pinion shaft. When the

proper pre-load is reached, 10 in.-lbs. of torque will start the shaft turning, and it will show 15 in.-lbs. of drag as it's rotated. Check the pre-load frequently as you tighten the yoke nut; if the pre-load is exceeded, it's difficult to back off with Loctite on the shaft.

When the pinion carrier is assembled and properly pre-loaded, it's ready to install in the differential housing. Pinion gear depth is adjusted by shims between the carrier housing and differential case. Pinion gear carrier housings are found in both cast and nodular iron, identifiable in the cast iron housings by spot-faced bolt holes, while nodular iron housings have fully machined flanges. Trial assembly of the ring and pinion gears calls for a .017-inch shim with a cast housing and, in this case, a .022-inch shim with the nodular housing. Shims are available from .010- to .026-inch to facilitate this adjustment. Leave the O-ring oil seal out during trial fittings. Torque the retaining bolts to 30 ft.-lbs.; final assembly calls for 45 ft.-lbs. After installation, check the bearing pre-load again. It should be the same; if it's not, something is in a bind, possibly a nicked or bent flange.

Next, install the ring gear and related Traction-Lok assembly. Lube the carrier bearings and install the carrier's outer bearing races over the matching bearings. Install the ring gear assembly in the differential case, carefully seating the carrier bearings in their saddles. Spanner nuts can now be installed in the saddles—make sure the threads are engaged. Tom recommends the use of his specially made solid spanner nuts. Install the bearing caps so that the spanner nuts turn freely.

Nodular iron bearing caps have an "N" molded in the crown. If you have a cast iron case with small carrier bearings, use the stock bolts and torque to 90 ft.-lbs. The C4AW-B cast iron case with large carrier bearings is fitted with nodular bearing caps after being drilled and tapped to accept longer and stronger bolts. Be sure the axle gear splines match your axles, as gears come in both 28 and 31 splines. Bearing caps should have a .001-inch crush to ensure proper securing of the outer races. The caps may have to be filed slightly, like rod bearing caps. Stock bearing caps often leave the races loose after being torqued down, allowing the races to spin under loading. Snug the bearing caps down just tight enough to permit the bearings to move from side to side with the spanner nuts, then snug up the spanner nuts.

To check the backlash (the play between the ring gear and pinion gear teeth), use a dial indicator posi-

20 When assembling the clutch pack, install the composite plate (one fiber-covered face) first, with the fiber face against the clutch hub.

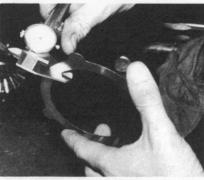
21 Measure the steel plates—they should be not less than .050-inch thick. Examine fiber-faced plates for wear; often only the fiber plates need to be replaced.

22 Stack fiber and steel plates on the hub alternately, beginning with a fiber one. Lubricate assembly generously with Tom's Posi-Lube.

23 Install clutch pack shims in case before installing the clutch hub and pack assembly. Shims come in various thicknesses and may have to be changed if there is too much or too little drag after a trial assembly of the carrier case.

24 There is a thrust washer between the clutch pack hub and the carrier case. Leave this washer out of the reassembly.

25 Align the clutch plate ears, and holding the pack together, install it in the carrier housing.

26 Drop clutch plate ear guides into the housing to prevent the steel plates from digging into the cast iron case.

27 With the side gear in place, the halves of the carrier are ready to be assembled. Offset Phillips screw retainers will ensure proper indexing of the halves.

28 Use Allen-head cap screws, large washers, and wing nuts to draw the carrier halves together. Note Phillips-head aligning screws are in place, but loose (arrow). Draw down evenly in a crisscross pattern.

29 Assemble carrier on a short section of axle. Unit should require a fair amount of effort to turn. If it turns too freely, or is locked solid, drag will have to be adjusted by changing the clutch hub shims (fig. 23).

30 After cleaning with acetone and blow drying, place a drop or two of BLUE Loctite in each bolt hole.

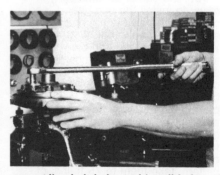
31 Align bolt holes and install bolts finger-tight. Torque to 50 ft.-lbs. in a crisscross pattern. Final torque is 75 ft.-lbs., using same torquing pattern. Be sure to double-check torque.

32 Check carrier bearing boss shoulders, and file or tap down any irregularities on the faces to ensure a solid bearing seat.

33 After wiping with acetone, apply a couple of drops of RED Loctite to the mounting boss and the inside of the inner bearing race.

34 Use an hydraulic press to seat the bearing solidly. Be careful; don't cock the bearing as it is pressed into place.

35 Apply a thin coat of Permatex No. 2 to the outer flange of the pinion shaft grease seal. Add a thin coating of white grease to the inner lip of the seal.

36 Install the grease seal in the pinion shaft carrier after the front bearing has been lubed and dropped in place. Seal can be hammered in, but Tom recommends the use of a press.

37 After the rear bearing has been pressed on the pinion shaft and secured with RED Loctite, apply more RED Loctite to the front bearing mounting area of the pinion shaft.

38 Slip the pinion carrier housing over the U-joint yoke, and drop the pinion shaft assembly through the housing and engage the yoke splines. Bearings are mated to outer races, pressed in the housing.

39 A new nut is being held with a flex-handle, braced against the vise, while Tom turns the yoke with a pin-face spanner wrench, pulling the shaft into the bearings. Draw the shaft in until it is just snug. Use GREEN Loctite on the nut threads.

40 Bearing pre-load is measured by rotating the pinion shaft with an in.-lb. wrench. Shaft should start to turn at 10 in.-lbs., and take 15 in.-lbs. to keep it turning. Take frequent readings, don't overload the bearings, and sneak up on the setting.

41 After pre-load is set, stone the mounting flange with a fine-grit flat stone to remove burrs and dings.

42 This nodular iron housing takes a .022-inch shim for trial assembly. Cast iron housings call for a .017-inch shim.

43 These are the identifying codes molded in the housing and bearing caps. C4AW-B shows in the case, with an "N" on the crown of the bearing caps, to indicate nodular iron housings.

DIFFERENTIAL

tioned at 90 degrees to one of the ring gear teeth. Backlash must be set with the side bearings pre-loaded. Use the small in.-lb. wrench to rotate the pinion shaft while tightening the spanner nuts against the carrier bearings—still retain some degree of backlash between the gear teeth. You already have 15 in.-lbs. of rotational resistance in the pinion shaft bearings, so now tighten the spanner nuts to increase this resistance to between 22 and 25 in.-lbs. The resulting difference will be in the carrier bearing pre-load, between seven and 10 in.-lbs.

Now check the backlash. Tom likes about .004- to .006-inch of backlash on new gears, and .006- to .008-inch with used gears. If you have too much, move the ring gear toward the pinion gear by adjusting the spanner nuts, and at the same time retain the proper bearing pre-load. Conversely, if there's too little, move the ring gear away from the pinion gear. Check the backlash at several points around the circumference of the gear. You may have to settle for a compromise setting between .004- and .008-inch of backlash.

At this point, the tooth contact pattern should be taken. Brush a marking compound on both sides of at least four ring gear teeth, and pass the marked teeth back and forth through the pinion gear teeth several times, using a wrench on the ring gear. Don't use the yoke to turn the gears, as this will smear the pattern. Repeat this procedure at several points around the ring gear and the pattern will be ready to read. Tooth orientation is defined by these terms: "toe" is the tip of a tooth at the inner end of the gear's small circumference, "heel" is the outer end of the tooth, "root" is the base of the tooth, and "top" is self-explanatory. The vertical side of the tooth is the "drive" side, and the sloping side is the "coast" side.

Ideally, you should have a fairly large, oval-shaped contact area in the center of the tooth, with the drive and coast patterns being directly opposite each other. If the pattern is too close to the toe on the drive side, move the pinion gear away from the ring gear by increasing the shim thickness between the pinion shaft housing and the differential case. To center a heel pattern, decrease the shim thickness. A pattern close to the root will require the ring gear to be moved away from the pinion gear, and a high pattern will require moving the ring gear closer to the pinion gear.

The entire operation is a delicate balancing act, trading adjustments off against each other, while retaining the proper backlash and bearing pre-load. If you must compromise, set the pattern low and toward the toe, as the contact point will move back and up under heavy loading. New gears have a manganese phosphate coating to prevent rust and facilitate run-in, but as this coating wears off, the backlash will increase slightly while the contact point will move toward the heel. If you have to remove the pinion carrier housing to change shims, mark the spanner nut on the ring gear side and back it off one turn. This prevents the gears from hanging up as they are separated, and allows you to return the spanner nut to its previous setting. Torque nodular iron bearing caps to 100 ft.-lbs. in 20-pound steps.

When everything is right, rotating the pinion yoke smoothly should produce a soft, steady, shussing sound; if there is any chatter, it will be worse in the car. Install the O-ring in the pinion carrier housing, retorque to 45 ft.-lbs.; add the spanner nut locks attached to the bearing caps.

With the assembly installed in the car, fill the rearend with oil, preferably with Tom's own SAE 140 gear oil, which has been compounded to his specifications by the Torco Oil Company. Otherwise, use any SAE 140 gear oil specified for Ford limited-slip differentials. Change the oil after the first 500 miles to remove wear-in debris; after that it only needs to be changed after every 30,000 miles.

Here's a list of the parts that may be needed to rebuild a nine-inch Ford Traction-Lok differential: *M*

Composite plate	C80Z-4A325-B
Steel plates	C802-4947-A
Friction plates	C802-4945-B
Pinion carrier shims	C80Z-4A324-A (2-.005/4-.010)
31-spline Traction-Lok assembly, complete	D4TZ-4026-A (4-pinion)
28-spline Traction-Lok assembly, complete	D3SZ-402-A (4-pinion)
31-spline 4-pinion empty case	D3TZ-4204-A
Short cross shafts	D3SZ-4211-A
Long cross shafts	B7AZ-4211-A
Right-hand side (axle) gear	C80Z-4236-A (31-spline)
Left-hand side (axle) gear	C80Z-4236-B (31-spline)
28-spline (axle) gears, (both)	C9AZ-4236-A
4-pinion (spider) gears	C80Z-4215-A

44 *Proper case preparation is crucial. Tom grinds off all the casting flash, and radiuses or chamfers all the edges and shoulders. He then smooths surfaces with 180 emery paper.*

45 *Redrill and tap the nodular iron cases to take three-inch Grade 8 Allen-head bolts to provide added strength in securing the nodular iron bearing caps. Bolts are quite a bit longer, as shown here.*

46 *With the pinion gear assembly in place, carefully lower the ring gear and Traction-Lok assembly into the case. Keep bearing races mated to the bearings.*

47 *Install the spanner nuts, being sure to engage the case threads properly. Install the bearing caps and seat so the spanner nuts turn freely.*

48 *Bearing caps should have .001-inch crush to hold the outer races. Snug caps down and tighten spanner nuts against the bearings with a spanner wrench. Check preliminary backlash by rotating U-joint yoke back and forth.*

49 *While retaining a small amount of backlash, tighten the spanner nuts until the in.-lb. wrench indicates 22 to 25 in.-lbs. of rotational drag. Tom's apprentice Dan Muhlenkamp takes the reading.*

50 *Read backlash with a dial indicator set at 90 degrees to a tooth face. Rock the ring gear back and forth. Indicator should show .004- to .006-inch of play between gear teeth. Bearing preloading must be retained while setting backlash.*

51 *Apply marking compound to both sides of at least four ring gear teeth.*

52 *Dan rocks the marked teeth back and forth through the pinion gear several times using a wrench on the carrier. Do not use the yoke to rotate the gears, as it will smear the pattern. Take readings at several points around the ring gear.*

53 *This contact point on the coast side of the tooth is too high and too far toward the toe. Install a thinner shim between the pinion carrier housing and differential case to move the pinion toward the ring gear and center the contact area.*

54 *Drive-side pattern is close to correct here. Setting is a balancing act, where one adjustment works against another, while the bearing preload and backlash are retained.*

55 *Drive- and coast-side tooth contact areas are about centered, and directly opposite each other. Pattern can be slightly toward the toe and low, if you wish. Loading and wear will center pattern.*

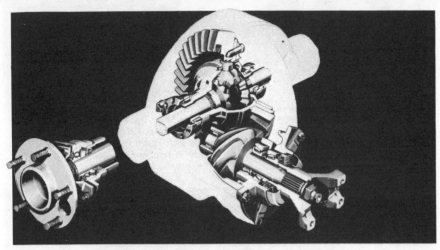

Removable carrier type

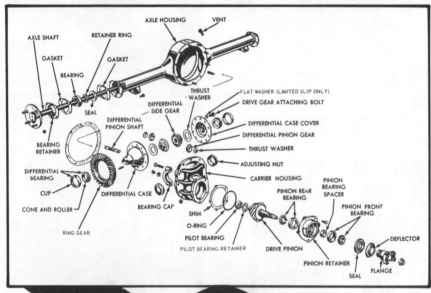

BY GEORGE RUTLEDGE

For many Mustang enthusiasts, trying to select just the right rearend equipment can result in aggravation, mistakes, and wasted expenditure. Countless rearend assemblies and parts were manufactured by Ford and various aftermarket manufacturers for the 1964 to present Mustangs. Hence, incalculable confusion exists concerning their identification, repair, and selection. A basic knowledge of these components is imperative before attempting any repairs or modifications.

From 1964 to 1970, two basic types of rearend assemblies were installed in Mustangs: the integral-carrier type and the removable-carrier type. The integral type is a one-piece casing, so removal of any part must be done underneath the car. The removable carrier type has a removable center section which contains the pinion gear, ring gear, and associated bearings and equipment. This makes servicing far easier than for the integral since the entire unit can be removed and supported on a bench fixture.

Beginning in 1965, integral units were installed when 6-cylinder or low-output 8-cylinder engines were ordered, and removable units were used for high-performance and 8-cylinders. After 1967, virtually all Mustangs were equipped with the removable type except for the 6-cylinder models. Obviously, since the integral carrier does not have the strength, versatility, or ease of maintenance of the removable carrier, it is undesirable for high-performance applications. Therefore we will be discussing identification of only the stock parts of this carrier. Since the majority of Mustangs came with the removable carrier assembly, which has admirable performance qualities, discussion of the identification of high-performance parts for competition will be confined to this model. But now let us further identify the various differential systems available on the removable and integral assemblies.

CONVENTIONAL (Open differential)

This is the oldest type of differential which is still commonly used today. With the conventional, the wheel of the car which first grips the underload (the load in this case being the road surface) transfers the power to the opposite wheel. This is never noticed in normal driving where both wheels share the load equally, but during hard acceleration, cornering, or less-than-desirable driving surfaces (snow, ice, or gravel), one wheel will grip the road and the other will spin. This slippage

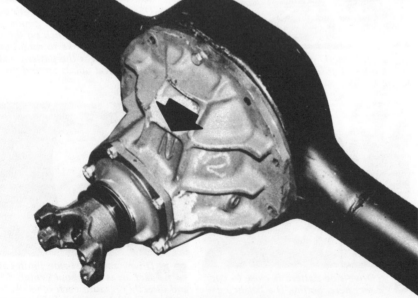

9-inch nodular case (note "N")

makes the conventional differential inadequate for high-performance use.

This assembly was available with either Ford's integral or removable carrier assemblies. Generally, Ford integrals with conventional differential can come equipped with 7¼ through 8-inch ring gears (years '65-'70), while removable models used ring gear sizes from 7¾ to 9 inches.

LIMITED SLIP (Closed differential)

This type of Ford differential uses four steel clutch plates which are locked into the differential cover. Three bronze-bonded clutch plates are splined to a clutch hub, which, in turn, is splined to the left-hand axle shaft. A beveled spring plate provides constant pressure between the steel and the bonded clutch plates, assuring that the clutch is always engaged. This provides equal disbursement of power to both wheels. Differential action between wheels is accomplished through clutch plate slippage.

Limited-slip differentials were available on a few integrals with 3.20:1 or 3.50:1 gearing. Generally, gear sizes of 7¼ through 8 inches were utilized. However, as stated before, this type of rear is not really suited for true performance work. By contrast, the removable carrier was commonly equipped with the limited slip and generally uses gear sizes of 7¾ through 9 inches, in conjunction with gear ratios of 2.80:1 through 4.30:1. Differences in the ring gear sizes occurred depending on the engine size used and the year of the car (1965-1970).

At this point, it is time to mention that although there are several gear set sizes available with removable carrier cases, the 9-inch ring gear is considered the "ultimate" from a high-performance, competition standpoint. However, if your removable carrier unit possesses a smaller than 9-inch ring gear, don't panic! Even the smaller sizes (8 through 8¾ inches) are tough enough for the stock engines that were originally installed with them.

TRACTION LOK DIFFERENTIAL

This type, although very similar to the Ford limited-slip differential model, has some important differences. Both types employ a multi-clutch plate system for positive locking action. In turning, the limited slip model allows differential action by slipping the clutch plates. This produces a noise level higher than conventional types.

But the Traction Lok differential uses a pre-load spring plate and center block between pinion gears and side gears. It has pre-loaded tension springs which release the pinion gears to rotate only under precalculated side gear loads. Therefore, the clutch plates remain engaged at all times, and are never required to slip for differential purposes. The result is a much improved, quieter operation during turns. Traction Lok is considered the best all-around street rear for Fords. Beginning in 1969, the Traction Lok differential system was available on removable carrier assemblies only. It cannot be inserted into the integral carrier. All Traction Loks utilized the 9-inch ring gear.

DETROIT LOCKER

Whereas the standard 9-inch Ford removable carrier is completely adequate for street machines (even when the stock engine is slightly modified), constant racing usage requires something extra in the area of strength and durability. The Detroit Locker is designed for racing purposes . . . *period!*

The Detroit Locker uses a super-strong splined ring-clutch system which provides positive engagement at all times. Differential action is accomplished via a ratchet tooth-jumping mechanism which is primitive yet entirely effective. This mechanism produces the clunking noises heard in turns which have made the locker famous. Considering that an optional limited slip differential or Traction Lok will accomplish virtually everything a Detroit Locker does, lockers are really not practical for street uses. The locker

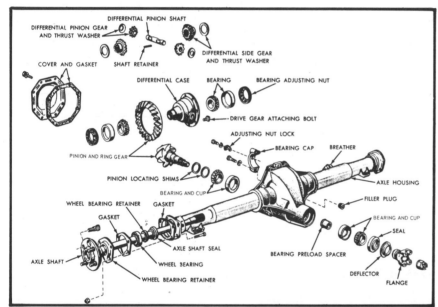

Integral carrier type

ALL PHOTOS, DIAGRAMS & CHARTS COURTESY FORD MOTOR COMPANY

Integral carrier type rear

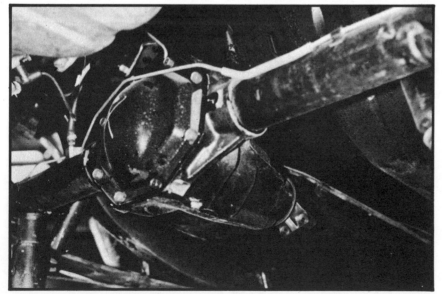

ID tag	ring gear dia.	diff type[1]	axle ratio :1	no. of teeth ring gear	pinion
WCY-F	7¼	conv	3.50	35	10
WCY-AC	7¼	conv	3.50	35	10
WDJ-D	7¼	locking	3.50	35	10
WDJ-H	7¼	locking	3.50	35	10
WCY-T	7¼	conv	4.00	36	9
WCY-AB	7¼	conv	3.20	32	10
WCY-E	7¼	conv	3.20	32	10
WCY-AD	7¼	locking	3.20	32	10
WCY-L	7¼	locking	3.20	32	10
WCY-R	7¼	conv	2.83	34	12
WCY-AF	7¼	conv	2.83	34	12
WCY-N	7¼	conv	2.83	34	12
WCY-AG	7¼	locking	2.83	34	12
WCY-AA	7¼	locking	2.83	34	12
WCZ-M	8	conv	3.00	39	13
WCZ-F	8	conv	3.00	39	13
WDJ-G	8	locking	3.00	39	13
WDJ-C	8	locking	3.00	39	13
WCZ-A	8	conv	3.25	39	12
WCL-K	8	conv	3.25	39	12
WCZ-K	8	conv	3.25	39	12
WCZ-G	8	conv	3.50	35	10
WCZ-N	8	conv	3.50	35	10
WCL-J	8	conv	3.50	35	10
WCU-B[2]	8¾	conv	3.50	35	10
WDJ-D	8	locking	3.50	35	10
WDJ-H	8	locking	3.50	35	10
WDK-B[2]	8¾	locking	3.50	35	10
WCU-C[2]	8¾	conv	3.89	35	9
WCZ-H[2]	8¾	conv	3.89	35	9
WCU-D[2]	8¾	conv	4.11	37	9
WCZ-J[2]	8¾	conv	4.11	37	9
WCZ-L	7¾	conv	2.80	42	15
WCL-N	7¾	conv	2.80	42	15

1966—REMOVABLE CARRIER

ID tag	ring gear dia.	diff type	axle ratio :1	ring gear	pinion
WCZ-E	7¾	conv	2.80	42	15
WDJ-B	7¾	ltd slip	2.80	42	15
WCZ-F	8	conv	3.00	39	13
WDJ-C	8	ltd slip	3.00	39	13
WCZ-S	8¾	conv	3.50	35	10
WCZ-R	8¾	conv	3.89	35	9
WDZ-A	7¾	ltd slip	2.80	42	15
WDW-C	8	conv	3.25	39	12
WDW-E	7¾	conv	2.80	42	15
WDW-A	7¾	conv	2.80	42	15
WDW-D	8	conv	3.50	35	10
WDZ-C	8	ltd slip	3.25	39	12
WDW-B	8	conv	3.00	39	13
WDC-B	8	ltd slip	3.00	39	13
WDE-B	9	conv	3.00	39	13
WEB-C	9	conv	3.25	39	12
WED-C	9	ltd slip	3.00	39	13
WED-A	9	slip	3.25	39	12
WDY-B	8	conv	3.25	39	12
WDY-C	8	conv	3.50	35	10
WEA-B	8	ltd slip	3.50	35	10
WDY-A	8	conv	3.00	39	13
WEA-F	8	ltd slip	3.25	39	12
WEA-A	8	ltd slip	3.00	39	13
WEC-A	9	conv	3.00	39	13
WEC-B	9	conv	3.25	39	12
WEE-A	9	ltd slip	3.25	39	12
WEE-C	9	ltd slip	3.00	39	13

1966—INTEGRAL CARRIER

ID tag	ring gear dia.	diff type	axle ratio :1	ring gear	pinion
WCY-R	7¼	conv	2.83	34	12
WCY-AA	7¼	ltd slip	2.83	34	12
WCY-E	7¼	conv	3.20	32	10
WCY-AJ	7¼	conv	3.20	32	10
WCY-L	7¼	ltd slip	3.20	32	10

1967

ID tag	ring gear dia.	diff type	axle ratio :1	ring gear	pinion
WCY-R1	7¼	conv	2.83	34	12
WCY-E1	7¼	conv	3.20	32	10
WCY-AJ1	7¼	conv	3.20	32	10
WCZ-F1	8	conv	3.00	39	13
WDJ-C1	8	ltd slip	3.00	39	13
WDV-A	7¼	conv	2.83	34	12
WDV-B	7¼	conv	2.83	34	12
WDV-C	7¼	conv	3.20	32	10
WDV-E	7¼	ltd slip	3.20	32	10
WDV-G	7¼	conv	3.20	32	10
WDV-H	7¼	ltd slip	3.20	32	10
WDW-K	8	conv	2.79	39	14
WDW-B	8	conv	3.00	39	13
WDW-C	8	conv	3.25	39	12
WDW-D	8	conv	3.50	35	10
WDW-J	8	conv	2.79	39	14
WDW-F	8	conv	3.00	39	13
WDY-A1	8	conv	3.00	39	13
WDY-B1	8	conv	3.25	39	12
WCZ-V	8	conv	2.79	39	14
WDY-C1	8	conv	3.50	35	10
WDZ-B	8	ltd slip	3.00	39	13
WDZ-C	8	ltd slip	3.25	39	12
WDZ-E	8	ltd slip	3.00	39	13
WEA-A1	8	ltd slip	3.00	39	13
WEA-B1	8	ltd slip	3.50	35	10
WEA-F1	8	ltd slip	3.25	39	12
WEB-B5	9	conv	3.00	39	13
WEB-C5	9	conv	3.25	39	12
WEB-E5	9	conv	3.00	39	13
WEB-F5	9	conv	3.25	39	12
WEC-A5	9	conv	3.00	39	13
WEC-B5	9	conv	3.25	39	12
WEC-D5	9	conv	3.00	39	13
WEC-E5	9	conv	3.25	39	12
WED-A5	9	ltd slip	3.25	39	12
WED-C5	9	ltd slip	3.00	39	13
WED-D5	9	ltd slip	3.00	39	13
WEE-C5	9	ltd slip	3.00	39	13
WEE-D5	9	ltd slip	3.00	39	13
WES-F	9	conv	3.00	39	13
WES-G	9	ltd slip	3.25	39	12
WEB-G	9	conv	3.89	35	9
WEB-H	9	conv	2.75	44	16
WEB-J	9	conv	2.75	44	16
WEC-F	9	conv	2.75	44	16
WEC-G	9	conv	2.75	44	16
WES-H	9	conv	3.50	35	10
WES-J	9	conv	3.89	35	9
WES-K	9	ltd slip	3.50	35	10

[1] Two-pinion unless otherwise noted. [2] Used with 289-4V high-perf. engine. [3] Conventional four-pinion.

1968

Code	Size	Type	Ratio	Ring	Pinion
WCY-R1	7¼	conv	2.83	34	12
WCY-E1	7¼	conv	3.20	32	10
WCY-AJ1	7¼	conv	3.20	32	10
WCZ-F1	8	conv	3.00	39	13
WDJ-C1	8	ltd slip	3.00	39	13
WDV-A1	7¼	conv	2.83	34	12
WDV-B1	7¼	conv	2.83	34	12
WDV-C1	7¼	conv	3.20	32	10
WDV-E	7¼	ltd slip	3.20	32	10
WDV-G	7¼	conv	3.20	32	10
WDV-H	7¼	ltd slip	3.20	32	10
WDW-K1	8	conv	2.79	39	14
WDW-B1	8	conv	3.00	39	13
WDW-C1	8	conv	3.25	39	12
WDW-D1	8	conv	3.50	35	10
WDW-J	8	conv	2.79	39	14
WDW-F	8	conv	3.00	39	13
WDY-A1	8	conv	3.00	39	13
WDY-B1	8	conv	3.25	39	12
WCZ-V	8	conv	2.79	39	14
WDY-C1	8	conv	3.50	35	10
WDZ-B1	8	ltd slip	3.00	39	13
WDZ-C1	8	ltd slip	3.25	39	12
WDZ-E	8	ltd slip	3.00	39	13
WEA-A1	8	ltd slip	3.00	39	13
WEA-F1	8	ltd slip	3.25	39	12
WEB-E6	9	conv	3.00	39	13
WEB-F6	9	conv	3.25	39	12
WEC-D5	9	conv	3.00	39	13
WEC-E5	9	conv	3.25	39	12
WED-A6	9	ltd slip	3.25	39	12
WED-D6	9	ltd slip	3.00	39	13
WEE-D5	9	ltd slip	3.00	39	13
WES-F	9	conv	3.00	39	13
WES-G	9	ltd slip	3.25	39	12
WEB-G	9	conv	3.89	35	9
WEB-H1	9	conv	2.75	44	16
WEB-J1	9	conv	2.75	44	16
WEB-K	9	conv	3.25	39	12
WEC-F	9	conv	2.75	44	16
WEC-G	9	conv	2.75	44	16
WES-H	9	conv	3.50	35	10
WEZ-A	7¼	conv	3.20	32	10
WEZ-C	7¼	conv	2.83	34	12
WES-M	9	conv	3.25	39	12
WES-N	8¾	conv	3.00	39	13
WES-P	8¾	conv	3.25	39	12
WES-R	8¾	ltd slip	3.25	39	12
WES-S	9	conv	2.75	44	16
WES-T	9	conv	2.75	44	16
WCY-R1	7¼	conv	2.83	34	12
WCY-AJ2	7¼	conv	3.08	37	12
WCZ-F1	8	conv	3.00	39	13
WCZ-V	8	conv	2.79	39	14
WDJ-C1	8	ltd slip	3.00	39	13
WDV-B	7¼	conv	2.83	34	12
WDV-G	7¼	conv	3.20	32	10
WDW-H	7¼	ltd slip	3.20	32	10
WDW-B1	8	conv	3.00	39	13

1969-'70

Code	Size	Type	Ratio	Ring	Pinion
WDW-C1	8	conv	3.25	39	12
WDW-F	8	conv	3.00	39	13
WDW-J	8	conv	2.79	39	14
WDW-K	8	conv	2.79	39	14
WDY-A1	8	conv	3.00	39	13
WDY-B1	8	conv	3.25	39	12
WDZ-B1	8	ltd slip	3.00	39	13
WDZ-E	8	ltd slip	3.00	39	13
WEA-A1	8	ltd slip	3.00	39	13
WEA-F1	8	ltd slip	3.25	39	12
WEB-F6	9	conv[3]	3.00	39	13
WEB-F6	9	conv[3]	3.25	39	12
WEB-H2	9	conv	2.75	44	16
WEB-L	9	conv[3]	3.50	35	10
WEB-M	9	conv[3]	3.00	39	13
WEB-N	8¾	conv	3.00	39	13
WEB-P	9	conv[3]	2.75	44	16
WEB-R	9	conv	3.00	39	13
WEB-S	9	conv	3.25	39	12
WEB-T	9	conv[3]	3.25	39	12
WEB-U	8¾	conv	3.25	39	12
WEC-D5	9	conv[3]	3.00	39	13
WEC-E5	9	conv[3]	3.25	39	12
WEC-H	9	conv[3]	3.00	39	13
WEC-J	8¾	conv	3.00	39	13
WEC-K	9	conv	3.00	39	13
WEC-L	9	conv[3]	3.25	39	12
WEC-M	8¾	conv	3.25	39	12
WEC-N	9	conv	3.25	39	12
WEC-R	9	conv[3]	3.50	35	10
WES-F	9	conv[3]	3.00	39	13
WES-G1	9	ltd slip[5]	3.25	39	12
WES-M	9	conv[3]	3.25	39	12
WES-N	8¾	conv	3.00	39	13
WES-P	8¾	conv	3.25	39	12
WES-S1	9	conv[3]	2.75	44	16
WES-T1	9	conv	2.75	44	16
WES-U	9	conv[3]	3.50	35	10
WES-AA	9	conv	3.00	39	14
WES-AB	9	conv	3.25	39	12
WES-AC	9	conv[3]	3.00	39	13
WES-AD	9	conv[3]	3.25	39	12
WFA-A	9	trac lok[4]	3.25	39	12
WFA-C	9	trac lok[4]	3.25	39	12
WFA-D	9	trac lok[4]	3.25	39	12
WFA-E	9	trac lok[4]	3.00	39	13
WFB-A	9	trac lok[4]	3.25	39	12
WFB-C	9	trac lok[4]	3.25	39	12
WFC-A	9	trac lok[4]	3.50	35	10
WFC-B	9	trac lok[4]	3.91	43	11
WFC-C	9	trac lok[4]	4.30	43	10
WFC-D	9	trac lok[4]	3.91	43	11
WFC-E	9	trac lok[4]	4.30	43	10
WFC-F	9	trac lok[4]	3.91	43	11
WFC-S	9	trac lok[4]	3.50	35	10
WFC-K	9	trac lok[4]	4.30	43	10
WFC-G	9	trac lok[4]	3.00	39	13
WFD-A	9	trac lok[4]	3.50	35	10
WFD-B	9	trac lok[4]	3.91	43	11
WFD-C	9	trac lok[4]	4.30	43	10
WFD-H	9	trac lok[4]	3.25	39	12

[4] Torque-sensitive locker (four-pinion). [5] Limited-slip four-pinion.

BRINGING UP THE REAR

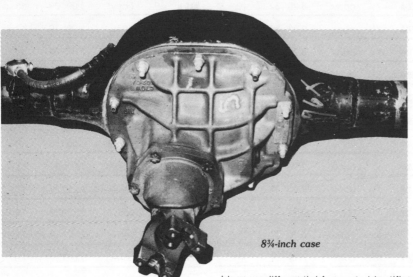

8¾-inch case

was an over-the-counter replacement assembly which could be installed at a Ford dealer. They were designed for the 9-inch removable carrier assembly only and cannot be interchanged with integrals.

Those are the four basic types of differential assemblies available in Mustangs from 1965-1970. As the illustrations show, these various assemblies consist of a multitude of different parts, some of which may still be available from Ford or auto part stores. While it is far easier to identify these parts when they are out of your car, most of us would rather not spend a whole Saturday disassembling a rearend just to identify certain pieces.

There is another, quicker method of identification *if* your Mustang still has its factory differential identification tags. Originally, all Ford products came with rearend identification tags. If your Mustang was lucky enough not to have been tampered with, the tags are probably still there. These aluminum tags were fastened to whatever bolt the assembler fancied, usually the integral cover bolt (integrals) or a carrier bolt (removable carrier). A tag will yield the original gear ratio, gear size, and the place of its manufacture (see charts for each year, 1965-1970).

Unfortunately, many Mustangs have been heavily modified during their lives and have parted with their tags long ago. In this case, there is only one way to be sure of what you have: disassem-ble your differential for parts identification. Once removed, identification is a relatively simple operation. Just compare the clutch system (or lack of) and number of gear teeth with the illustrations given here. Without disassembly, an approximate figure for the axle ratio can be obtained by observing the number of tire revolutions for one revolution of the driveshaft. Also, by driving the vehicle in question, one can observe whether it is equipped with a locking or open differential.

9⅜-inch unit (Though larger than the 9-inch unit, it's not as strong.)

Detroit Locker limited-slip differential exposed

As a general rule, all big-block Mustangs came equipped with the removable carrier type using gear sizes of 8¾ or 9 inches (1967-1970). The 428 and 427 engines were always mated to 9-inch ring gears (all years) while some 1967 and 1968 390 GT Mustangs came through with 8¾-inch ring gears, and others used 9-inch gears when an optional gear ratio was ordered. High-performance 289, 302, and 351 Windsors all used removable carrier rears with ring gears ranging from 8¾ inches (1965-1966) to both 8¾ and 9 inches in the later years (1967-1970). Standard 2-barrel, 289, 302 and all 6-cylinders used ring gears varying from 7¾ to 8¾ inches, and, as previously stated, some combinations used integral rears.

SPECIAL FORD DIFFERENTIAL CARRIER CASES

Not all Ford removable carrier cases are of the same casting quality. In 1965, Ford, realizing that racing would subject standard parts to abnormal abuse, designed a special nodular iron case for such conditions. It is known affectionately as the "N" case. This name refers to the letter "N" stamped on top of the case between the two top vertical ribs. This special case utilized a finely-controlled nodular iron grain structure casting process and included additional webbing which was thicker, deeper and closer-spaced. This provided much improved rigidity and greater strength over the standard production unit. It was designed around Ford's excellent 9-inch ring gear differential assembly. Unfortunately, this part is no longer available from Ford, but there are probably some still available in various Ford-oriented parts shops. A small batch of special aluminum "N" carrier cases were cast by Ford in the late '60s for their various racing programs, but they are extremely rare.

Generally speaking, the "N" case was strictly an over-the-counter item or dealer-installed option. After 1967, most high-performance, big block/small block case castings were cast with the same type of process and alloys, but, the distinctive webbing of the "N" case is not used on any other Ford differential casing. This extra webbing makes it strong enough to hold up under the most punishing racing applications. However, it should be kept in mind that this casing would not be necessary for most street machines.

So there you have it! You have just been taken through a basic course in identifying Ford differential components offered from 1965-1970 on Ford Mustangs. While we can't make any claim that this is all you need to know on the subject, at least from this point on you will be talking the correct language at your next swap meet. 5M

THEY PART OUT DEAD HORSES

...DON'T THEY? HOW TO SAVE MONEY WITH PARTS CARS
BY BRUCE CALDWELL

It's a terrible realization for Mustang diehards that not every Mustang ever made can be saved for posterity. Attrition is a fact of automotive life; that's what keeps Detroit in business. The best way to console oneself concerning the demise of Mustangs is to keep in mind that their good parts will help keep other collectible Mustangs on the road.

Finances can also play a big part in your Mustang involvement. It takes money to own and maintain, as well as build up, a car. If you can save money by using a parts car, that makes the hobby much more affordable.

Economics play a vital part in the decision of whether a Mustang gets saved or scrapped. A thrashed coupe that isn't a GT or anything special is often worth more as a parts car than as a whole model, because the cost of restoring it is more than the car would be worth. If kept long enough, almost any Mustang could be worth a lot of money, but the cost of storing and maintaining it, plus insurance and the original restoration costs, make saving it financially unsound. It's better to save the best cars and make constructive use of the wrecked ones.

PROS AND CONS

Parts cars can be a great way to save money on your next Mustang project, but they can also be a big headache. If finding a parts Mustang and taking it apart were super easy, everyone would do it, and there wouldn't be too many wrecking yards in business. Parting out a Mustang is messy, dirty, and ultimately time-consuming. You

1 This '69 Mustang coupe is typical of a good parts car. The neglect and abuse is extensive, yet there are many usable parts left.

2 The engine is a 351 Windsor that has been stripped of some parts and hasn't run for a long time. Don't expect much of an engine like this.

trade your time and labor for a cash savings, but only you can set a value on your time.

We're certainly not against wrecking yards; in fact, we're all for them. For most people, they're probably the best bet because they provide a lot of valuable services for their higher prices. They do the dirty work, and all you do is pick up the part. Many of their parts are already cleaned, reconditioned, and have some type of guarantee or exchange privileges. Wrecking yards have lots of reference books and knowledgeable employees to help you get just the part you need. If they don't have a part in stock, they can get it quickly through their network of cooperating wrecking

3 The interior of our parts Mustang looks like a breeding ground for strange diseases. It's moldy, dirty, and ripped to shreads.

151

4 *This fastback is far from mint, but it probably should be saved. Weigh the costs of fixing a car before parting it out.*

5 *Wrecking yards have knowledgeable staffs and many valuable reference sources. They know how to find the right part, not just one that comes close.*

6 *Yards are equipped to store lots of Mustangs in various states of disarray. They are well fenced and zoned for this activity.*

yards. They're also set up and zoned for large quantities of wrecked cars, so they don't have to worry that neighbors will complain about an unsightly mess.

If wrecking yards provide so many attractive services, why part out a Mustang yourself? The biggest reason is to save money. A parts car can be an excellent way to keep costs down when building a similar Mustang, and you might even make a few dollars on the parts car. The other big advantage is that you can take the car apart just the way you want. You can use every nut, bolt, clip, light bulb, and trim item available. A wrecking yard is really only interested in selling the major components. Little items aren't worth their time to remove, and few yards let customers

7 *Wrecking yards have the storage facilities for tons of parts. If they don't sell a part immediately, they can wait; private parties don't have this luxury.*

remove their own parts because of high insurance premiums. The neighborhood junkyard where you could remove your own parts and haggle over the price has almost totally been replaced by modern supermarkets or recycled parts. The high cost of real estate, labor, and insurance have all but eliminated the traditional wrecking yard.

Since Mustangs are so popular and collectible, there are many businesses devoted solely to those particular parts. Many semi-professional swap meet vendors are also keenly aware of the value of used Mustang parts. Standard wrecking yard operators take note of market trends, so they know Mustang parts, and price them accordingly.

This activity can contain elements of fun besides the financial benefits. If you like cars, it's fun to part out a car. If you ever want to know how a certain item on a Mustang works, you can tear it apart and find out for yourself. If you decide to sell some of the salvageable body parts, cutting up the car with an air chisel, cutting torch, or body saw is sanctioned destruction that appeals to the kid in all of us.

THE BEST MUSTANG PARTS CARS

Obviously, the best parts cars are the ones with the most usable parts at the lowest possible price. If you have specific requirements for a Mustang project, then you'll have to find a wrecked one that has the parts you need. This is particularly true when it comes to body pieces. If your main need is mechanical parts, a wider range of Mustangs and even other Ford products could suit your needs.

Since Mustangs are so highly sought after as both collector's cars and just good transportation, only the really thrashed cars make sense to part out. Body style is an important factor; a convertible of any year would have to be badly damaged and/or severely rusted in order to be a parts car. A coupe is the prime candidate for a parts car since there's an abundance of them.

We demonstrate how to use a parts car with this '69 coupe. It was wrecked and poorly repaired several times, then abused some more. The interior is an unpopular blue and looks like the inside of an old garbage can. The engine doesn't run (and hasn't for quite some time), and it has parts missing from it. The car doesn't have any luxury options, the glass is mostly cracked, and almost every corner has some form of damage. We just traded a little bodywork for it, so the price is certainly right. The cost of restoring such a mangy Mustang would be prohibitive, so it's a perfect car to part out.

If your main need is mechanical parts such as the engine, transmission, rearend, brakes, or radiator, you might consider a Cougar, Maverick, Comet, or Fairlane as a parts car. There's a great deal of "interchangeability" between various Ford products, and using almost any non-Mustang is cheaper than getting the same parts from a Mustang. As a general rule, big cars such as station wagons and four-door sedans are priced less than smaller cars, yet many Ford products of this size have usable mechanical parts for Mustangs.

WHERE TO LOOK

Parts cars are everywhere, but it takes extra initiative on your part to find the best buys. This is particularly true with Mustangs, since they're so desirable. Insurance companies deal almost exclusively with established wrecking yards, so you'll never get a chance at some of the "choicest" wrecks. Many private parties with a wrecked car just call the wrecker rather than go to the trouble of placing an ad in the newspaper. On cars like this, you need to get there before the wrecker. If you happen to see an obviously wrecked Mustang in someone's driveway, ask them if they would like to sell it, or leave a note for them. Chances are you'll pay more than the pro, but the owner might not have thought about selling it to a private party.

The parts section of the want ads can produce good cars, but in big cities the competition for these cars is high. The resourceful Mustang parts seekers know just where to get the earliest editions of the newspaper, and they quickly call any Mustang ads. Some people advertise individual Mustang parts for sale, but these aren't particularly cheap. The person with the Mustang parts for sale already has the parts car you wanted.

Another source is the regular "Mustangs For Sale" column. The cheapest Mustangs are often damaged ones. Call on ones that even seem a little high, because maybe the car is damaged and the seller will have to lower his price. It also pays to check the Ford section since some Mustangs get advertised in the wrong section. The harder you look, the more good deals you're apt to find.

When looking seriously for a Mustang parts car, establish a budget and have the cash on hand. The minute you get a good lead, grab the cash and go. The best parts cars go very quickly. Having the ready cash can make the car yours while another potential buyer tries to get to the bank before it closes. If you don't like keeping cash around the house,

consider getting traveler's checks, or keep enough cash for a good deposit and deal with a bank that has an after-hours cash machine.

Many cities have vacant lots or parking strips that are known as places to park cars for sale, and they're often a fine place to find good deals. It also pays to look for "For Sale" signs in cars in your neighborhood or other parts of town. Successful parts car finders develop an extra sense for spotting potential buys in back yards, alleys, and side streets. They ask about the car or leave a note on the windshield, regardless of whether the car has a "For Sale" sign or not. The best buys are usually the ones where you take the initiative. Let the owner think you're helping him by taking the tired Mustang off his hands. The object of getting a good buy is to avoid a competitive bidding situation.

TRANSPORTING A WRECKED MUSTANG

A car wrapped around a tree isn't a big deal for a professional wrecker. They have both the equipment and the experience to handle any situation. Be-

8 *The most desirable parts are stripped as soon as a new Mustang comes in. Front sheetmetal and doors are stored for later sales.*

9 *Wrecking yards use gas-powered cut-off saws to make nice clean cuts when removing items such as quarter panels.*

10 *The hood is usually one of the first parts to be removed for easy engine access. Good hoods are valuable resale parts, but this one is ripped.*

11 *Even though the hood is beyond repair, the hinges are a good swap meet item.*

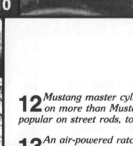

12 *Mustang master cylinders can be used on more than Mustangs. They're popular on street rods, too.*

13 *An air-powered ratchet and an impact wrench are great aids for quickly dismantling a parts Mustang.*

14 *The radiator must be removed in order to pull the engine. Good radiators are always in demand.*

PART OUT

fore you buy a wrecked Mustang, make sure you can get it home.

Along with ready cash, your ability to quickly remove a wrecked car is often very important to the seller. Be sure you have a trailer or big flatbed truck you can use before you offer to buy the car.

A winch is often needed, especially on cars with heavy front end damage. Sometimes you may be able to remove enough damaged sheetmetal to get the car rolling, or a Porta-Power may push away enough damage to get it going. Often, a wrecked Mustang will have one or more flat tires, so bring a couple of spares, an air tank, or a tire pump.

Another good precaution is to call a few local towing companies and get their rates. Depending on the hook-up charges, it might be cheaper and easier to have a damaged car towed by professionals.

Even Mustangs that appear towable can often have expired license plates, and you may have to buy a one-way trip permit to avoid a ticket. Flat-towing a car should always be done with a towbar, not a chain or rope. Remember that in most states, it's illegal to let someone ride in a towed vehicle.

SELLING THE SPARE PARTS

A key element to any parts Mustang is a clear title. If the car doesn't come with the proper paperwork, stay away from it. You must have a legal title to even give the hulk to the crusher in most states, so check the regulations in your state before you buy any car.

After determining that you can legally dispose of the parts car, do some more checking before you remove any parts. Make sure there's a market for the parts you don't want. It's not a bad idea to place an ad in the paper for the parts before you do any dismantling, so the demand will dictate how you take the car apart. Many people want a left front fender, but you might do better to sell the complete front clip. Someone might want a rear quarter panel, but a good body shell with the quarters intact might be worth more to someone who's building a race car.

Once you place a want ad, you need to sell as many parts as quickly as possible. Running a lot of ads will cut into your profit, and all the calls can be a nuisance. Since you don't have the luxury of time (people always know where wrecking yards are, but they don't know to call you for Mustang parts), go for the bigger sales first, and don't worry about the $5.00 items. Don't ruin an expensive part to sell a cheap one unless you feel you can't sell the larger item. An example is selling brake drums instead of selling a complete rearend.

If you'd like a little more time to sell the parts, consider placing notices on bulletin boards. Many auto parts stores offer them free for the use of their regu-

15 *This engine doesn't run, but it still has many usable parts such as cylinder heads, exhaust manifolds, intake manifold, and power-steering pump.*

16 *A heavy-duty engine hoist and a cart for moving the engine and trans makes the dismantling process easier.*

17 *Our parts Mustang had a decent right front fender, so it was sold. The headlight buckets are also good sellers, but our car didn't come with any.*

18 *Small items, such as this hood latch, can add up if you sell them at an old-car swap meet.*

19 *One method of removing a rearend is to unbolt the shocks and rear shackles so it can be lowered onto the springs and pulled out by one person.*

20 *Good Mustang doors are easy to sell. They're heavy, so always have two people remove them.*

PART OUT

21 *The driver's door was badly dented, but the glass was still salvageable. Remove interior panel to access the window channel.*

22 *We even saved the hinges on the damaged door.*

23 *The Mustang only had one good quarter window glass, so we removed it for possible sale. The windshield is actually the most valuable glass item.*

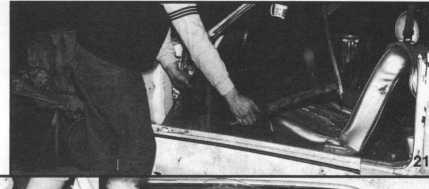

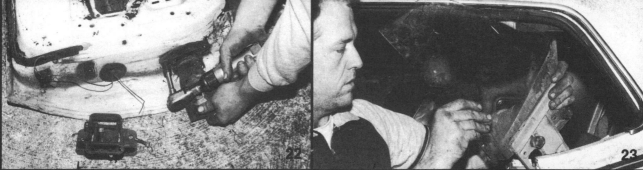

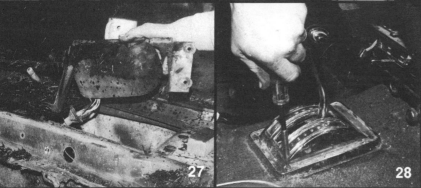

24 *Cowl vent panel is rust-free, so we removed and saved it.*

25 *Windshield is cracked, but the trim moldings are still good. This window trim removal tool is available at most auto parts stores; it makes easy work of trim clips.*

26 *The lower windshield trim piece on our Mustang is held in place with trim screws. The screws are easy to get to after the cowl panel is removed.*

27 *The windshield wiper motor is good to keep. Just unplug the wiring harness.*

28 *Mustang automatic shifter units are popular swap meet items because many street rods and kit cars use them. Remove all the linkage with the shifter.*

29 *We removed the steering column from our parts Mustang, but unless it's a tilt column, it's not too valuable.*

30 *Dashboard items such as gauges and clocks are good swap meet items. Our dash still has decent wood-grain trim, but the dash pad is badly cracked.*

PART OUT

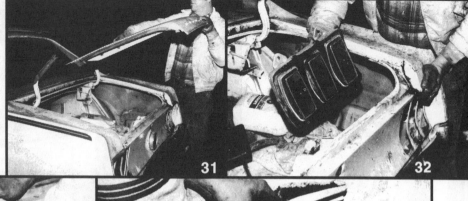

31 More cars are damaged in the front than the rear, so trunk lids don't have as much value as hoods, although Mustang fastback trunk lids are relatively valuable.

32 Taillights are easy to remove. Many buyers will only want the lens, but it's just as easy to remove the whole unit.

33 An undented, rust-free gas tank can be sold. Never leave a gas tank in place when cutting off a quarter panel.

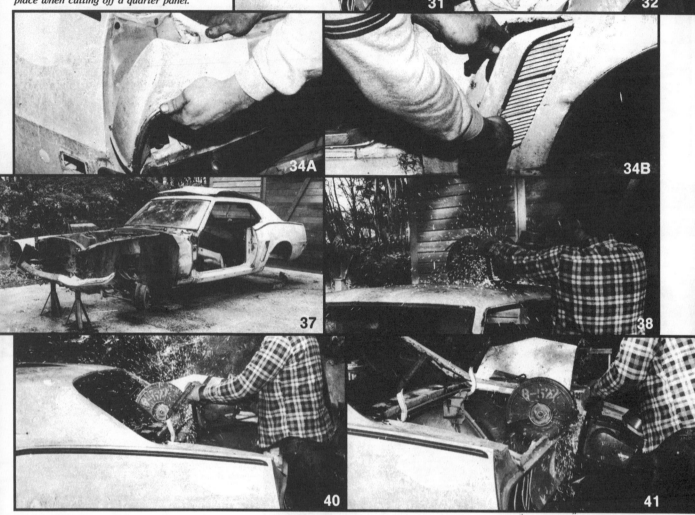

lar customers. You might also consider taking the spare parts to a swap meet, but this method is labor intensive, and you might end up bringing the parts back home. The smaller trim items seem to sell better at swap meets than big items, since many potential buyers aren't equipped to take an engine home.

If you have a lot of *mechanical* parts left over, don't overlook the street rod market. Mustang parts such as master cylinders, steering boxes, disc brakes, and nine-inch rearends are very popular with street rodders. Mustang II independent front suspensions, small-block Ford engines, and C-4 transmissions are other Mustang parts that are in demand.

Inevitably, you'll have leftover parts,

and you should keep them for future use or trading stock. Hopefully, you bought the right parts car and you won't get burned by the unneeded parts.

DISASSEMBLING

A parts car can be very messy and a real eyesore, so pick a good spot for your dirty work, preferably somewhere where the neighbors won't see the car. Parting a car in your front yard could be against local ordinances, so keeping the junk out of sight is the best policy for a happy neighborhood.

When you pick a place to dismantle it, give plenty of thought as to how you'll remove the hulk. Don't get the car trapped in a side yard without any suspension.

Safety is another important aspect of

taking apart a Mustang. Old cars are heavy, they have broken glass, knife-sharp pieces of metal, and they can be fire hazards. Always wear safety glasses, gloves, a long-sleeved shirt, and steel-toed shoes. Keep a fully charged fire extinguisher handy.

It's a good idea to leave the suspension pieces intact as long as possible, and it's much easier to roll the car around on wheels and tires as long as you can, too. Support the car with heavy-duty jackstands whenever you crawl underneath, and also when you remove the suspension parts. Be particularly careful with springs since they're stored energy.

The engine and transmission will probably be the first items you remove. If possible, run the engine while it's still

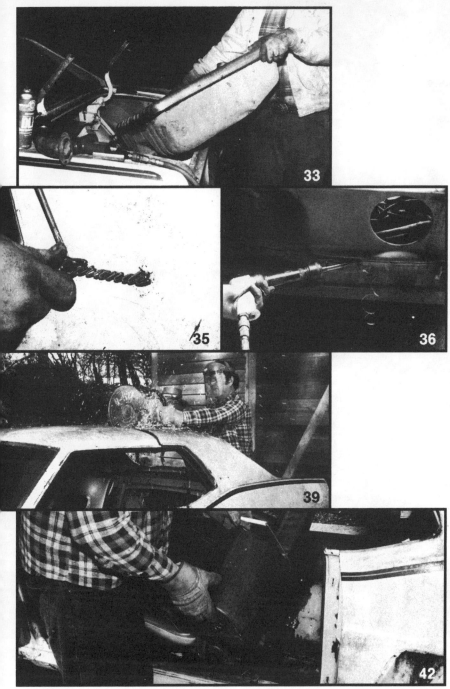

in the car, since it's easier to determine its condition that way, and you can also check out any accessories.

You can dismantle a car with an adjustable wrench and a screwdriver, but air tools are a real time and effort saver. Rusty bolts come off a lot simpler with an impact wrench, especially when there are so many fasteners to undo. Spraying the fasteners with a rust penetrant or silicone spray will also make your work easier.

Get a selection of coffee cans and boxes to sort and separate the various parts and fasteners. Use masking tape and a marking pen to identify parts and their order of assembly; you'd be surprised how quickly you can forget which bolt goes where.

If you plan to sell items such as rear quarter panels, taillight panels, or cowl sections, you'll need some kind of cutting equipment. The cleanest cuts are made with a body saw, which can be rented. These gas-powered cut-off saws send out a shower of sparks, so wear eye protection and heavy clothes. A cutting torch can also be used, but beware of possible fires caused from cutting through gas lines, brakelines, or cutting near any upholstery or carpeting. An air chisel will easily cut sheetmetal, but it can be difficult to remove double-wall panels with one.

DISPOSING OF THE HULK

Before you get too carried away with a sledge hammer on the hulk, make some calls to be sure you can even give the remains away. Depending on the current price of scrap metal, someone may come and get it, or possibly even pay you a few dollars for the remains. If the price of scrap metal is depressed, you might have to pay for pickup service, or even deliver the hulk yourself. This means some additional planning when dismantling the car.

If you want to haul the hulk to the crusher yourself, the biggest problem is getting it on a trailer. If you leave the rearend in until just before the car is loaded on the trailer, it will be a lot easier. One good method is to put the main part of the car on the trailer, then remove the rearend. This way you can push or winch the car all the way on the trailer.

Once you get the hulk to the crusher, they have plenty of equipment to unload it. If it's still on wheels, most crushers will pick the car off the trailer with a big forklift so you can remove your wheels and tires.

Parts cars aren't for everyone, especially if you're fond of clean hands. If you don't mind a little extra work, and some hardcore "hands-on" experience, they're an excellent way to get the parts you need at an extremely affordable price.

EDITOR'S NOTE: Some "brand X" cars are used in the accompanying photos. Sure we know what Mustangs look like, but we also know it's somehow easier to see a bow-tie bomber crushed than a Mustang. *M*

34 *A&B Small items such as quarter extension caps and '69 side scoops are often damaged, so they're easy to sell.*

35 *If you can remove trim items like this Grande script without damaging them, do so. Badges and nameplates are always in demand.*

36 *You can use an air chisel to remove body panels, but they don't work well on double-panel areas. Watch out for the sharp metal scraps.*

37 *Always use heavy-duty jackstands to support the car. Never cut corners on safety.*

38 *We were able to sell the quarter panels of our beat-up coupe. We rented a body saw to make the cuts, starting with one across the roof.*

39 *We made the second cut from the middle of the roof to the rear of the car. Remove the rear glass before making this cut.*

40 *Make the next cut through the package tray. Always wear safety glasses, a face mask, heavy gloves, and a long-sleeved shirt for protection from the sparks.*

41 *Remember to remove the gas tank before making the cut down the taillight panel.*

42 *You need a cutting torch to make the floor cut, so pour water over the old carpet to prevent a fire. Keep a fire extinguisher handy as well.*

Going, Going,

EXPERT ADVICE ON MUSTANG AUCTIONS
BY JERRY HEASLEY

Strange things often take place at car auctions. Just last month at the one-day Kruse International classic car auction in Hot Springs, Arkansas, a '66 289 coupe with new upholstery and carpets, an automatic transmission, and standard wheelcovers sold for $2100. The car was in semi-restored condition (no visible rust, fair paint, a few dents in the chrome trim), but what a buy at this price! The owner must have been in a selling mood as $2100 is well under market value. Imagine the ecstasy of that lucky buyer.

Perhaps you've been skipping national collector car auctions because you've heard so much about

the $21,500 auction Mustang, or you think classic car auctions are for prewar vehicles. The truth of the matter is that more than 50 percent of collector cars attending classic car auctions are postwar vehicles, and as far as high prices are concerned, there are far more $2000 Mustangs. Occasionally, a $20,000 exotic comes along, but there are always some great buys popping up at every sale. What's important to Mustang lovers is that almost every classic car auction is sprinkled with Mustangs, from '65 coupes and convertibles to '67 Shelbys, early Mach Is, Boss 302s, and 351s.

Beginning to sound better? Here

are the facts you need to know before getting involved in the auction action.

ENTRY FEES
The seller must pay a consignment fee (usually at least $100) to ensure some money for the promoters to run the vehicle through the sale. It's a necessary charge when you consider the rent for the building and the money spent on ads to attract both buyers and sellers to the event. Try to consign your Mustang early, and send along a picture; the auction company may advertise your car in the national hobby press and in their mailing brochures.

BIDDER'S FEES
The usual charge is $10-$20 for a

GONE!

bidder's number. Bidders are signed up and can be quickly identified, stopping normal bystanders from unwisely jumping into the action. This service also protects sellers from selling their car to someone without cash.

At Von Reece sales, you pay a $100 bidder's fee which is refunded at the end of the day if you pay what you bid for each car. Kruse International, the largest national collector car auction company, offers a one-time sign-up fee for the year.

Another benefit of signing up for a bidder's number is it places you on the company's mailing list to receive auction brochures. These include pictures and descriptions of

The famous "K-GT" '65 convertible, bid to a world's record $21,500 at Jimmy Leake's collector car auction. This Mustang was untouched since new.

159

GONE!

This '68 California Special has new maroon paint, white stripes, and wire wheel covers. The reserve was a reasonable $3500, but it was bid to a no-sale at $2800.

A '69 Boss 302 on the revolving auction block at the giant Las Vegas collector car auction. It's silver with black stripes and in excellent shape, but was a no-sale at $5000.

A rare and extremely desirable Mustang is this '67 GTA convertible with a 390 four-barrel engine, automatic, console power top, and GT wheels. It was a no-sale at $6400.

This '70 Mach I has the Windsor 351 two-barrel engine, and was bid to $3500 in 1982. No sale here.

This converted coupe has been made into a "Ranchero." Classic car buyers like tastefully modified Mustangs such as this, and it sold for about $6000 in 1983.

This '72 Mach I sold for $5600. Although it had a lower performance 351-2V engine, it had many extras, 77,000 one-owner miles, and it was in excellent condition.

This '67 Shelby GT500 is about to be driven onto the auction block at the July 1983 Las Vegas collector car auction.

This '66 Mustang convertible had a six-cylinder, automatic, no air, and spinner wheel covers. The turquoise rag top was bid to a no sale at $4350.

The premier auctioneer of classic and special interest cars is Dean Kruse of Kruse International. Dean is auctioning a Mustang at the Grand Old Cars museum close-out sale in 1983 in Arizona.

This Mustang sold for $2100 in Hot Springs, Arkansas, in March 1984. It's a 289 coupe with new upholstery, new carpets, automatic trans, and standard wheel covers.

At the 1984 February in Albuquerque collector car auction, this '65 Mustang with six cylinders, three-speed trans, and only 14,000 original miles was bid to an honest $21,000. The owner turned it down!

A '67 Shelby GT350 gets attention, even in average condition. One with 18,000 miles and a Paxton supercharger really makes people sit up and take notice.

A close-up shot of the Paxton supercharger in Reggie Jackson's GT350. In December 1982, the car was bid to a $19,000 no-sale.

vehicles to be sold at upcoming events.

COMMISSIONS & PAYMENTS

The usual commission fee is 10 percent charged to the seller, and the maximum commission is generally set around $3500. At the popular Rick Cole auctions in California, the buyer and seller split a 10-percent sales commission; each pays five percent of the selling price. If the car doesn't sell, there isn't a commission.

BANK LETTER OF CREDIT

Bidders must decide ahead of time whether they will pay by cash or check. A bank letter of credit is required for checks, or the buyer must be convinced the check is good.

The owner is paid directly for his car the day it's bought, and the auction company acts as the middleman by handling the transaction. However, some sellers request a check from the auction company, rather than a check from an individual. In any event, it is easier to bring cash.

TITLES

The procedure for changing titles varies from state to state, but in any state the title and the registration slip are needed. To be safe, bring all the papers for the car to the auction.

Only tax-exempt dealers don't have to pay state sales tax as part of the title changing procedure. Since the auction company will probably be based out of state, a local dealer handles the title changeovers and is responsible for getting a valid title for the car. However, out-of-staters who will be registering the car in their home state should request a "demand" title. This title remains in the previous owner's name, and the new owner takes it to the Department of Motor Vehicles in his state for the title change. Taxes are paid in the state where the title is registered.

ADMISSION

Bidders and consigners are admitted free, while spectators pay between $3.00-$5.00. However, many newcomers mistakenly plunk down admission, then pay their $20 registration fee inside. Auction companies hand out VIP passes to registered bidders, so just tell the ticket sellers at the gate you want to register. It's the same procedure for consigners of auction cars.

AUCTION POSITION

The best auction positions are usually around the early to middle part of the day, and it's first come, first served. Early consignment means a better position in the sale. The auction company can't guarantee an exact time of day, but they will allow you to select from the remaining numbers.

SETTING A RESERVE

When you fill out your auction contract, you'll also have to fill in what is known as a reserve, or the minimum price that you will accept for your vehicle. Most experienced sellers set a high reserve ($7000 for a car worth $4500-$5000). Once the bid passes the written reserve on the contract, the owner is obligated to sell his car. Since the reserve isn't announced to the crowd, the owner can accept any bid that he wants. When your car crosses the block, one of the auction ring men will confer with you on your low dollar, or what you would accept for your vehicle.

A word of warning on setting a reserve ridiculously high: the auctioneers may not take you seri-

GONE!

Some bidders will crowd around a car while it is on the block. Usually it's the ring men who are closest; they're looking for bids and coaxing higher offers.

During the preview time, it is a good idea to have your car well-displayed with the hood and trunk open so potential buyers can make a thorough inspection.

If you display a "For Sale" sign in a car's window and park it in the auction parking lot, you risk having the car towed away as the promoters want to sell the auction cars.

Here is a Mustang prior to the start of an auction. It's a good time to stick near your car and field questions from potential buyers.

This seller is cleaning up his '73 351 Cobra Jet convertible prior to the giant 1983 Sun City, Arizona, sale. A well-detailed car is a must for top prices.

A '71 Boss 351 at the Pate Museum of Transportation collector car auction in 1982. Today, this car would bring about $7,000 easily, if in excellent condition.

ously as wanting to sell, and quickly no-sale your vehicle with a dummy bidder.

TRANSPORTATION
There is a large car-hauling industry built around the collector car hobby, and these companies set up booths at classic car auctions. You can pay to have a car hauled anywhere in the country (or have a car trailered to a sale). One of the largest haulers is Frank Malatesta's Horseless Carriage Carriers, Inc. (61 Iowa Ave., Paterson, NJ 07503, 800/631-7796). Their rates are 70 cents per mile plus a $20 loading fee, but short hauls can be expensive as the minimum fee is $462.50 for under 600 miles. It's a good idea to pick an auction close to home and cut down on transportation costs.

FINDING THE AUCTIONS
Our suggestion is to pick up a copy of Old Cars Weekly on the newsstands; it has a listing of the collector car sales around the country. One will come to your area sometime during the year.

STOCK VERSUS MODIFIED
Generally speaking, the modified Mustangs don't sell for as high a price at a classic car auction as the stockers and the low-mileage origi-

nals. But a tasteful modified can do quite well.

CHECK-IN TIME
Cars are checked in the day before the sale, and this is a good time for buyers and sellers to mix with car owners fielding questions from potential buyers. Remember that no rules restrict or prevent a thorough investigation, even to the extent of a test drive, and this may be possible on the day before the auction.

You will see '65 and '66 Mustangs, Shelbys, high-performance Boss 302s, and Cobra Jets. Handy reference books such as the Mustang Data Plate Decoder (available for $4.95 from Mustang Publications, 410 Brannen Rd., Lakeland, FL 33803) allow you to decode both warranty plates (1964½-1969) and vehicle certification labels (1970-1973) to check for originality.

Another useful pocket-sized reference is the Mustang Black Book, which lists current values of '64½-'73 Mustangs, plus vital facts on production figures, engines, and annual body style changes. This book is available from the same publisher, also for $4.95. Be sure to fully check out the codes. If the owner represents his Mustang as a high-performance 289, check for the "K" code on the warranty plate and the VIN under the hood. If it's supposed to be a GT, then make sure it has the right engine for a GT. By using this book, we found a 351 Cobra Jet convertible, and the owner was unaware that his Mustang was a Cobra Jet!

It's important to take time to decide the value of a car, and set a price limit. Keep in mind the various expenses, such as transportation, state taxes, and even the five-percent commissions charged to the seller at some auctions. Check for large areas of repair on freshly painted Mustangs with a small magnet wrapped in tape to protect the car's finish.

If you're selling, make up a professional-looking sign to set your car apart from the others, and let buyers know your car's special features. If you have any documentation of your Mustang's originality, bring the proof. An original window sticker, a copy of the original title, or an old invoice will do.

Get to know the buyers and sellers; they are fellow collectors and investors who can help you check out a certain car for authenticity. For example, at one sale a '67 GT looked like a real GT from 10 feet, but word quickly spread that it was a converted GT, not a factory GT. Take advantage of this strength in numbers, and if you bring a converted GT to auction, be sure to list it as such.

THE BIDDING BEGINS
You should have your homework done by now, whether you are buying or selling. Buyers should know their bidding limit, and sellers should set a minimum price.

Usually, the auctioneer asks for a high opening bid, then drops down to the first offer. For example, he may ask $15,000 for a '65 Mustang convertible, see an eager hand at $5000, and from here the bidding moves on up.

It is widely known that "shills" are sprinkled throughout the bidding audience, and while everyone resents competition from a fake bidder, shills do perform a worthwhile function. Let's say you have a '71 429 Cobra Jet Mach I, easily worth over $5000, and it's one of the stars of the show. It would be embarrassing to take a $1500 top bid simply because there are no '71-'73 Mustang enthusiasts in the crowd. Crazy low bids stymie sales, dampen spirits, and create the domino effect of a large percentage

of no-sales. It's simple to counteract bidding against a dummy bidder: know what you will pay for the Mustang you want.

If you are selling, come to the podium when your car crosses the block so you can work with the auctioneer and any buyers. Also, if you are selling a Mustang convertible, work the power top up and down to draw attention to the car.

BUYING OR SELLING AFTER THE BIDDING
Auction regulars know that some of the best deals are made after the bidding ends. Often a seller has a change of heart after getting his $150 public appraisal, and he realizes he was asking too much for the car.

If you want a certain Mustang and the owner turned down a high bid, follow the car off the auction block. After a few minutes, walk up to the owner and make an offer. If the high bid was $7000, but you think the car is worth five, offer it to the owner. He may accept it. The $7000 bid may not have been a "real" bid; since the owner had an inflated value placed on his car, the auctioneers had to pump bidding up to come close to the reserve. If a car is sold after bidding, the 10 or 12-percent commission must still be paid to the auction company.

MUSTANG AUCTION TRENDS
In the last two years we have seen the auction crowd show interest in the '67 and later Mustangs. From 1975 through the end of 1981, the '65-'66 Mustangs drew almost exclusive attention at the big sales.

Interest in the '65-'66 series apparently peaked in 1981 at the James Leake collector car auction in Tulsa, Oklahoma. It's one of the world's largest and most prestigious classic car auctions, and an unrestored '65 "K"-engined GT convertible with 21,130 miles went for a record $21,500.

In early 1982, interest in the '67 390 GTs and GTAs came about. Prices hit $6000 on restored cars, and some sellers hung onto these cars with reserves of $7500! At that time, it was thought that interest would simply move up through the model years, finally encompassing the '68-'73s. However, interest jumped right through that era, with any special Mustangs getting recognition and bidding that had been held back for years. A '71 Boss 351 with 18,000 original miles sold for $8750. A '72 Mach I fastback with a low-performance 351 2V sold for $5500, a respectable price

at auction.

What we have today on the auction scene is a situation where just about all of the '64½-'73 Mustangs are accepted and known quantities. Interest still remains high for the '65-'66 series, although prices have now stabilized except for very special cars. *M*

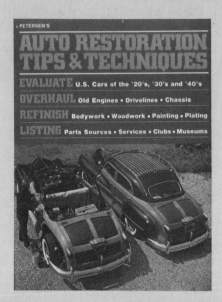

PETERSEN'S

AUTO RESTORATION TIPS & TECHNIQUES

EVALUATE U.S. Cars of the '20's, '30's and '40's

OVERHAUL Old Engines • Drivelines • Chassis

REFINISH Bodywork • Woodwork • Painting • Plating

LISTING Parts Sources • Services • Clubs • Museums

AUTO RESTORATION TIPS & TECHNIQUES